R. Dennis Shelby, PhD

People with HIV and Those Who Help Them: Challenges, Integration, Intervention

*Pre-publication
REVIEWS,
COMMENTARIES,
EVALUATIONS . . .*

"**P**eople with HIV and Those
Who Help Them is a wonderfully wise, compassionate, and helpful account of what it means for men to become HIV positive, the issues posed in dealing with the diagnosis, and the course of time from initial diagnosis through conversion to illness. Shelby provides a wealth of information regarding the meaning of the HIV-positive diagnosis for the lives of these persons and those who live with and care for them, and important information regarding psychological intervention. It is must reading for health professionals and all those who are concerned with the psychological significance of HIV for our society."

Bertram J. Cohler
William Rainey Harper Professor
of Social Sciences, The University
of Chicago

"In this book, Dennis Shelby shares vitally important knowledge he has gained from the first decade of the HIV epidemic. He listens to gay men with HIV and brings their voices to the page. In addition, he applies his seasoned clinical skills and self-psychology theory to distill the meaning of their experience, their 'new reality.' All are helped by Shelby's unflinching attention: those with HIV who strive to make meaning of their lives and those who strive to help them sort out the meaning.

As an acute observer, theorist, and clinician, Shelby is an explorer and cartographer in the wilderness which HIV can be. His research takes us deep into that jungle of intense emotion of gay men with HIV. He finds common themes in their experience and establishes signposts which orient us. . . . In the last part of the book, he successfully applies the self-psychology model in order to further illuminate the meaning of the experience using several complex case examples.

There is a deeply therapeutic experience to be had in reading this book: an 'Ah Ha!' experience of, 'That's right. That's what it is. He's got it right. He understands.' Shelby extends the healing art of therapeutic intervention into the written word. To hold this book and read it is to feel held and understood, which is what we all need in order to find meaning and to survive in this Age of AIDS. Those with HIV experience will recognize themselves in this book. Those without will be better prepared, guided, and accompanied when they do."

Steven Cadwell, PhD
Private practice, Boston;
Co-Editor of *Therapists on the Front Line: Psychotherapy with Gay Men in the Age of AIDS*

The Harrington Park Press
An Imprint of The Haworth Press, Inc.

People with HIV
and Those Who Help Them
Challenges, Integration,
Intervention

HAWORTH Social Work Practice
Carlton E. Munson, Senior Editor

New, Recent, and Forthcoming Titles:

People with HIV and Those Who Help Them

Challenges, Integration, Intervention

R. Dennis Shelby, PhD

Harrington Park Press
An Imprint of The Haworth Press, Inc.
New York • London

Published by

Harrington Park Press, an imprint of The Haworth Press, Inc., 10 Alice Street, Binghamton, NY 13904-1580

Library of Congress Cataloging-in-Publication Data

Shelby, R. Dennis.
    People with HIV and those who help them : challenges, integration, intervention / R. Dennis Shelby.
        p.   cm.
    Includes bibliographical references and index.
    ISBN 1-56023-865-8 (pbk.)
    1. HIV infections–Psychological aspects. I. Title.
RC607.A26S4916   1995
616.97′92–dc20   94-33087
                                                  CIP

CONTENTS

ABOUT THE AUTHOR

R. Dennis Shelby, PhD, is a Licensed Clinical Social Worker and a Board Certified Diplomate in Clinical Social Work. He has worked with and studied HIV-related problems since the epidemic first began to impact Chicago. Dr. Shelby has published numerous articles on clinical work with HIV-related problems and psychotherapy with gay men, and is the author of *If a Partner Has AIDS: Guide to Clinical Intervention for Relationships in Crisis* (The Haworth Press, 1992). He is a faculty member at the Institute for Clinical Social Work in Chicago and maintains a private practice.

Foreword

Adversity and misfortune threaten the integrity of the self and challenge fundamental constructions of life experience, anticipated future, and personal meaning. As the neurologist Oliver Sacks reminds us in his reflections on personal narrative in health and in sickness, each of us *is* a story, *is* a biography, constructed continually out of our feelings, thoughts, and actions, in our experiences of self and of others. Inevitably, the effort to restore a sense of coherence and continuity in sense of self and life experience following trauma assumes the form of narrative: stories are ways of organizing experience, interpreting events, and recollecting self. "To be ourselves," Sacks observes, "we must *have* ourselves . . . possess, if need be re-possess, our life stories" (Sacks, 1985).

In this new study, Dennis Shelby moves beyond the traditional social-psychological perspectives that have shaped our assumptions and beliefs about stress, coping, and adaptation over the last quarter century and makes use of narrative and phenomenological methods in his continuing efforts to understand the experience of HIV seropositivity. Drawing on the relational methods of naturalistic inquiry in the human sciences, Shelby seeks to understand shifts in the experience of self, others, life events, and anticipated future following discovery of HIV seropositivity, independent of widely accepted stage models of adjustment and adaptation. In presuming not to know, he realizes, we preserve the possibility of discovery that may help us see, and understand, and act in generative ways.

By way of background, as we review the outcomes of risk research carried out over the last three decades, we realize that we have come to know more about determinants of dysfunction and psychopathology . . . in brief, why people fare badly . . . than we have learned about the capacity to cope, to remain resilient, to grow and develop in the face of adversity and misfortune. In large measure, as critics have emphasized, social psychological research on life-threatening conditions has proceeded on the assumption that distress and depression are inevitable reactions to trauma and critical elements in achieving adaptation. Perceptions of beneficial change or reports of growth and development are not expected; frequently, they are interpreted as signs of denial or maladaptive defenses, or viewed as indications of latent psychopathology.

And yet, as clinicians in health care settings have long realized, many persons deal with adversity and misfortune far better than conventional theoretical formulations or empirical reports would lead us to expect. Most people manage to restore prior levels of functioning, following realization of life-threatening conditions; what is more, a surprising number would appear to grow as a consequence of adversity and report enduring beneficial change following life-threatening illness and physical disability. As Shelby recognizes, such observations challenge the prevalent view that reactions to unexpected life events are uniformly negative and call into question the validity of universal stage models of adjustment proposed in current formulations of adaptation.

Shelby's study shows how the discovery of HIV seropositivity often leads to a reconsideration of what matters most in life. The possibility of illness and loss strips life to its bare essentials, as the subjects of his study continually remind us, and the experience may lead to consolidations in sense of self and identity more commonly than we realize. Ongoing interpretations of events and experience, continuing recollection and repossession of the self, may help one realize opportunities gained and lessons learned, and live life more fully. Shelby's work, informed by more than a decade of clinical experience with gay men, extends our understanding of the psychological and social experience of HIV seropositivity and promises to assist health care professionals in continued development of psychosocial assessment approaches and therapeutic intervention with this growing population.

–William Borden, PhD
Associate Professor, School of Social Service Administration;
Department of Psychiatry, University of Chicago;
Faculty, Institute for Clinical Social Work

REFERENCE

Sacks, Oliver (1985). *The man who mistook his wife for a hat and other clinical tales.* New York: Harper and Row.

Acknowledgements

Many people were helpful during the long process of conceptualizing, interviewing, analyzing the data, and writing up the results of this study. Again, Thomas Kenemore was there encouraging–at times challenging–me all along the way. The much-appreciated mirroring by many members of the faculty and fellow graduates of the Institute for Clinical Social Work helped keep me going during the many times I was sure this topic was too complicated for me to attempt.

An important factor in the success of this project was the recruitment of participants. Thanks go to Tom Klein, MD, Ross Slotten, MD, and Andrew Pavalatos, MD, for referring their patients to the study. The Test Positive Aware Network was very responsive to my request for help and allowed me to observe meetings and to recruit men from the organization. Deep gratitude goes to the men who have shared their lives with me–the men who participated individually, the ones who were members of the group, and my individual clients. A wonderful surprise that went with the project were the many friends and strangers who spontaneously shared their experiences of being HIV-positive when they learned of the study I was working on.

This work is dedicated to the many gay men who are living with and have lived with HIV. They have much to teach about living and growing, of continuing to find meaning in a world that often does not make sense. And to my friend of 20 years, John McCollum. I was deeply moved by how delighted John was by the publication of my first book, *If a Partner Has AIDS*. He urged me on to complete this one, a topic so near to his experience. John died suddenly several weeks before the book was completed. I will miss his presence in my life. And to my family, my partner, David Prentice, and "the kids"–Maggie, Wynona, Winnicott, and DeeDee. While they have presented me with many challenges over the years, they have also offered a great deal of delight and reassurance that life continues to unfold.

Chapter 1

The Challenge

HIV disease presents an infinite number of challenges to infected people and to the efforts of institutions and individuals who provide the vast range of treatment, research, and services needed to meet human need in the wake of the HIV epidemic. This book is an effort to understand and conceptualize the many challenges that people encounter as a result of HIV infection. It is also an effort to present a framework for clinical intervention based on mens' ever-evolving and challenging experience of being infected with HIV. It is the result of a series of dialogues between myself and the HIV-positive men who have helped me to understand their experience.

The first challenge for an effort such as this research project is to define or in some way conceptualize what it means to be HIV-positive. Because the human mind is multifaceted and our ways of conceptualizing the human mind are equally as multifaceted, many ways of defining the psychological impact of knowing that one is HIV-positive are possible. For example, Borden (1992) uses a number of terms to describe testing HIV-positive: "Traumatic experience"; "negative life events"; "crisis" "adverse circumstances"; "Stressor Condition"; "a departure from the social clock of the life course." These evocative terms and concepts establish the framework from which Borden listened to and understood the experiences of the men in his study. Similarly, Cohen and Abramowitz (1990) stated AIDS "precipitates a profound destabilizing crisis for the self." This conceptualization set the framework from which they understood the experience of the people they worked with in a clinical context.

Funding for this project was provided in part by The Institute for Clinical Social Work, Chicago, Illinois.

1

A much broader conceptualization of the meaning of testing positive is needed for this book as a whole to make sense philosophically. The methodology employed, compiling the results of the inquiry into the experience of testing positive, and the framework for clinical intervention must be considered in order to achieve a consistent organizing perspective. The basic conceptualization of testing positive employed in this work is a new reality. It is a reality that individuals who know they are infected must attempt to make sense of in light of the basic ways they have come to previously know and understand themselves, and the complex social meanings that AIDS and HIV have acquired in the past decade. In many ways, and as the results illustrate, people who learn they are HIV-positive may feel that they have to get to know themselves all over again.

Kohut (1984) pointed out that once the theory of perspective was introduced, we began to see the world differently. This to me is the nexus of the experience of testing HIV-positive. At some point people feel differently about themselves, the world appears different, time and the future take on very different meanings. And it hurts.

Though it represents an ontological position different from that of this book, one that essentially states that there is no reality at all, rather that all "reality" is created, the story of Schrodinger's cat concerns the nature of multiple realities and comes by way of quantum mechanics. Though seeming far removed from the realm of living with HIV, it offers an evocative perspective for the experience of wondering and worrying, deciding to be tested, and being informed of the results. Lincoln and Guba (1985) relate the story in this way:

1. A closed steel case containing one radioactive atom. The atom has a half life of one hour, that is, in a large sample of such atoms half of them would remain after the passage of an hour while the other half would have decayed. Thus, after one hour, the probability of finding the atom still in the case is .5.

2. A photocell sensitive to emitted radiation. If the atom decays the resulting radiation trips the photocell, which in turn releases a deadly gas.

3. A live cat is introduced into this cage at the same time that precisely one atom of radioactive element has been released in it. Question: at the end of an hour, what we will find on opening the case, a live cat, or a dead cat?

Wolf points out that according to quantum mechanics, *you* control the fate of the cat if you are the one to open the cage. After one hour there are two equally likely scenarios regarding whether the cat is alive or dead. Wolf (1981, p. 189-191) observes: "In a certain sense, the universe has become *two* universes. In one, there is a living cat and a happy you, and in the other, there is a dead cat and a sad you." If you did not reach over and to open the crate and thereby disturb it, these two universes would go on forever, side by side, indefinitely. When you open the cage, you *create* the reality that you find. Until then there is only potential. (p. 85-86)

Contemplating this argument from the perspective of a clinician and a clinical researcher, one could argue that there are three, not two potential realities: worrying indefinitely about the fate of the cat, opening the door and finding out the cat is dead, or opening the door and finding out the cat is alive. Many of the men in this study spent a considerable period of time worrying whether they were positive or not. Many became used to this state of worrying and did not investigate the situation in a way that would give them a definitive answer. Many men to this day choose not to find out. At some point and for various reasons, the men in this study made the decision to find out, to open the door and face what was inside.

This book is about the psychological experience of opening that door, of having one's blood tested and finding out what one's antibody status actually is. Men are then faced with the complicated task of constructing what that test result means. We have an event—being informed of one's antibody status as indicated by a laboratory procedure. We then have the complicated, dynamic, and ever-evolving process of people attempting to make sense of their world in light of the test results and changing medical status. As Lincoln and Guba (1985) point out: "Events, persons, objects are indeed tangible entities. The meanings and wholeness derived from or ascribed to these tangible phenomena in order to make sense of them, organize them, or reorganize a belief system are *constructed realities"* (p. 84).

Conceptualizing the psychological impact of testing HIV-positive as a new reality may seem a bit broad and loose to clinicians and researchers accustomed to quantitative research that endeavors to offer definitive answers. However, this approach enables us to look at the general range of human experience, the meanings that evolve, and perhaps most important, a longitudinal perspective–how the experience changes over time. If this work helps a future researcher formulate and design an effort to closely examine a particular aspect of the experience of testing HIV-positive, then great. If this approach helps people arrive at an appreciation for the complexity of the experience, be it their own, their client or patient, their partner, friend or relative, then all the better.

The narrative account presented in Chapters 4 through 10 discusses how gay men construct the reality of knowing they are HIV-positive. First the men encountered the potential of being infected with the HIV virus. Then they made the decision to find out if they indeed were infected, and dealt with making sense of the results of the test. Constructing–or perhaps reconstructing–the many assumptions and meanings that influence our perceptions of the world in the face of HIV is a complicated and evolving process. Over the years many HIV-positive men have in various ways rhetorically asked me, "I don't lock myself in the house because I am afraid of being hit by a truck and killed as I cross the street. Why do I sometimes get so afraid of moving ahead with my life because I am HIV-positive?" My usual response is along the lines that it is because no representative with the status that we culturally ascribe to the scientific medical community has told you that sometime in the future, you will be hit and killed by a truck as you cross the street.

Several years ago, a friend "read" my palm. Her assessment was basically threefold: "You have the mark of the healer" (good). "You will not find true love until you are in your fifties" (not so good). She then appeared very concerned and adamantly stated, "Be aware of head injuries; you are at great risk" (not good at all). To this day I find myself feeling anxious riding a horse or motorcycle without a helmet.

AIDS and HIV infection have been a tragic aspect of the reality of the lives of gay men for the past decade. When I think back over the years there were many times when I thought this was all just a bad dream, one that we would collectively wake from, and the awful reality would be over. Obviously it is not. The reality of AIDS and HIV continues to unfold. Indications are that it will continue to do so for some time. If we think back on the last decade our understanding of the disease has changed and evolved considerably. Our understanding and response to HIV disease, and the consequent meanings for infected individuals may be very different ten years from now. In many ways this book is an historical document. It is about how gay men experienced HIV infection in the years 1989 to 1993.

The challenges of living with HIV are many: to find ways to modulate the often intense and overwhelming feeling states; to find people that understand the impact of being positive and offer the reassurance of a sense of belonging; to feel that one is engaged with one's life–and what is most fundamental, to keep finding meaning in life even though it may seem that all meaning has been whittled or blasted away. While living with HIV is a fine motto to live by, it is not always easy to do. Living with HIV is challenging. It is not always tragic; many triumphs are to be found. But there will be many valleys when despair is dominant, death feels imminent, and confusion reigns. Hopefully the results chapter of this book will help in the process of making sense of the complicated process of living with HIV. It is a collective account about what it is like to live with HIV. It is a potential reassurance that living with HIV is a challenge for everyone that many have experienced, are experiencing, and will experience.

For clinicians the challenge is to find ways of working with people in such a way that they are helped to continue to find meaning in life. We must also continue to find meaning as we work with people as they cross several stages of HIV infection. For me, seeing and participating in the often tremendous growth people encounter in the face of HIV has been a central, humbling, inspiring, and encouraging experience. Hopefully, clinicians who read this book will get ideas of their own, or conceptualize a puzzling aspect of the experience of infected people so that their ability to intervene is enhanced.

For friends and relatives of people living with HIV, this book may help you to understand the person you love. It may often be challenging to be with positive partners, friends, children, or sibs in such a way that feels comfortable and sustaining for all. Hopefully it will assist you in your sometimes challenging efforts at being there for those you love by giving you an empathic perspective of their world.

Chapter 2

Methodology

RESEARCH STRATEGY

The central question for this study, "What are the experiences of gay men who test positive for HIV antibodies?" lent itself to the construction of a research design based in the methodological and philosophical approach to systematic inquiry of qualitative research.

Lincoln (1992) defines qualitative methods as:

> . . . generally those non-quantitative methods that attempt to grasp phenomena in some holistic way or to understand a phenomenon within its own context or to emphasize the immersion and comprehension of human *meaning* ascribed to some set of circumstances or phenomena or all three. Qualitative methods are generally considered to be the methods of choice for most forms of anthropology, for much of sociology, for ethnography, or for any kind of research that emphasizes broad understanding and deep insight over shorthand or reductionist data. (p. 376)

A central assumption for this study was that the biological course of HIV infection (infection with the HIV virus, development of HIV antibodies, decline of T-cell counts and other laboratory indicators of the progression of the infection, development of opportunistic infections and eventually death) represents one model of conceptualizing the disease and its consequences. However another equally complex and compelling phenomenon exists. That is the human experience of knowing that one is infected with the HIV virus. This takes us into the realm of the meaning of disease and its consequences for human beings. Consequently, a model of systematic inquiry whose purpose is to elucidate the meaning for those infected individuals was indicated. Related to this was the assumption that the experience of being infected with HIV was dynamic and subject to transformation.

A design for inquiry into the phenomenon of testing HIV-positive was constructed that allowed the researcher to gather data through "*human-to-human* qualitative methods . . . includ[ing] interviewing, participant and non-participant observation and nonverbal communication" (Lincoln, 1992, p. 366). Given the assumption that the experience of testing HIV positive was subject to transformation, men who participated in the study as individuals were interviewed over the course of 12 to 14 months. The observation that gay men often sought help through support groups upon finding out they were HIV-positive led the researcher to be a participant-observer at several meetings of a large support/educational organization for infected individuals. In order to gather more refined data in the setting of infected men seeking help in groups, the researcher conducted a small ongoing psychotherapy group for infected men from which data were collected over a one-year period. An additional source of data included men in individual psychotherapy with the researcher.

Setting

Individual interviews and the ongoing psychotherapy group were conducted in the researchers' office in Chicago, Illinois. In order to recruit participants and to observe the workings of a large educational/support group for infected men, the researcher attended several meetings of Test Positive Aware also located in Chicago. The men who participated in the study were primarily from the metropolitan Chicago area. Additional data were acquired in a variety of social and professional settings when the researcher mentioned this study and men spontaneously volunteered their experience of HIV infection.

Characteristics of Participating Men

A total of 26 men formally participated in the study either as individuals or in the group. Sixteen men initially agreed to participate on an individual basis. In the course of the study three men died, and another three either dropped out of the study or moved and contact was lost. A total of ten men completed three interviews over a 12- to 14-month period. A total of ten men participated in the psychotherapy group while data were being gathered. Another 15 men contributed data either on an informal basis, i.e., spontaneously sharing their experiences with the interviewer, or the interviewer obtained data in the context of individual psychotherapy. Consent to use the data was obtained from each man regardless of formal or informal participation.

Each participant defined himself as a gay man who was infected with the HIV virus. At the time men contributed their experiences, they had known they were HIV-positive for several days to several years. Three of the men had experienced opportunistic infections and were formally diagnosed with AIDS. Several men were diagnosed with AIDS in the course of the study. Participants ranged in age from 23 to 58 years with the majority being in their late thirties to early forties. Several men who were partnered participated in the study as couples; all couples were both HIV-positive. Participants were primarily white, middle-class professionals or service providers.

Data Collection

Interviews with individual participants were tape recorded as was the psychotherapy group during the one-year period that data were collected. Data from the researcher's private practice or spontaneous interviews were written down as soon as possible following the interaction. For the formal individual interviews the basic question was, "What has been your experience as a gay man who has tested positive?" Additional questions and subsequent interviews were recursive (Schwartz and Jacobs 1979); that is, further questioning was derived from the content, questions, and answers of previous interviews. For the most part the researcher found that in subsequent interviews merely asking what had happened since the previous interview was enough to elicit rich and comprehensive accounts of the men's experiences. Participants were originally asked to contract to three interviews over a nine-month period. However, as the study grew in complexity, this was changed to a 12-to 14-month period. The majority of participants completed the three interviews. Several participants who were coupled chose to be interviewed conjointly.

The psychotherapy group was an unstructured, dynamic process. The group's stated goal was to collect data on the experience of testing positive within a small group format. General themes in the group centered around changes in the experience of self since testing positive, revealing one's antibody status to others, and adapting to life as a person infected with the HIV virus. Data from men in individual psychotherapy secondary to their HIV status were incorporated when appropriate as were the spontaneous data collected in the course of the researcher's private and professional life.

Data Analysis

Data were collected, organized, and analyzed according to the Grounded Theory method for qualitative research detailed in Glaser and Strauss (1967), Glaser (1978) and Strauss and Corbin (1990). The goal of this methodology is to construct theory that is grounded in observed data. In accordance with the Grounded Theory method, data collection, organization, and analysis occurred simultaneously. The methodology incorporates the Constant Comparative Method (Glaser and Strauss 1967, p. 5). According to the method, the taped interviews, group sessions, notes from individual psychotherapy sessions, or serendipitous encounters were broken down into quotes and coded according to categories, with a category representing a conceptual idea. Quotes from participants were constantly compared with previous quotes (Glaser and Strauss 1978).

During the process of coding, theoretical ideas were placed in theoretical memos. Theoretical memos are the theorizing write-up of ideas about categories and their relationship as they strike the researcher while coding (Glaser 1978). The memos then become the basis for delimiting the theory (Glaser and Strauss 1967, p. 109). As data collection, organization, and analysis continued, categories and their component properties became refined, the theory (reconstructed experience) developed, and coded quotes then became the tools for illustrating the theory (Glaser and Strauss 1967, p. 110).

The assertion by Glaser and Strauss (1967) and Glaser (1978) that categories came from the data has caused considerable controversy in some academic circles primarily because the conceptualizing phenomenon is a particularly human phenomenon, hence it could not come from "data" alone. Strauss and Corbin (1990) alter this position by stating that categories come from the researcher. However, this is not a complete explanation. It is more coherent to assert that categories evolve from the researcher's immersion in, and interaction with the data, and in the case of data collected in the context of human-to-human interactions, with the fellow human beings participating in the research endeavor.

Trustworthiness of the Study Results

The philosophical basis for this systematic inquiry into the experiences of gay men who test HIV-positive is firmly rooted in the constructivist paradigm as detailed by Lincoln and Guba (1985). As such, the questions are raised of whether the results (or the reconstruction of the participants, experience of testing HIV-positive) are trustworthy and authentic. The reader of this study should evaluate its method and results based on its *trustworthiness judgement* and *authenticity judgement.* Trustworthiness criteria include credibility, transferability, dependability, and confirmability. Authenticity criteria included fairness, ontological authenticity, and tactical authenticity (Lincoln 1992).

To help establish the trustworthiness of the results, the procedure of member checking was employed (Lincoln and Guba 1985). Participants in the study were offered the opportunity to review drafts of the study results as they emerged. The comments, suggestions, and criticisms were then integrated into the final document. In addition to member checking, the researcher engaged in "debriefing," a process of reviewing the collection, organization, and analysis of the data with an objective individual (someone more removed from the researchers' immersion in the experience under study) (Glaser and Strauss 1967).

In general the essential evaluative criteria for this inquiry rest on a consensus of individuals who read and utilize the results. This consensus must include those individuals whose reality is being studied, those individuals familiar with the participants' reality, and those removed from the phenomenon being studied so that the results are coherent, offer a reasonable and helpful conceptual model, and contribute to our understanding of the human experience. The extent to which the results are useful in understanding other similar phenomena (i.e., individual's experience of other chronic and terminal illnesses) will be subject to judgements of clinicians regarding the utility of the conceptualizations (Kennedy 1979).

Chapter 3

Introduction to the Results

When a gay man is informed that he is HIV-positive he enters an experience, a new reality that will occupy the very center of his existence for the rest of his life. For the vast majority of gay men, AIDS and HIV infection and its social and personal consequences have become an integral aspect of our reality over the past decade. When they are informed that they are HIV-positive many men eventually realize that the reality of their social milieu–the fear of infection, illness, and death–has now become their personal reality in a very profound way. Most men who test HIV-positive have already experienced the effects of HIV and AIDS in their social and intrapsychic world.

Many gay men have already seen a friend in the advanced stages of HIV disease, have lost friends and partners to the illness. They have made profound changes in their sexual behavior and their personal conceptualizations regarding the nature of sexuality before they approach finding out if they too are HIV-positive. Fear, sorrow, despair, terror, and a profound sense of the world having tilted on its axis are just a few of the human emotions that have accompanied the existance of HIV infection in the social milieu. Upon testing positive the virus is no longer "out there" in a world that has already become too frightening. It is inside; it is now a part of the self, along with the profound fear that it may very well bring about its demise.

Based on the analysis of data collected for this study, the experiences of gay men who test HIV-positive have been conceptualized in the form of a long and complex narrative account that consists of seven distinct areas of experience. Each of the seven chapters that follow have been devoted to an area or category of the experience.

Individual chapters are further broken down into properties or components that together form the distinctive qualities of the area. Given the nature of the human mind, many properties flow through several areas or categories of the experience, transforming over time.

Men enter the experience with THE GREAT DEBATE–the process of making the decision to be tested in light of the presence of the disease in the social milieu, knowledge of the infection and its routes of transmission, their personal sexual encounters and identifications with infected and non-infected individuals. TRUTH AND CONSEQUENCES encompasses the process and the individual's initial response to being informed of the presence or absence of the virus based on laboratory findings. THE TWILIGHT ZONE is the consequent response to being informed that one is positive. For many men it represents the demise of the self that one was accustomed to, the result of being faced with a new reality and the initial incoherence that it brings.

The next four areas of the experience roughly parallel the progression of HIV disease. THE LONG HAUL is the period of getting to know one's self again, making changes in the matrix of relationships, acquiring information to help make sense of and to help sustain the self in the face of the new reality. IT'S TIME encompasses the need to begin antiviral treatments and the meanings associated with disease progression and medical intervention. MOVING ON is an area of stabilization following the initiation of antiviral treatments and often the emergence of bothersome symptoms of HIV infection. The narrative ends with THE BIG BANG–the often long-awaited and feared diagnosis of AIDS. As this study focuses on testing positive and living with the knowledge of HIV infection, only the initial aspects of being diagnosed with AIDS are explored and elucidated.

Given the highly variable nature of human experience and disease progression, not all men will proceed through the areas in an orderly fashion. Some men will not experience the massive loss of coherence described in THE TWILIGHT ZONE until they are faced with the loss of a friend, the need to begin taking antiviral medication, the decline of T-cell counts into the 100 range, or some other triggering event. Some men will find out they are positive at the time of diagnosis. When this occurs elements of THE TWI-LIGHT ZONE and THE LONG HAUL are often observed as part of the initial and ongoing response to the diagnosis.

While the narrative endeavors to reflect the experience of testing HIV-positive as accurately as possible, it is still one person's construction or conceptual model about the experience. In reconstructing the experience, a decision was made to organize the data parallel to the prevalent model of disease progression in order to help guide and ground the reader. The data could have been organized independent of disease progression and indeed, one could conceptualize the experience as a series of fragmentations and the process of gradually regaining coherence. However, my experience as a clinician and a researcher indicates that infected men often have enough trouble placing themselves in relation to the disease and I did not want to present a model that may further compound the phenomenon.

Models of medical treatment of the disease continue to evolve. Some of the men in the study began antiviral medication when their T-cell counts approached the 200 range, while other men in the study began antivirals when their counts approached the 500 range. Prophylactic treatments for opportunistic infections are now a common aspect of treatment and continue to evolve. As the analysis and write-up of the data were concluding, the Berlin AIDS conference and the findings of the Concorde study created strong questions regarding the emerging paradigm of antiviral treatments and their effects on disease progression. Thus this model represents our understanding of HIV infection and the response of infected people in the years 1989 to 1993. Some aspects of the model may hold up over time, others may not. We will have to wait and see.

This book is intended to be read by professional and lay readers. How one reads the book and uses the information depends on the purpose for reading it. Clinicians are more apt to read the book straight through and may apply the conceptual models of the mind that they are most familiar with to the results and accounts of clinical intervention of men who experienced difficulty negotiating the experience of HIV infection. Friends and family of infected men are encouraged to read it from the vantage point of familiarizing themselves with the complex and often arduous experience of their loved ones. It may help them understand and be more empathically present for the evolution and transformation of the experience and how it is played out in relationships with people they know and love.

Men who know they are HIV-positive should read the book, especially the results chapters that follow. If it gets to be too much, put it down and take it up at a later date. I have learned that many of the men who read *If a Partner Has AIDS* approached the book in just that way. For some, looking to what lay ahead was too overstimulating, but as the experience progressed, they returned to the book to help understand what was happening to them. For HIV-positive readers, the hope is that the results chapters that follow will help in the struggle for coherence by offering a mirror of experience. I also hope they will provide a validation of its complexity and reassurance of the enormity of the psychological phenomenon that is being faced.

Chapter 4

The Great Debate

I had thought about it and dismissed it and thought about it and dismissed it. The whole cycle of trying to weigh the pros and cons.

Before actually being tested, gay men often have spent years wondering whether or not they are indeed positive. The AIDS/HIV epidemic has been an evolving, dynamic entity, and likewise the human mind is an evolving, dynamic entity. For many men, the debate began in the early 1980s, long before testing, when the media began reporting on the often gruesome illness that was affecting gay men. Many asked themselves, "Will I be next?" When it became clear that the disease was sexually transmitted, again the question of "me too?" was raised. The laboratory test for the presence of viral antibodies emerged several years into the epidemic and was initially designed to protect the blood supply, not as a diagnostic tool. At the time activists and the media urged gay men not to be tested for fear of reprisal. Medically, there was little to offer as well. While men watched friends die, the media reported on those urging quarantine and tatooing for those carrying the virus.

In the late 1980s, AZT came along and medical and political opinion began to shift. Early intervention with AZT appeared to offer prolonged life. Gay men were now being urged by their physicians, AIDS/HIV agencies, and the media to get tested; now there was hope. Initially AZT was licensed for those whose T-cell counts fell below 200. Several years later it was licensed for counts below 500. The campaign for testing began in earnest. The horror stories also emerged: children kicked out of schools, homes burned, men fired from jobs when their antibody status became known. The statistics also continued to climb. More men, more friends continued to die.

Against this background, private and public debates began, and anxiety ebbed and flowed. For some men anxiety reached enormous peaks, then declined into quiet resignation. For many, sadness mounted as friends succumbed and was mingled with anxious wondering about what would happen to them as the epidemic progressed. Men became less sure that they would be spared as more people became ill. Men also became more frightened and enraged as bigots vented their fear in the form of restrictive legislation or proselytizing that was often a mixture of homophobia and self-righteous indignation. Many times it was uncertain whether people were trying to protect the "general public" from AIDS or from homosexuality.

Deciding to be tested is a complicated and anxious process. Though men often debate privately for years, once the decision has been made, and they are on a trajectory for testing, it happens quite quickly when compared to the years of anxious wondering. The properties of this area, THE GREAT DEBATE, are:

- *Gathering Evidence*–the process of making assumptions of one's antibody status based on perceived similarity with infected or ill people;
- *Should I, Shouldn't I?*–weighing the pros and cons of finding out one's antibody status;
- *Established Dialogues*–when the debate takes place within established relationships;
- *Hard Evidence*–the emergence of evidence from physiological changes, medical sources, or actual contact with an ill or deceased person;
- *Conduit*–a person or persons serving to focus and channel anxiety and head a person on a trajectory for testing; and
- *Placing Bets*–individuals private assumptions regarding their status as they approach testing.

GATHERING EVIDENCE

What weighed on me was that I had been scared for a long time. First I had a friend die, then another. Then two months later I had two friends die.

When debating about testing, men often begin to collect evidence that may indicate whether they are infected or not. One source of evidence is identification–a perceived similarity with friends and in some cases, family: "Several old 'bar buddies' came down with PCP. I remembered all the carrying on we used to do. I figured if they had it, surely I did also." "When John became ill, I just knew I had it as well." For some men, the illness of family members indicates that it "is getting closer." "My brother died of AIDS several years back in the epidemic. At his funeral I kept wondering if I was next." "When Brian told me he had Aids Related Complex (ARC), I freaked; it felt like surely I had it if he did." These assumptions are based on perceived similarity, rather than on sexual contact or other risk factors with the ill or positive person. A lack of perceived similarity can help the person weigh evidence in the opposite direction. "He really carried on. I never had sex with all that many people." I latched onto the bit about 'frequent anonymous partners' and figured I would be okay." Other men may turn to other aspects of their history. "I was out of the country in the early eighties. That was the time it was going around and we did not know about it. When I came back, AIDS was in the news, and safer sex was the new thing. So I figured I missed it. If I had been here, knowing what I like to do, I would be very worried."

Men may gather considerable evidence that while terrifying, does not propel them into finding out if they are indeed infected. "I debated for years. I just was not ready to be tested." "Some friends had gotten tested and turned up positive. It scared me but that really did not matter–not enough to make me want to find out." The fear is not so much of being infected, but of finding out that one is dying. "I was scared to find out. I think it meant that I too would follow in their footsteps." "I did not want to find out that I was going to die–like Jim and Rich and, and, and." Often images of friends and their acute illnesses become the guiding force. "I watched friends–small infections here, there–then they increase and your body just disintegrates." "I kept looking at his history, how he fell apart, and wondering if that was going to happen to me."

SHOULD I, SHOULDN'T I?

A friend of mine and I talked about it a great deal. We were both so scared. Should we, shouldn't we? What are all the ramifications?

Part of the great debate is weighing the pros and cons. Rarely does the increasing evidence that early intervention in HIV infection often prolongs the length and quality of life outweigh the anticipated emotional impact. "I did not want to deal with the emotional trauma." Men may wonder: what is the point? "I felt there was nothing you could do. I am having safe sex–it won't do me any good to know." Men who have followed the progression and changing medical and political opinions regarding testing and treatment remember the days when the community was urged not to get tested. "Back in the eighties we were advised not to get tested because it could be used against you." They may recall media accounts. "The prejudice at that time was so high, you were considered a leper. The Jesse Helms of the world would have us all put in concentration camps." Men may also have encounters with professionals earlier in the epidemic that advised against testing. "My doc said he would do it, but that there was little he could do for me, and that I should think about all the worrying it may cause." "I got real worried reading about what was happening in New York and San Francisco so I went to Howard Brown and they asked, 'Do you do IV drugs? Do you and your partner play around?' I said, no, no, no. They said there was no reason to be tested, you're probably negative."

Clinical evidence began to mount that early intervention with AZT was effective in slowing the progression of HIV infection. Prophylactic treatments for PCP for people with T-cell counts below 200 emerged and became standard. Physicians who previously had not urged their patients to get tested until symptoms emerged "because there was not a whole lot that could be done," began to urge their patients to consider testing. Likewise the media and HIV/AIDS service organizations changed their stance.

Gradually many of the same people who had been actively discouraging were now encouraging men to find out if they were infected. Gay men now had a new set of data to consider. "You know, I think I longed for the days when we were told not to do it. Even though I am a health professional, and could distinguish between a medical argument and a political one, I took comfort in the political arguments. It took the pressure off me." The possibilites of prolonged life are balanced against the fear of trauma. "I read the articles urging people to get tested, that it could prolong life–somehow that did not mean as much as being traumatized by the news." "For me it was if I get tested and turn out positive, my self-worth would not be as great as it was. I went around and around on that issue for a year and a half."

Assurances of privacy that attempted to counter the horror stories in the media often offered little comfort. "I knew you could go down with an assumed name and get tested at a center, or my doctor kept a separate file–that no one would ever know. But hell, I would still know." Many men had the opportunity to find out for years before deciding they wanted to know. "I was in the Multi-Area-Cohort-Study (MACS) and was tested every six months. I had never asked for the results. I did not want to know." "I was in the MACS study for six years. I knew all along you could find out. I just never wanted to know."

Other men may cite other life considerations as indicating the need. "I was deciding whether or not to do a doctorate. I decided to get tested because if I was positive, there was no way I was going to put myself through that ordeal." "My company wanted to transfer me to Asia for a couple of years. I freaked. What if I got sick in Asia? All of a sudden I had to know." For some men anxiety and preoccupation increases until the anxiety of not knowing outweighs the anxiety of knowing. "I just got more and more preoccupied and worried. I thought everything was a sign of AIDS. Finally I had enough and decided to settle it." "After so many years of not wanting to know–of hemming and hawing–I just had to know. It was starting to make me crazy."

ESTABLISHED DIALOGUES

It was the debate, at times, argument in our household for quite awhile.

When gay men are part of an established relationship, the potential implications are felt not just for one man, but for himself and the relationship. The concern becomes not just for himself, but for his partner and their dialogue. People approach testing on highly personalized time lines. At times one man may be in a different place from the other. "I never really thought about it. I had a lover for one and a half years. He was very negatively into the idea of positive or negative. He was very paranoid. He would bug me about it–wanting us to go get tested together." "One day out of the blue he announced that he wanted to get tested and wanted me to as well. I freaked. I had always not wanted to know. I was afraid, but he kept hammering away at me." Knowing the way his partner handles stress may serve to make a partner reluctant to proceed with testing. "He was afraid he would be positive and that his life would go down the tubes. Knowing him, I was afraid his life would go down the tubes and I did not want to be a part of it." If one partner is more bent on getting tested, he may try ways to cajole the reluctant partner. "We had been playing very safe. I tried pointing out all the things we had not been doing, that we could do, if we were both negative. He did not buy it." Some partners may try to find ways of deflecting the issue. "My lover kept saying, 'We should be checked for AIDS.' I was very inappropriate with him. The first thing I said was, 'What, have you been fooling around on me?' "

One partner may point out evidence that the other does not want to see. "I pointed out that his ex had died of AIDS and that he may have picked it up from him, and he still refused." Conflicts around testing may become quite intense. "It makes me so angry that he refuses to deal with it." "He kept carrying on about it and I finally started screaming at him to leave me alone." The conflict may spill over and be understood and debated within the context of other relationship dynamics and conflicts. "It is just like him, always sweeping things under the rug." "I felt backed into a corner. When he decides to do something he just does it. I pleaded that this was not like getting a new car, or changing the color of the wall–this is our life."

Concerns for the relationship may be raised. "He was afraid that he would be positive and that I would be negative and that I would leave him–actually I was afraid of the reverse, and that he would leave me." The relationship may have reached a comfortable equilibrium, and the fear becomes upsetting the balance in the dialogue. "We had great plans. I thought about how happy I was, and we were–being together, making a family. I did not want to have it wrecked; I did not want that kind of trauma in our lives." "It really did not seem fair that we had to deal with this issue–one of us getting sick and dying, or worrying about one of us getting sick and dying." Often after some debate, the issue is resolved. "He pushed for it; I did not want to go. Finally we went together."

Some couples may approach testing as a part of establishing a relationship. "We had been together for three months and were both wanting to be a couple, to make it permanent. It was scary but if felt like the right thing to do." For some new couples, testing may be the first intense conflict they will face. "Out of the blue he said, 'Let's get tested.' I said I was not ready to deal with that. He got very angry and started carrying on about committment. I said, 'Committment–We have been dating for six weeks!' " Some couples may take comfort in the relationship and its capacity to sustain each other, no matter what the trauma. "We talked it over a great deal. The bottom line was that we loved each other a great deal, and felt secure that the other would be there, no matter what." Still others may take security in the relationship in such a way that they avoid testing. "My partner and I were already together. We were already in a commited relationship, so the consequences were what the consequences were. If one of us was positive, so was the other. If one of us got sick, the other would be there."

Some men approach testing in the wake of the breakup of a relationship. "I was just out of a relationship, and before I went on to meet new people I wanted to find out–to protect myself and them." "I figured that since I was going out on the market again, I probably ought to find out what my status was." Other men may approach testing in the context of self-esteem issues following a traumatic breakup. "I was miserable from a breakup. I guess I just wanted to make myself more miserable." "My lover of four years and I had just broken up. That had wiped out my self-esteem. I figured, what do I have to lose?"

For some men, the testing may be related to anger and resentment toward the former partner. "I broke up with him because I finally realized and faced the fact that he was a sex addict. I felt the son of a bitch was not only tricking out on me, but he probably gave me AIDS." "After we broke up I started to find out that he was fucking around all over town. I thought we were monagamous. I thought,

'Good God, what did he catch and give me, on top of making my life miserable?' "

Debates often occur in established friendships. "There for awhile everyone was talking about it–should we, shouldn't we, so and so says, my doc said–back and forth, back and forth." "It was a steady topic at a lot of dinner parties–back before people here started getting sick in droves." Some debates in friendship groups may become quite intense. "It got pretty wild a couple of times–the 'no testers' verses the 'go-out-and-do-it-tomorrow camp.'" Some debates may be more quiet and subdued. "It was a sensitive subject matter. No one really wanted to deal with it or face it, and they knew they were ultimately talking about themselves. Sometimes it felt like we were all walking on eggshells."

HARD EVIDENCE

I found myself feeling fatigued. A change in appetite, changes in body functions. It just seemed that something was not right, like an internal mechanism telling me that something wasn't right. It was time to get it checked out.

Some men may encounter a different kind of evidence: a seemingly clear indication that something is wrong with them; that their body is just not functioning as they are accustomed or that they have developed one of the many problems associated with immune deficiency. "I have always had eczema and psoriasis, but it became overwhelming–it was quite noticeable. I was getting more and more depressed. It was time to stop wondering." "I was developing thrush, but nothing that would stay around. After awhile, I was feeling worse and decided it was time to consult a professional." Other men may encounter evidence from other forms of testing. "I was in the MACS study and they were encouraging everyone to at least find out their T-cell count. Low and behold over the past three cycles I had a precipitous drop in my count–1400, 800, 500. They said it certainly looked like a trend."

Other men encounter evidence from the illness of men with whom they had past relationships. "I got a call from my ex who had moved to California. He had just gotten out of the hospital with

PCP. I kept going back and forth from being worried about him, to panicked about myself." "I opened the newspaper one day and there was the obituary of an old boyfriend of mine. We had had a wild, passionate affair. I thought, 'Oh Shit!'" Some may find the evidence in their current partner. "I got tested when it finally came about. At the time my partner was ill with AIDS. He died four months later." "Stan had just been diagnosed and I was in shock. They said I should take this test. I did and then–boom!" For some men, the evidence may come from multiple directions. "In the wake of the drop in T cells I decided to wait and see what the next count would be. While waiting I got a call from a woman in Seattle saying that a former lover of mine had died of AIDS. So between that and the decline in T cells I went into a real panic." "Several former lovers had died, plus I had these rashes that would not go away."

CONDUIT

I went in to see my doc just for a routine checkup for work. He started talking about HIV testing. I had been worrying on and off for years and resisting, but just the way he said things–the anxiety declined and it felt like the right thing to do.

Many men encounter a person or persons who serve as a conduit. They help channel the debate, at times defusing the anxiety, and head the person on the trajectory for testing. The people who serve as conduits can be physicians, therapists, partners, or friends, usually someone with whom the person has a trusting relationship. "I came down with gonorrhea. My doc looked at me and said, 'You know, you better get tested.'" "I was at the doctor's office for something else. He calmly said that it would be a good idea. There was no indication that I was positive, but that in case I was, we had therapies now that could help a lot. All of a sudden it seemed the right thing to do." Some men after considerable debate may ask their doctor. "His stance was that you should know as much about it as you can so you can take precautionary steps to protect yourself. I think I was struck by the novelty of his approach. I had been so worried about being discriminated against that it never dawned on me that it was self-protective. Anyway, I decided to go ahead and do it."

Some men may find out via a change in policy in one of the many ongoing studies of gay men. When people feel forced into testing they often feel anger and rage, while considerable anxiety is often present, but the anger dominates. "When I joined the study, we had the option of finding out our test results or not. Midway through, I got a letter saying that the powers that be had decided to make finding out your antibody status a condition for remaining in the study. I was told I had to be told. I was furious and freaked." Men in these predicaments may seek out someone to serve as conduit for their mixed anger and anxiety. "I talked to a guy at the clinic a number of times over the phone. He went on and on about monitoring and drugs; I went on about confidentiality. Finally I gave in."

Just as two men in an established relationship may serve to guide each other into testing, friends may also serve the role of conduit for men who do not know their status. "My friend was literally blown away when he came back positive. I was giving him a lot of support. That is what tipped the scales–our interaction around his experience." "One friend came back negative, another came back positive. They were both interested in having me test." Some friends can be quite insistent. "A couple of friends of mine had both tested positive. They kept saying I should go in. They finally wore me down, but I went in kicking and screaming." And some friends join together the way partners often do. "A friend of mine and I went back and forth. Finally we decided to go and be tested together."

Men who are in ongoing psychotherapy may use the therapist as the conduit. "I knew it was something I should do. My therapist made it easier to physically go and do it." Sometimes the dialogue between patient and therapist may be quite long and elaborate. "He was pretty patient. I went around and around on it for months. I would make an appointment to get tested, then cancel it. Finally I got there."

Still other men may feel forced into testing by insurance companies. "I applied for life insurance. They wanted blood tests and all of that, so I went ahead. When I was denied the insurance I knew what was going on." When men feel forced by insurance companies and the inherent threats to privacy, anger is again mixed with anxiety. "I was moving into private practice and applied for insurance through the National Association of Social Workers. The year before I had applied and was accepted right off the bat, but I had a change of plans and did not need the insurance. The same medical history as the year before, only this time they wanted me to be tested. I was furious. I felt forced into it. I had myself tested first to see if I wanted to send in the samples for the insurance company. I raised hell all up and down NASW. The president was mighty angry and appalled. Everybody else sounded concerned but just said tsk, tsk, tsk. I finally found out the truth. All of those bleeding-heart social workers at NASW wanted to protect the integrity of their insurance program, and if that meant denying insurance, that is what it meant."

Other men may be tested due to non-HIV-related medical necessity. "I was involved in a major car wreck and in critical condition. I had to go on dialysis. Part of their testing for that was HIV–they said to protect the next person who used the machine. I wanted to live, so I said go ahead."

PLACING BETS

In the back of my mind there was a maybe–maybe I wasn't. But I didn't think that it was much likely.

As men come close to being tested they often begin to place bets on whether they are positive or negative. More often than not, men tend to assume they are positive. In a very real sense, being tested is also testing one's assumptions about antibody status. "I just sorta knew I was positive before being tested–just because of my lifestyle." "I figured I was positive, so I guess I was going in to find out that I was, indeed, positive."

The prime source of evidence for the assumption of positivity is past sexual encounters, the timing of the activity, and preferences for sexual acts considered to be the highest risk for contracting the HIV virus. "I was a real slut at one point in the glorious seventies." "I was pretty promiscuous–and anal receptive. I came out in 1979, and I figured with the kind of things I had done, the chances were good." For some men, the assumption of being positive is quite strong. "I was 99 percent sure I was positive." "I went ahead and was tested, though I had strong suspicions I was positive because of my past sexual history."

However, a few of the men in the study did assume they were negative. "I was 99 percent certain I was negative because all I ever had was oral sex." Interestingly, only one man referred to the test as an it–a result on a piece of paper–versus *I*. "I was assuming it would be negative; I was very careful." The power of the information goes far beyond a test result. "It is not just a test. It's your life–or death."

Despite one's assumptions, the evidence, the illness of friends, men often hold out for some hope that they will indeed be negative. "It was only 1 percent but I hoped that the 1 percent would be true." "I really hoped that I would be one of the lucky few who escaped."

Chapter 5

Truth and Consequences

While waiting for the results, I was preparing myself for either answer–walks on the beach and so on.

TRUTH AND CONSEQUENCES encompasses the period of time between being tested, waiting, and being informed of the results. Depending on the testing site, the wait tends to be from 48 hours to several weeks. For many men the wait is an anxious one. Along with the anxiety are attempts to modulate the fear, until the answer is known. The properties of TRUTH AND CONSEQUENCES are:

- *Waiting*–the period while waiting for results to come back;
- *Reviewing the Evidence*–further attempts to determine chances of being positive or negative;
- *The Messenger and the Message*–the conveyance of test results;
- *Positive*–the initial responses of men who test positive;
- *Negative*–the initial responses of men who test negative; and
- *I Think I Am Still*–the experience of testing negative as subject to change.

WAITING

The couple weeks waiting I was scared shitless.

The period between the time the sample is drawn or in the case of ongoing studies, the appointment to find out what one's antibody status has been all along, is often an anxious one. Men find their anxiety growing, "I was terrified" and find their own unique ways of modulating anxiety such as walks on the beach as in the opening quote of this chapter, or other ways. "I am a writer. I was so scared that I started keeping a diary. I thought, at least if it is bad news I could write about it, and maybe put it to good use."

Men often sense the enormity of the information they are about to receive and a strong forboding may emerge. "It felt like one of those crossroads in life." "I knew my life was going to be different after I found out–enormously so–but how to prepare? Part of me wanted to don a monk's robe, and meditate in an ancient monastery with Gregorian chants echoing through, until I was called with the verdict–gee, kinda sounds like the last judgement doesn't it?" Questions often race through men's minds. "Who do I tell? What about my partner?" Men may feel their situations are quite precarious. "I am a freelancer. How will I make a living? I had no savings. What about insurance?"

The differences in waiting times can be experienced as a burden or a blessing. "Two weeks was just too long. Too much time to think. At first I thought it would be plenty of time to get my head together, but then it just wore on." In contrast, a shorter time may feel too brief. "When the doc said the results would be back in forty-eight hours, I was relieved, but as soon as I got home, I panicked. I did not have enough time to prepare."

REVIEWING THE EVIDENCE

I was making myself crazy. My entire sexual history passed before my eyes–what was the answer going to be?

While waiting for test results, men may find themselves reviewing the same evidence they had previously reviewed while debating whether or not to be tested. "I tried to think of every time I had anal intercourse, with who, and if they were still healthy." "I found myself thinking, 'there was Chuck the time we stayed at the B&B in Michigan, that hot high school football coach. . . .'" Some men may feel comfortable once they believe they have accounted for all past experiences only to find another piece of damning evidence. "Oh shit, I forgot about Key West." "The football coach was from San Jose; I bet he went to San Francisco a lot!" For some men, reviewing the evidence can become a highly consuming activity.

"It's not just further attempts–it's *concentrated*. You remember those times in Key West and a shudder goes through your body."

Reassuring evidence is also reviewed. "I did not do all that much." "I was mainly into oral sex." Men may also turn to statistics. "I thought: let's see, they estimate fifty percent positive in San Francisco, thirty percent positive in Chicago. I don't recall having sex with anyone while I was in San Francisco, so that leaves Chicago. That means I had a seventy percent chance of being with people who were negative."

Men may also find guilty ruminations. "I don't know where my head was at. Going to Key West, partying around the clock, wondering who I would meet next." Some men may also fear they are about to be caught. "I thought: well, all your sleaziness is about to catch up with you."

Superstitious thinking may also evolve. "I really thought I would be negative, but then I thought: you better not be too sure, else you will be positive." "I finally decided I should just keep it in the middle, perhaps then it won't hurt so much." Men who have considerable direct evidence for infection may be soundly assured they are positive but still hold out. "Bart's test came back positive, so I knew what I was going to be, but I held out for that tiny possibility." Some men in relationships feel it would be betrayal to wish that they would be spared. "I found myself hoping I would be negative, then I was horrified. How could I think that with John positive and having to start AZT?"

As they approach finding out lab results men enter with a range of assumptions regarding their status. Some are convinced they are positive. "The day I went in for my results, I knew. . . ." Others are certain that they are negative. "I really thought: no problem, you're safe." Others are somewhere in the middle. "Bottom line, I felt it was fifty/fifty."

THE MESSENGER AND THE MESSAGE

It really was not handled well at all. He just very casually said, "You're positive."

Men rarely experience that the person who informs them of their seropositivity is being empathic enough. Clearly some people are able to break the news more gently than others, and some are quite bumbling. But in general, one often sees a confusion between the messenger and the message, especially when the news is not that the person is negative. Clearly the news is traumatic, and some messengers add to the trauma with the manner in which they convey their message. "The doctor said to me as casually as if I had a cold, 'You're positive; you are contaminated.'" When men feel forced into testing via a change in study policy or by insurance companies, the rage they felt at being forced is often focused on the messenger. "He said, 'You're positive.' I wanted to throw him up against the wall." "I got a letter back from the insurance company saying that I was rejected. I knew what was going on; I wanted to blow up their headquarters." Though there have been attempts to legislate procedure for informing people of their status, it appears that rarely is it followed. "There was no counseling. It was, 'Here is your information; You're positive. You have a count of 890–nothing to worry about. Good-bye.'"

The results tend to be conveyed in a variety of ways depending on the agency or situation. "I went in and there was the guy with an envelope that contained my testing results since the study began. I was supposed to open it in front of him. It all felt very strange." "I am sitting there with this stranger and the envelope. I thought: gee, the first time in my life an envelope is being opened to see if I am a winner, and this is what it is about."

Men tend to feel horribly abandoned and enraged when the messenger fails to spend time with them, to empathize with their distress, or actively avoids them. "He came in all cheery and said, 'Hi, I am Doctor Bob' but he was more anxious than I was. I don't know who wanted to get out of there faster, me or him." Men also become angry if there is another agenda for the messenger. "When I went in, he said they were doing a study, and that before he gave me the results I had to answer a few questions. The last one was, 'Do you think you are positive or negative?' I said I did not know and he got very pushy and said he had to have an answer. I got pissed and said, 'Okay, I think I am negative. Now will you give me my results?'" If their distress is not handled appropriately anger can again result. "This idiot was supposedly a psychologist. I am sitting there devastated and he says, 'You're not suicidal or anything are you?'"

For some men, the news was totally unexpected, and was conveyed outside of the context of deciding to be tested. "I was going in for the next procedure of plastic surgery. The day before I was to have it done, the surgeon's office called me on my car telephone and said that my bloodwork indicated that I was HIV-positive and that they were canceling the procedure." Unexpected encounters can be horribly disorganizing. "I went to this dermatologist for this rash I was having. He took one look at it and said, 'You're HIV positive. This is HIV related.' I freaked. I subsequently found out that he is notorious for doing that to people." It can be especially traumatizing when the messengers are totally unaquainted with HIV and make their anxiety known, and even more so when the message is accompanied by a rejection. "I was in the hospital after a car wreck. They called me into this meeting and there were seven people sitting around the room. One of the doctors I had seen for a total of ten minutes. I did not know who the rest of them were, or why they were there. They brought me in, sat me down, 'We have something to tell you. You are HIV-positive, and you have to leave the hospital by six o'clock tonight–you do not have any insurance.' Well, I did have insurance and tried to say so, but that was it. The meeting was over, and they all got up and left."

For some men, the relationship with the messenger is never quite the same. "My doctor called me and told me my results. I was really upset and angry. He left kind of abruptly. After that it never felt comfortable with him. I decided to switch doctors." "I met with this therapist at the clinic before and he gave me the envelope with my results. I kind of liked him the first time. After I got the results he gave me his card and said to call him, but I just did not want to face him again." For some men who had a long-standing, comfortable relationship with their physician, this may be the first time they felt traumatized by him. "It took me awhile to get comfortable with him again after that. I kept worrying that he was going to have more bad news."

Other men reported quite different experiences with the messenger–one that they felt helped to minimize the impact and provided them with an idealizable figure from the start. These men tend to have fond memories of the messenger, rather than anger. "The lady who told me that I was HIV-positive also told me that she was dealing with terminal cancer. We talked for an hour–even went out and had lunch a few times." "He told me and it just seared right through me. But he talked with me, told me about TPA, and got me hooked up with a good therapist. I have always appreciated the way he helped me out right from the beginning." "My doctor spent a lot of time with me and said he wanted to see me next week. When I came back, he came in with an armload of information for me to read."

POSITIVE

It opened up a nightmare.

For many men, no matter what the preparation or level that they have reconciled to being positive, being informed that tests indicate one is indeed positive is devastating news. Men report feeling intensely sad: "I cried." "I was crushed." "I was devastated and panicked." "When I was not crying, I was freaking out." Some are not able to contain their sorrow. "We left the doctor's office and I sat down on Michigan Avenue and cried."

Some men feel that their life has come to an abrupt end. "I had a lover, the house. We pretty much had everything we wanted. Then there was an abrupt stop to all of it." Some men find the way in which the message was delivered dominates their experience. "He said I was 'contaminated.' That absolutely freaked me out. The word stood out–*contaminated*–like a dirty object. For months I kept remembering him saying the word, and feeling every bit like a contaminated thing."

Men often have intense fears of being rejected. "The fears I had up front were that someone would discover this and I would be denied my insurance rights." Men who actually were rejected upon being informed are relieved when someone is able to respond appropriately to them. "So they kicked me out of Loyola Medical Center. As I was packing up, crying and confused, a nurse came in and said, 'They are real homophobic here. I'm really sorry this is happening.' Then the ambulance took me to Northwestern and the Doc in the emergency room said that what they did really stunk, and yes I had insurance and they admitted me."

Some men go into a high degree of confusion. "I must have gone into shock when the Doc called me on Thursday. I called him back on Saturday and said, 'I thought you were going to call me with the results.' He said, 'Barry, I already told you the results.' " Others look to life situations they are currently involved in and wonder how they will make it. "I thought: What is next, Lord?" "I was just out of a relationship, my son had just moved in with me, and *then* I found out I was positive." Some may initially question whether to continue with ongoing pursuits. "There I was in graduate school. I wondered: Is all of this really worth it?" Other men may not believe the results. "I got tested three more times before I finally believed that I was positive." Some men find out in the wake of their partner being diagnosed. In these instances, men often table their concerns. "I just put it on the shelf. Brad was real sick, and there were more important things to worry about."

NEGATIVE

It was a great relief. I promptly went out and got drunk.

When men test negative there is often a great sense of relief. "Whew, I really had managed to convince myself that I was positive." "My doctor called me when I was with a client. When I heard his voice I looked across the room at the person I was working with and panicked. I said I would have to call him back. When I got him he said, 'You are the second person today I get to tell that they are negative.' "

Many men feel that they have to contain their relief. "I told several of my straight friends first. I did not want to risk offending anyone." I was so happy but then I felt guilty. My roommate had tested positive, and had been a mess for months. I really did not want to tell him." Some men find that friends who are positive have trouble with the news. "I told Bill and he just said, 'Oh.' " "I really found myself wondering who it would be appropriate to tell."

After several weeks of anxious wondering men find their lives returning to their usual concerns. "All of a sudden I was back to my usual worries." "Well, I guess I do not have an excuse not to go back for my doctorate."

A kind of existential crisis may emerge as men ponder why they have been spared. "It is mysterious, yet another former lover has AIDS. If I made a list of all of my serious relationships, the majority are dead, or dying. I do not know–I have always been pretty healthy–guess I have a good constitution. I never got amoebas, but everything else–syphilis, gonorrhea, crabs, hepatitis–but not this." While men who test positive often struggle with the psychological impact, men who test negative may have to struggle with, "Why was I spared?" "Several weeks after I tested negative, I was out partying and ran into an old boyfriend. He took me aside and told me that he had been diagnosed several months earlier. I was devastated for him, but it also threw me for a loop. He was on my list of possible 'transmission episodes.' He was sick, and I was negative and he fucked me. I felt like there had been bullets flying around me for years, and for some reason they had missed me. Fortunately, a friend of mine who was also negative happened to call while I was still spinning. He knew exactly where I was coming from."

Once they have taken the first step, some men make regular testing a part of their routine. "I get tested every six months. It is just something I do." For these men, testing appears to have a calming and reassuring effect. "I have lost so many friends, even exes and continue to lose people or hear about people being sick. I get tested regularly." "I kept getting tested every three months. I play very safe and never liked–in fact I hate–anal intercourse. Top, bottom, condom or not. Finally my doc asked me why I kept doing this." In sharp contrast to those who debate for years, some men cannot tolerate not knowing. "I want to know. I have to know for certain. I do not get just the Elisa; I get the Polymorphase Chain Reaction test–the one that tests for DNA. It is a lot more expensive, but it is the most accurate."

I THINK I AM STILL . . .

Well, I think I am still negative.

Men tend to think of being positive as a "steady state" that cannot be taken away, no matter how hard they wish. They are stuck with it. They are on a trajectory that they cannot get off. In sharp contrast, testing negative is often not viewed as such a sure thing, especially if the person is sexually active. "I got a high fever, and flu symptoms that would just not go away. I started worrying all over again. I have played safe for a long time, but there is always the possibility." "I get tested every six months to make sure I am still negative." Some men may find the whole cycle repeating itself. "I really should go back in and be tested. I am wondering about it all over again. I do not want to face being positive after all of these years." "I find myself thinking about the times that there could have been a leak in the condom." As the epidemic progresses, men often encounter the loss of still more friends and the wondering and anxiety again emerges. "I guess it is weighing on me again. The other night I dreamed that I had eight T cells."

Chapter 6

The Twilight Zone

It's like living in the twilight zone.

After testing positive, many men enter a period of great turmoil. Anxiety, fear, and confusion often dominate their experience. What seemed real, certain, and predictable before, now appears foreign. The basic experience of self is changed. Profound fear and vulnerability, a strong sense of being damaged, isolated, and terminally ill can come to dominate the person's experience. As the above quote states, many men describe the upheaval in this area as living in a twilight zone. The sense of future–the assumption that life is an ongoing, unfolding, infinite progression is lost. Men may feel that death and illness are imminent. Men may be so caught up in the experience that they do not realize the extent to which their experience of self and the world has changed. What they are aware of is the chaos that can come to dominate their lives.

The emergence of the chaotic experience of self so central to THE TWILIGHT ZONE does not necessarily proceed in an orderly temporal sequence. Some men will experience the constellations of feelings and thoughts immediately after being tested. Entry into this area may be delayed for months or years for some men. The central psychological experience of this area is the loss of the familiar ongoing experience of self and the need to reconcile the interjection of being positive and its implications.

The properties of *THE TWILIGHT ZONE* are:

- *Waking Up*–the emergence of the constellation of feelings and thoughts of this area,
- *A Great Fear*–the fear of dying that often comes to dominate one's experience;

- *Alone in the Storm*–a profound sense of isolation;
- *Damaged Goods*–the sense of being less than, of being diminished;
- *Nightmares Revisited*–the reawakening of and comparison to past traumatic events;
- *Loss of Future*–the loss of the sense of future;
- *Spinning Wheels*–the state of disorganization and attempts to calm;
- *Despair*–the profound feeling of hopelessness that can emerge;
- *Sexual Dialogues*–the often profound changes in the experience of the sexual self;
- *Helpers*–interactions with people that help calm, soothe, and reassure; and
- *Spoilers*–interactions with people who by their actions stir up affect, enhance damaged self-esteem and uncertainty.

WAKING UP

I did not really go through wondering and truth and consequences. About six months after Stan died, I woke up in the middle of it.

Men who were tested in the midst of the illness of a partner or close friend often do not experience the two preceeding areas. "After Stan was diagnosed, his doctor wanted me to be tested. I was positive, but I was more worried about Stan." "I was Cal's closest friend and took care of him while he was sick. We both had the same doc and he wanted me to be tested also." "In these situations the focus is often on the partner or friend. I really did not think twice about it. There was so much going on with trying to take care of Stan, and being so devastated that I was going to lose him." "It was such a nightmare–so much to try and set up for him, trying to care for him in between hospital stays."

For these men the emergence of this area often occurs about six months into the mourning process. "I was just starting to feel a bit more stable after Stan died, then one day I woke up and realized that I was positive, that the same thing was going to happen to me." "I never had asked what my results were. Back then there was no AZT so I did not bother and I told my doc I did not want to know. Six months after Cal died I started wondering and getting scared. I asked if I was positive and Wham! I just lost it."

Men who enter the experience in this manner are faced with mourning their partner and trying to make sense of being positive at the same time. "I really was a mess for awhile. Stan was dead; I was positive. My life just seemed to be constantly falling apart." "There were many times I was not sure what was going on. Was I freaking out over the loss of Stan, or freaking out because I was positive?" For these men the loss of the partner will be a powerful image as they negotiate their own experience of being positive.

A GREAT FEAR

There was a really short period when I was angry. It quickly turned into tears and a great fear.

Fear is often highly prevalent, if not dominant in the twilight zone. "I was sacred shitless." The fear of following in the steps of so many others: friends, partners, the faces on the obituary page. The fear of becoming ill and dying and just how soon it will be. "I found out in March. I knew I would not make it until Christmas." Men may feel they have been sentenced. "This is a death warrant for me. Just as the judge would tell a convicted prisoner—you are going to be executed." Being informed that one is positive is often experienced as a confirmation of the fear of becoming ill and dying. The messenger has confirmed the fear, and the person is now on a terrifying journey, for which there is only one way out. "As soon as I found out I was positive, I realized how horrendous it was. That I was going to get sick and die." "It is the ultimate. You are going to die in that prison, one way or the other."

While testing positive is often initially perceived as a death sentence, it is a sentence without a definite date of execution. Men may search for markers, signs of the beginning of the end. "At least the condemned prisoner knows when he is going to die. I don't. I live with the fear every day. A pimple, is this the beginning of my downfall? Is this pneumocystus or just a cold, or is it some other of the twenty opportunistic infections that will attack my body?" "Shortly after I tested positive, I got bronchitis. I was so afraid that it was beginning already–that this is what my life would be like from now on." The fear may only be enhanced as men look to their previous experience with friends who tested positive. "Everybody who is HIV-positive that I know eventually dies of the disease. If there were just *one*–I would be a little more hopeful." Men may find fear at every turn. So much so that they long for a retreat. "There are times when I wish I could go and hide." Some men anxiously anticipate the future. "I spent a lot of time trying to figure out what my life would be like until it ends."

ALONE IN THE STORM

I just felt like I could not touch anybody. I felt more removed from the center of society. I felt out of it, alone.

Men often find themselves feeling very much alone. A profound sense of isolation can ensue. Some men who have struggled throughout their lives with feelings of aloneness, of being different, now find these feelings returning with a vengeance. "I have felt alone and outcast a great deal of my life; my own mother did not want me. But never this intense."

The sense of isolation is often far reaching from the broadest social context, to established relationships. "I felt like a social outcast, an untouchable, like I had been banished to an island in the middle of nowhere." "All of a sudden, I felt like a minority within a minority. A lot of gay people do not want to deal with this, they want to pretend it does not exist."

Men may feel cut off from established friendships. "I felt like I no longer fit in." "I was at a dinner party with some long-time friends a few weeks after testing positive. I found myself feeling like a stranger, that they were strangers. What would they say, think, do, if they knew I was positive?" If the confirmation of seropositivity comes in the wake of the breakup of a relationship, then the isolation can again be compounded. "Over the years of my relationship, my friendship circle condensed considerably. We broke up, then I tested positive. All of a sudden I found myself in a situation where I felt incredibly alone." If seropositivity was a factor in the breakup, and the person is not comfortable revealing his status to friends, then again the isolation is compounded. "What really brought it to the surface was when I broke up with Ed and I could not tell anyone the real reasons. I could not tell my story."

Men who are used to the companionship of an ongoing relationship, but now are without that dialogue, may find themselves yearning for it. "I feel more alone now without anyone at my side than I have ever felt in my life—and I have felt very alone in my life." "Most of my last twenty-five years has been spent in relationships. I don't think it is just the HIV, it is also that there is not another person to share with and get some satisfaction out of life."

Men who are single may now feel that the possibility of a relationship—a sense of family—is cut off from them. "I was walking along a beach. I would see families—parents and children playing together, and I thought, 'Gee, I will never have that.' But I did not really want that; I wanted some aspect of it." "When I first tested positive, there was this knee jerk thought that I was now cut off from meeting anyone with whom I could develop a relationship." Men may abandon efforts that they were engaged in that were in the service of establishing a relationship. "The primary goal of my therapy was to straighten out my whatever so that I could find a good relationship. Well, I thought: I am HIV-positive, ready to die, looking for a relationship; this is ridiculous. So I terminated treatment."

Men in established relationships may also feel isolated. "I tested positive, he tested negative. I really felt cut off from him, that he did not understand what I was going through." "After a couple of weeks of being a mess, I could tell that he was starting to get impatient. On one hand I was angry, feeling that he did not care; on the other I was frightened that he was going to drop me."

The social stigma of HIV and AIDS often compounds the isolation and deprives people of social support. "One of my coworkers just came down with MS. In a way I am jealous. He has been getting all of the sympathy. He can announce it." "My boss developed a brain tumor. The whole office knew about it every step of the way—the diagnosis, the surgery, his recovery. I wondered what would happen to me if I announced that I was positive." Societal messages may come at any time. "I was at the funeral of a friend who had died of a brain tumor. I overheard his parents say, 'Well at least it was cancer and not AIDS.' How can you say that about your child?"

For some men, testing positive can serve to confirm societal messages about homosexuality. "It was an extension of the 'bad' things about being gay. It was like I heard these words, 'If you are going to be gay, this is the kind of thing that is going to happen to you.' You end up not having a disease, but being a 'bad' person who got what he deserved."

DAMAGED GOODS

I feel like there is this bug crawling around in me, and who wants damaged goods?

Men may find a deep sense of being damaged, of being less than, evolving. This sense of being flawed, and infectious, can become a painful aspect of self-experience. Often it emerges in the context of relationships–that "no one would want to have anything to do with me." "Now that I am sick, positive, whatever . . . who would want me? I would be afraid to give this to someone." Men may find themselves feeling like lepers. "It is the leprosy of the nineties. And I have it." The sense of being damaged can reach profound levels. "I felt like a filthy, wretched piece of shit. I had sort of lost any humanity about myself."

Long-standing or past feelings about being damaged, or not good enough may reawaken. "When I was a kid I found out I had epilepsy, that something was wrong with my brain. It was a family secret. Now this feels just like the epilepsy, only worse." In childhood homosexual men were often subject to being labeled as different and at times attacked. "As a kid I was always being made fun of, called a sissy, a fag. I finally learned to feel comfortable with myself and feel like I belonged. Now any good feelings have been taken away."

The sense of being infectious can come to dominate with the messenger's message coming to be the central metaphor. "The doctor's words kept going around in my head, 'You are positive; you are contaminated.'" It can also emerge at unexpected times. "The other night I masturbated. Afterward, I looked at my cum and thought, 'It is full of virus, it's poison. I could kill someone.'" An intense prohibition against sex, and an assumption of unworthiness may evolve. "I want to be in a relationship, but that has been taken away. I feel that it is not allowed."

NIGHTMARES REVISITED

There were some traumatic events in my past–but this is it. This is the worst event. It has changed my life.

Men may find past traumatic events in their lives being reawakened. The feelings and memories of the events may be evoked and compared. "I sort of knew the worst thing in my life was Vietnam–watching friends get killed–having their blood and pieces of their flesh splatter on your face. When I found out I was HIV-positive, I realized it was not." "When I was twenty-one, I got caught in a machine. I had eighteen operations on my hand."

Invariably, these events have been past experiences, lived through, and though at times men may have been certain they were going to die, or be maimed, men have lived through them; they have survived. "In Vietnam, I was lost in the jungle for a few days. Talk about a horrifying experience. There are leeches, ants, snakes, and people that can and will kill you. But I survived. I made it out. There is no way out of this." "Before I went into surgery, the doc said I would probably lose three fingers. I came out with all five. That was the bleakest period of my life. But I made it."

LOSS OF THE FUTURE

Getting sick and dying feels like it is right over there.

As human beings we are accustomed to a sense of future. A bedrock assumption that life is an ever-unfolding process. We plan ahead, we anticipate future events, we have goals, plans for reaching them, and we have dreams. When this sense of future is challenged, as in the case of seropositivity, the mind tends to assume that life could be over at anytime. The sense of future seems to be (save perhaps in later adulthood) an all-or-nothing proposition. Life and the future is either infinite, or could abruptly end at any time.

After testing positive, men often find their sense of future suddenly contracting if not disappearing. "I remember when I first got my test results I was certain I was going to die next month. I was ready." "I felt like life was just over for me–that this was the end." Just as men may assume that the possibility of a relationship and sense of family are cut off from them, other dreams and plans lose their appeal. "I would just start crying. I felt like, well, why am I bothering to finish this house? I am HIV-positive. I am going to die." "There I was slaving away in grad school. What is the point, you're dying. You're spending all of this time and money. I may not even be able to finish."

The loss of the sense of future can have a subtle to profound impact on the experience of life. "I felt trapped and put into a corner. It speeds everything up–there is a reality change." "Life does not change, but your perception, your involvement in life changes." The loss of future is a key element in the experience of being seropositive. Over the course of the experience one hears about the sense of future initially imploding, then gradually expanding. This sense tends to expand and contract over the course of the experience. "I would settle down and think: I am ok, everything is going to be all right–then bam!" "Initially the doors close and everything comes rushing forward like a time compression. Then it eventually opens back up." The experiences that facilitate the expansion and disruption of the sense of future will be explored in the next chapter, *THE LONG HAUL.*

SPINNING WHEELS

There was a point that I felt that I had lost control.

The hallmark of THE TWILIGHT ZONE is the often intense disorganization that tends to occur following testing positive. Some men will not experience this disorganization immediately. For some men the disorganization will occur farther into the experience–in the wake of the death of a friend, the need to begin antiviral treatment, or in some cases, not until diagnosis. The sudden loss of the sense of future which often provides us with a great deal of traction in life, and its replacement with the fear of impending death, can lead to a massive shift in perspective. "Life does not change–but your perception, your involvement in life changes." "It's terrible because your mind plays all kinds of terrible tricks on you."

This property describes the disorganization brought about by this sudden shift. "I felt like I was dying. I was an emotional wreck. It took me six months to come out of that hole." Affects are often intense and volatile. Men may abandon endeavors that provided them traction, at times self-destructive behavior may emerge, or re-emerge. Men may also become preoccupied with their bodies, frequently checking for signs of illness. One can understand this as attempts to organize affects, and to regain a sense of traction. There is a tendancy to underestimate the potential impact of testing positive and the initial disorganization that ensues. "The doctor, my friend, and I all underestimated a very, very large factor about being tested. The ramifications."

Affects are often intense, and unpredictable. "I was having anxiety attacks–I was just not coping well." "I became so anxious I did not sleep at night." Some men may find themselves becoming overwhelmed with sadness, sometimes when they least expect it. "I would be on the bus on the way to work and just get crazy." "I cried a lot." Confusion and questioning may also emerge. "It brought into focus things that were irrelevant before. What is this going to amount to? What am I going to amount to? It all went up in the air."

Men who are accustomed to negotiating their life in an organized manner now find their functioning considerably diminished. "I would sleep for a few hours then be wide awake and have to function all day." "My mind was gone. I pulled out in front of another car on my way to the office." Men may find their functioning in their career impeded. "At work I become disorganized. I have been doing it for a long time, but I had to start writing things down–making lists. I had to try to organize myself." In the wake of the disorganization little in life may seem predictable. "I feel like I have been turned around and upside down. I know I have to figure it out. Where to go from here. What to do." Everyday experience may come to be dominated by HIV and trying to understand the disorganization that has come to dominate. "It took over the forefront of my experience–professionally and personally."

Men can quickly come to view themselves as ill. "I saw myself as sickly and ill." With this perspective shift often comes a preoccupation with searching for signs of illness. Testing positive can become confused with a diagnosis and the preoccupation with illness can become intense. "The first six months after I was diagnosed–I mean tested positive–I would interrupt my work four to five times an hour to go to the washroom and look at the spot on my face in the mirror to see if it had changed, or gone away." "I check myself over for lesions every day." Things that were previously ignored now become alarming. "Every little bump and rash sent me through the ceiling." Men tend to look for signs that they are as ill as they feel or reassurance that they are okay. "If it had grown more, it meant that I was real sick. If it had gone away–I wasn't." "I kept running to the doctor's office for every little thing." Periodically, the despair behind the search emerges. "It becomes a downward spiral. Checking the thing on my head forty-five times in the rearview mirror on the way to work. It's like–Jesus, why even get out of bed?" Fantasies that accompany the downward spiral may be frightening. "I would see myself as sickly and ill–and the next thing you are a bag man on the street. Your friends and family have rejected you, your insurance company has cut you off. . . ."

Men may find themselves ruminating about and chastizing themselves for their past sexual behavior. "I changed my sexual behavior around 1983 because things were happening. I guess it was too late." "All of the things I had done experimentally for years–all of a sudden added up to something–I was sick." Internalized homophobia may become mingled with societal perceptions about the illness and become entwined with fear of humiliation. "It's more than being a gay man. It is that you are a promiscuous gay man. I am a whore!" "I felt like I had been caught with my pants down–that all of the world would now know that I went around having dicks stuck up my butt."

Men may also engage in seemingly self-destructive behavior during this time. These activities may also be understood as attempts to manage the intense anxiety and radically different experience of self and the world. "I was really nervous, drinking a lot, and I began smoking again after eleven years. I couldn't believe I was doing all of this–but I was. I would come home and drink by myself. It was totally out of control." "After I found out, for three to four months, it was nothing for me to go out and drink $30-$40 worth of beer every night." While some men may completely cut off sexual contact, others seek it out. "I would go out, get drunk, and drag people home. It's scary looking back on it. I let them do whatever. I felt it did not matter." Others turn to food. "I gained fifty pounds the first year after I found out." Other men may lose interest in ongoing pursuits that were aimed at enhancing their lives. "The week I found out I was HIV-positive was the week I terminated therapy. I thought, what was the point?"

Other men may turn to their financial status as a sign of security. "Initially, I kept going through the books to find out what my net worth was." Others may lay plans for future disability that may be not all that realistic. "I had heard about how government programs say that you cannot have any money. I pulled all of my money out of savings and hid it in books around the house."

Some men do not feel the disorganization initially. Some men feel the initial sadness. "I cried a lot for a couple weeks but that was it. It did not hit home until much later after a close friend died, then wham!" Other men focus on activity. "Everything was going okay, then boom–it all blew up. I had moved, tested positive, joined a group and felt on top of things. Then someone vandalized my car, and it all came falling down."

DESPAIR

I wake up some mornings and I go to get out of bed and I say, 'Why?'

Men often feel intense despair, a sense of deep hopelessness. Often the despair is voiced in the nature of the illness and the lack of a way out. Initially the possibility of, or a plan of action for, beating the disease or prolonging health and life until a cure is found is illusive. "I entertain no thought that in my lifetime–no matter how long or short it may be that they will find a cure." Some men may feel there may be hope for others but not themselves. "I have heard of people who have been positive for ten to fifteen years and have no symptoms–but that is one out of ten people. The odds are definitely against me." For many men the despair is compounded by their experience with friends. "I would look at my address book, all of the names of men that are now gone. All of the horrible deaths. Then I think, why bother?" Others see themselves as all alone. "So I get sick, who will take care of me when I need it? Will there even be anyone left to come to my funeral?"

For some men, the questions of "Why me? What have I done to deserve this?" may dominate. "It's a terrible injustice. All my life I was a good citizen. Building, learning, volunteering. I fought for my country in Vietnam. I worked hard for twenty years, only to die this way." "It brought back the old catechism fantasies of if you do not follow the straight and narrow something bad will happen. I found myself wondering what I had done, if this was God's retribution for something evil I had done."

SEXUAL DIALOGUES

I played safe–at least I thought I did. I now feel that there is only one safe sex practice–masturbation. If you are alone.

The experience of one's self as a sexual being is often radically changed. Initially men often feel cut off from sexuality. Sexual contact and past sexual experiences are now viewed as the culprit that got them into this mess. Where before sex may have been a source of validation, it is now viewed as the source of the current trouble. Tremendous blame may now accompany sexuality. Rarely do men blame others for the situation, rather they blame themselves. "I have what I have not because somebody did it to me. I was a consenting adult–participant–partner. No one threw this at me and I caught it. Somewhere along the line I agreed to go to bed with somebody and this is the result of that."

The gay community has been saturated with warnings and encouragement to follow safer sex guidelines. Men who know or assume that they contracted the virus in the face of this information are left feeling that it was all their fault. "I felt so stupid as far as how you can contract it." "I really felt stupid. I had seen all of the posters that say, *'Is this the body to die for?'* but still it happened."

Men may find themselves feeling a great deal of contempt regarding their past sexual encounters. "I thought I was dating, but it was only tricking." "I still probably have not learned what a loving gay relationship is. I know what two guys meeting and heading for the rack is, because that is all it has ever been." Men who have been heavily engaged in exploring and acting out their sexual fantasies now view their endeavors quite differently. "All the sexual exploration I used to do. It had quite a grab on me. I used to think of it as a great adventure. Now I think: 'This is what you got out of it. You got sick.'" "I think of all the wasted time–and money. The drugs, the fantasies, the bars, the baths. Vacations planned with meeting hot men in mind. You know there always was this voice that kept saying there are more productive ways to spend your time. As exciting as it once was, it now seems like a giant waste. A waste of my life." If disappointments were encountered in pursuit of relationships then feelings of rejection can become intermingled with the self-blame. "You meet someone, go home, have sex. Then you see them three days later and it is like nothing ever happened."

The previously described sense of being damaged can also affect men's sexual life. Sexual encounters or the possibility may become tinged with fear. "I felt dirty–as though I did not belong. It really affected my sex life." Men often become highly fearful of infecting someone else. "My sexual life plundered to nothing. I just did not want to do anything. I was afraid. I was afraid like my penis was just–if I took it out of my pants I would contaminate the other person. I just felt dirty."

Men may feel initially trapped by their sense of being damaged and by moral duty. "I felt I should tell people before they went to bed with me, but I was just not ready to take the risk of being rejected. So I opted to not even bother." And some men may find even their fantasy lives impeded. "I would try to masturbate–but it kept intruding into my fantasies–infection–exposure. I could not even enjoy sex by myself."

Men continue to seroconvert at this late stage of the epidemic. Men who find themselves testing positive in the face of so many years of safer sex education may find the shame compounded. "I

feel speechless. There is no excuse for this; I brought it on myself."
"I think I know exactly when it happened. I was in a kind of depressed, who-cares mood. I took the risk in the heat of the moment. The crazy thing is that several months later I am out of that way of thinking, and I get hit with the results. Bam." "Bottom line is that I feel pretty god-damned stupid."

REVELATION

I was really devastated. I was not sure where to turn with the problem.

Revelation is a complicated process that flows throughout the entire experience. In this area when men are often feeling confused, vulnerable, and needing to protect their damaged self-esteem, revelation is often approached with a good deal of apprehension. Some men may find their anxiety and fear about revelation encouraged. "I went to the hospital today for some tests. My doctor had written HIV-positive as the diagnosis. The girl at Admitting looked at it and said, 'You don't want me to put that on here do you?' It struck me, bless her, she is trying to protect me. Then I thought: 'What is she trying to protect me from?' Now I am scared."

Men tend to begin the process with their friendship system. If friends were a part of the process of deciding and being tested then often they are the first people that men reveal their status to. "I came out of the room and there was Joe. He could tell by the look on my face. I took one look at him and started to cry." "My friends had pushed me into getting tested–so they were all calling and wanting to know." Some men find it fairly easy to tell their closest friends. "I told a number of my close friends right away. Just because they were my close friends and it was something I wanted them to know."

Other men may feel more reluctant. They sense that they need to tell others but are hesitant to do so. "I want to tell people. I have to tell people but I am reluctant to do so. Once that information is out, it is out there." The problem becomes developing a supportive matrix, which requires revelation. "How do you get a support system going when you are afraid to tell people?" Some men may be surprised when they reveal. "I finally began to tell my friends and it turned out that several of them were positive also."

People outside the friendship matrix are often approached with a great deal of apprehension and are rarely informed during this area of the experience. Parents and people in the workplace are often viewed with a great deal of apprehension. "If I had leukemia I'd tell everybody at work. But I won't tell them I am positive for fear of reprisals. Even though I trust them. I do not know where this will go." Men often view the revelation of their status as a double or triple revelation. "It's not just a disclosure that you are positive; it's that and that and that. . . . Assumptions that you are gay, an IV drug user, promiscuous. . . ." If insurance claims are handled in house, then men may be reluctant to use their benefits. "I will pay for my lab work and when the time comes. I will pay for AZT out of my own pocket. We have to give all of our claims to a woman in personnel and God only knows what would happen with the information." Some men may be encouraged to not reveal and their worst fears heightened. "I told my manager because he is also a good friend. He told me not to tell the owner because if I did I would be out of here the next day." For men in the health care field the thought of revelation is especially frightening. "All this talk of forced testing for health care workers scares the shit out of me." "I love what I do. I am very careful, I know about infection control. But hospitals are so PR oriented, I could just see them firing me."

Parents tend to be the last people that men reveal their status to. Though they may long to–revealing to parents is often viewed as complicated and overwhelming. "I really want my parents to know what is going on with me and to feel closer to them, but I am just not ready to tell them." Men often anticipate that revealing to their parents will be a highly charged emotional experience, one that at this point in the experience they feel little prepared for. "I know it is going to be an emotional scene–and I just do not want to face up to that right now." Men may feel that their parents just would not understand. "They are from a small town–kind of like the one where they burned that family's house."

Again the revelation may be viewed as a double or triple revelation. At this point in time, men often feel that they are actively in the process of dying. Hence the thought of revealing often includes that they are dying, not that they are positive. Homosexuality, illness, and death often become fused together at this point. The fear becomes that parents will also fuse them as well. "They do know that I am gay. So it would be telling them that I am gay, am positive, and going to die of AIDS, and that I was promiscuous–I got caught with my pants down around my ankles." Past homophobic messages from parents may come to haunt. "My mother once said that she would die if she had a gay son. After I came out I said, 'Well you are still alive, aren't you?' Now I have to go and tell her that I am the one who is dying because of homosexuality."

Some men who reveal at this point find themselves having to field questions. Questions that they themselves are very uncertain about. "Isn't there anything they can do for you?" "My friend came up to me the other day and said, 'So you are going to be all right. They have medications and everything now, don't they?' I almost started to cry. I said, 'No, I am dying.'" Some men may feel that they have to manage their friend's anxiety when they are having a hard enough time managing their own. "My friends come up with this hesitant look in their eyes and ask, 'Are you okay?' I say, 'Sure.' But inside I am falling apart."

Understanding the impact and implications of testing positive is a two-way street. Both the person who has tested positive, and the people he is revealing his status to are trying to understand, to make sense of the frightening information. "As you try to make them understand and realize what your dealing with, you're also doing for yourself, making yourself realize it."

HELPERS

It was liking walking into a gay bar for the first time and you realize, my God! There are so many people like me. That feeling that you're not alone–and–you do not have to be alone.

Helpers are people who calm, reassure, and assist men in their efforts to stabilize, to find their way in a world that feels so dramatically different and frightening. Physicians, group experiences with other positive men, and at times therapists all serve to help stabilize, to modulate the intense feelings of isolation, and sort through the often myriad, intense feelings so prominent in this area.

While some men may find that when their physician informs them that they are positive it is disruptive to the doctor-patient alliance, other men may find it solidifies the relationship. One often observes intense idealizing relationships developing with the physician if the recently informed individual feels his distress is emphatically responded to. "He was great. He did not have to counsel me, but he sat with me for a good while and actively invited me to talk." Some men will develop a relationship with a physician after they have been informed. Again if the physician is empathic, responsive, and helps to contain and organize affect, then the idealization begins to develop. "I have no idea how I got the doctor I got, but I would not trade him for any other. He always spends plenty of time with me discussing options, showing me copies of articles."

While explaining and answering questions about the disease process, the physician is often the first to begin to point the way for men, to suggest ways to help negotiate the impact of testing positive. "As soon as I found out, he started telling me about all the things that were available–groups, therapists. He set me up with a therapist right away." "He told me the one thing he insisted on was that I join a support group." Just as the unempathic statements of the informer can haunt men for some time and leave memories of the experience as a stark reminder, the empathic stance of physicians and other initial helpers can be a soothing, reassuring reminder that people can help. "He did not have to, but he listened to me a lot. He took time."

Some men may have to search to find groups, others to work up the courage to join groups that they may have heard about, but hoped they would never need. "I scanned the newspaper to see what support groups were available. I joined a group at Horizons' which is one of the best things that happened to me." "It was two and a half months before I found them. I had sheets of paper looking for help. I found all kinds but not specifically what I was looking for–they were all for people who were very ill." For many men, the initial phone call inquiring about a group is a very important experience. "I called Test Positive Aware (TPA) and talked to someone named Bob. He answered three million questions, explained what TPA was all about. He said, 'Tell you what–we are having a meeting Tuesday night. Why don't you come by?'"

Many men find groups to be an important aid in helping them calm down, begin to reorganize, and to feel more in control of their lives. "That ten-week group at Howard Brown saved my ass. I was on the edge of losing it, but I really calmed down." "I really started to settle down after going to TPA." Some men report that they felt dramatically better after several weeks in a group experience. "After a month at TPA I was back on track."

An important element in the group experience is that men begin to once again feel a part of the world. Many find the isolation rapidly disappearing. "I likened it to when I was coming out and first went to the Bistro. It was like wonderful! All of these people and they look normal! And I literally began to feel that way." "You come into this room and everyone is just so friendly. There is a feeling of togetherness. We are all in this together and we are going to work it out together." Men are often surprised to encounter people they already know. "I even saw people I knew from other places. That was reassuring. The same people that I had been seeing and associating with in the bar scene for years were also in that room."

Some men find themselves feeling radically different in group meetings. Where before they may have felt anxious and out of control, they find a different constellation of feelings evolving. "It was just a different sort of feeling; it was comforting. I could feel the acceptance. If you want to cry, that is just fine." If the group is an open format, many men will find themselves initially spending a great deal of time at meetings. "At first the high point of my day was going to meetings and sitting between two people who were also positive and would accept me." For some men, the group experience will be the first time they feel reassured since finding out their status. "I was aware of my condition for six weeks. When I first joined the group was the first time I felt comfortable since I found out." Men not only get information in group settings but they often begin to understand, accept, and tolerate their emotional upheaval. "When someone else is telling me what is going on in their life, it helps me understand some of what is going on in mine."

However, groups are not for everyone and some men may not be able to use a group experience. Instead of feeling accepted and reassured, they find that their anxiety rises, that their shaken self-esteem becomes even more tenuous, and that their fear of illness becomes exacerbated. Some men have to tolerate these feelings for a few weeks, but then begin to feel more comfortable. "I felt so stupid, so ignorant the first few times at TPA. I did not know half of what they were talking about." While many men identify with how "well" and "normal" group participants appear, others immediately identify with the "ill" and not so "normal-looking" men. "I was blown away the first time I went because I thought I was asymptomatic. But there were a lot of sick guys there so that upset me a lot. It lasted a week, then I went back." Different men will experience the same group in radically different ways. "It was just such a downer. Why all the doom and gloom? To me a support group is supposed to be just that–not beat you while you are down."

Other men will not be able to contain these feelings at all. "I can't go back there. There were all of these sick guys in the room. It just freaked me out more." Other men fear exposure. "I can't go there. If it got out my business would be ruined." And some men may find themselves overstimulated. "I only went once. It felt like a meat rack. I got propositioned a couple of times. I did not feel that they were interested in helping me, just laying me." Some men will find individual therapy to be the most comfortable. "A group? It is hard enough for me to talk to my shrink about this, let alone a bunch of strangers."

SPOILERS

About six weeks after I tested positive, I broke a crown. I went to the dentist I had gone to for years. I told him I was positive. He would not even look in my mouth. He said that I could not be treated in his office anymore. I flipped out. I was devastated.

Spoilers are people who by their interactions with men, or statements in general are experienced as rejecting and unempathic. Often the greatest fear for positive men is rejection because of their status. The actions of spoilers exacerbate affect, concerns over rejection, and can often leave men in a state of disorganization. While later in the experience men may find themselves becoming angry and confrontational with these people, in the twilight zone when the

self is acutely vulnerable the result is often disorganization and
further damage to self-esteem.

As related in the previous chapter some men may encounter
spoilers in the medical professions. "I wanted to be honest with my
neurologist. A month or so after I found out. I went in to have my
blood work done and I told him. He called me several days later to
say that his office staff was not comfortable drawing my blood. I
pointed out that I had been seeing him for fifteen years. He said,
'I am sorry' and hung up." The sense of rejection, hurt, and betrayal often runs very deep when the relationship is long and established. "I could not believe it–fifteen years and zip." "I was devastated I had not been to a dentist for three years since it happened.
When I finally found a new dentist, I could not sleep for a couple of
nights fearing that it would happen again."

Men often hear the thoughts of others as they go about their lives.
"I was flying home from burying Ken and a woman boarding the
plane said, 'I'll sit anywhere as long as the person who sat there
before did not have AIDS.'" "On the bus one day a group of kids
were horsing around and saying, 'Ewww! You have AIDS' to each
other."

Some forms of spoiling may be less direct. Men may find themselves overstimulated by media reports. "A couple of weeks after I
tested this newscast came on announcing that AIDS deaths had
topped the 100,000 mark. I freaked." Accounts of out-and-out rejection are especially sobering. "It wasn't too long after I tested that
they burned that family's home in Florida. I thought: 'Great, maybe
you do have a reason to be paranoid.'" Some men may encounter
evolving AIDS policies in their workplace. "A few weeks after I
tested we all got the new AIDS policy. It said that anyone who was
positive was supposed to report it to the head of infectious diseases.
All of a sudden I felt like I was in Nazi Germany."

Some men may find a spoiler present in the group that they
thought was safe. "The other night this guy came in and said, 'Boy
this is a pretty up group for a bunch of guys who are dying.'"
Others may find themselves being exposed to the anxiety and concern of acquaintances. "Most of my friends have been great, but
then there are a few that are ready to go out and start carving my
tombstone."

Chapter 7

The Long Haul

You have to learn a different whole. *All the way around. But where do you go? How do you do it?*

For many men who test positive, the THE LONG HAUL will be the longest and most complex area of their experience. The turmoil of THE TWILIGHT ZONE gradually subsides and men begin to feel more grounded. THE TWILIGHT ZONE may have felt like a shattering of hopes, dreams, and familiar ways of feeling about one's self and others, an experience of life being torn apart. THE LONG HAUL is a process of rebuilding, of maintaining, and often, of considerable growth. Despite initial fears, weeks often turn into months and months into years. The advent of antiviral treatment earlier in the disease may prolong life and provide a degree of hope.

However, the medical ability to potentially slow the progress of HIV infection prolongs the basic underlying uncertainty of being positive. Many men will make a number of changes in their lives. Support groups may become an integral factor. Often men find their experience of themselves fundamentally changed. Activities and/or dreams that once held a great deal of importance may no longer seem so imperative. Monitoring health, finding a sense of calm and purpose, managing the intense anxiety and sadness that periodically awaken become central aspects of their lives.

The complications of this area include the ongoing process of revelation, making decisions based on the changing medical approaches to HIV, and maintaining health insurance coverage. Many men will make a number of new friends in the course of seeking support and a group of people they feel a part of. Oftentimes men who are positive will encounter the deaths of many of the people who were the bedrock of their support system. Some positive men will encounter the deaths of their partners. Men who are single may venture into dating; some will find partners.

What men soon discover is that many of the ground rules for life are changed now. A way to sum up the experience of testing positive and negotiating life in the wake of the knowledge is that it is a fundamental change in the person's reality. As the above quote indicates, the sense of self is often so fundamentally changed that one has to learn a different approach to life. Many of life's experiences and perceptions are now understood in this new context. Men find themselves more vulnerable to different circumstances and events than they were accustomed to.

Testing positive is not a steady state; it is dynamic, evolving, and changing. Many men find their sense of future gradually expanding again. It will most likely be shaken in the wake of the loss of friends, decline in T-cell counts or other reminders of the potential progression of the disease. Yet life continues. Decisions must be made and people often find ways of continuing to be involved in life, despite the often powerful pulls toward isolation. In many ways being positive can subtly erode self-esteem and confidence. However, the need to tend to the ongoing stress of being positive can lead men into pursuits that tend to long-standing painful aspects of themselves. Some men will experience considerable psychological growth and self-acceptance despite the ongoing hardship of negotiating HIV infection.

The properties of THE LONG HAUL are:

- *Decline of Preoccupation*–the tendency to be less preoccupied with being positive;
- *A Great Fear*–the continuing fear of illness and death tends to be less dominant, but at times is exacerbated;
- *Damaged Goods*–the sense of being damaged may also recede but periodically be activated;
- *Helpers*–the supportive matrix tends to evolve and becomes an integral component for men managing the psychological impact of HIV;

- *The Game Plan*–the often elaborate plan of action that emerges for remaining healthy;
- *Looking for Traction*–the emergence of T-cell counts as a reference point;
- *Revelation*–the ongoing process of revealing one's seropositivity;
- *Sexual Dialogues*–negotiating dating and establishing sexual relationships;
- *Calming Down*–the return of a less anxious state of mind;
- *Loss of Future*–the ongoing struggle to keep living in the face of a highly tenuous view of life ahead;
- *Planning Ahead*–the alterations in the usual future planning to which men are accustomed;
- *Losses*–negotiating HIV infection in the wake of multiple losses in the friendship matrix;
- *Balancing*–the ongoing efforts to maintain the sense of psychological balance;
- *Meltdowns*–the experience of the loss of balance and the plunge into despair; and
- *Transition to AZT*–the experience of decline in lab values and the beginning of anti-viral treatments.

DECLINE OF PREOCCUPATION

It is continuing to bother me, but not the way it did.

During THE LONG HAUL, men often find that the preoccupation with HIV that is so prevalent during THE TWILIGHT ZONE declines. Checking the body for signs and symptoms, fearing exposure, and an acute sense of vulnerability tend to be less dominant. They are often still present, but men tend to be less aware of them. "Gee, I just realized, I haven't done my daily (KS) Kaposi's sarcoma, hairy leukoplakia and candidiasis check for quite awhile." "I still check every day, but it is more like a routine, a ritual. I am not as panic stricken as before."

The degree of preoccupation with being positive as with many other properties in this area rises and falls. Events or new data can trigger an increased preoccupation. "A friend of mine came down with KS and I started becoming worried about getting it also. What would happen to me? Would I get them on my face?" "Every now and then I get anxious and start going over my books to see just how much money I have–how many assets–to see how long I could live without working."

A GREAT FEAR

I fear two things–a diagnosis and death.

The intense fear so prevalent in THE TWILIGHT ZONE also tends to decline somewhat and become more focused on anticipated events. Fear also is subject to rises and falls, suddenly emerging then quietly receding until it is again triggered. As in the above quote, a central fear in this area is being diagnosed with AIDS–developing a defining opportunistic infection. "I find myself wondering what it will be like." "I get terrified–not being able to breathe–the hospital–the medications." "It is so hard to describe. It's like I feel my life is finally back into some kind of order and bam! an explosion, and it all comes crashing down. I am diagnosed and it's all over." The fear of diagnosis can be expressed in many ways. "I have a great dentist. I am afraid to go to him because he is going to look in my mouth and go 'Oops, you have got thrush' and bam–he has got me. On the way out of his office I am going, 'Thank God, he did not find anything.'" The disease process and the feeling that one is progressing toward it becomes an ongoing theme. "It seems like this disease picks at the very basic things–so much of us. It makes your appearance ugly, and for a lot of people it affects their minds. It is just an ugly disease." "Sometimes the feeling of ugliness gets generalized into all of me, not just HIV."

Some men will find that the ongoing fear has an erosive effect. "I just get so tired of it sometimes. I think the fear of getting it just makes you feel horrible." When they reflect on the often intense fear of becoming ill, men may wonder if they are capable of dealing with the hardships of illness. "It's depressing and very scary. Because you look at those people and think God, you know, I don't know if I can cope with being in that situation. My friend with KS lesions all over his body has almost died three times."

For some men, as they encounter more experience with friends who have been diagnosed, the fear shifts somewhat. "It's not the dying I am afraid of, it is the process, being helpless, being so sick day in and day out." And for some men as their experience with ill friends continues, the fear of illness may shift as well. "I am sure as you reach that stage your mind sync changes and you're not as freaked out. At least that is what I have seen in my friends."

Insurance, jobs, and health care often become basic concerns for men who are positive. "I have a lot of fears–right now my job and insurance." "They are making cuts again at work. If my job goes, there goes my insurance. Sure I could COBRA it, but then I have to worry about pre-existing conditions." Men who have worked hard to conceal their status may fear exposure. "I called an airline for an application and they said among other things, 'And we do test for HIV.' I said, 'thank you,' and did not pursue them." Men may also wonder if they will receive adequate health care or if the system will be so overwhelmed with others that they will be shunted to the side. "I am afraid we have too few gay doctors trying to take care of too many HIV and AIDS patients." "I wonder how my doctor does it, if he will be so discouraged by the time I get ill that he won't be aggressive enough."

Men also fear the disruption of important bonds. "I have a great fear of this disease. I have a fear for my family. I have a fear for my mother because she and I have been very close–and I know it would just destroy her to see me go through this." Some men fear losing what they have obtained psychologically and professionally. "I am getting to the point in my life where I am feeling comfortable with myself. I am a master at what I do professionally, but now it looks like I am going to lose it all."

Over the course of THE LONG HAUL, the fear may decline considerably and men may reflect upon periods of intense fear and question themselves. "I think I developed a lot of unrealistic fears and phobias about being positive." Other men become so involved with other aspects of being positive that fear is not so dominant a part of the experience. "It's not that often that I sit back and acknowledge that I am scared sometimes."

DAMAGED GOODS

I tend to see the world through this filter of "I'm HIV-positive."

The sense of being damaged rises and falls as well. Many men will find these feelings declining during this time. "I know I am different, I felt for awhile like a leper. But I do not feel that way anymore." However, the sense of being damaged, infected, ill, or an outcast can be triggered and become dominant. "It pops up at strange times. All of a sudden something will happen and I feel infected." These feelings are not always triggered by external events, rather they can occur as a part of everyday processing. "It happens at the oddest times, reading in bed, daydreaming, then boom–an HIV thought . . . infected . . . dying . . . yech!"

Some men will be highly aware of the erosive effect that being HIV-positive has on self-esteem. "What bothers me is the subconscious devastation. It colors everything. Its not just that I am HIV-positive, and it colors every day. I wake up with this attitude–it's in my system, and everything becomes an effort–who cares–then this general depression sets in. That is the scary part; it sneaks up." For some men the sense of being damaged will be one of the most painful aspects of the experience, one that they will have to assert considerable effort to manage. "I have to remind myself that I am a good person despite the fact that I have this disease. That I am not an awful, dirty, sleaze-bag guy." "My self-esteem is pretty shot to hell." Some will be aware of its subtle to profound impact on the way they present themselves to other people. "You don't feel so good about yourself–so you sell yourself hard."

Some men will find that the sense of being damaged is deeply involved with their body integrity. "My blood is not a symbol of life anymore. It's this poisonous substance." Given the modes of transmission, semen can now be experienced as dangerous. "My cum–I look at it and see HIV virus. My cum could kill someone." Men who understand and read up on advanced biology may find other metaphors. "It is so microscopically involved with me now–down to my DNA. I feel this poison thing strongly." At times the thoughts may be so intolerable that men long to be able to get it out, to rid themselves of the virus and its impact. "When I was a teenager and had zits, I could always squish them and force the poisons out of my body. I always felt cleaner after that–force the bad stuff out. With this there is no way to force the bad stuff out."

Some men will feel the sense of being damaged in more of a social sense, not so much in terms of their own body and basic self. "Other people have said that, but I really do not feel all that bad about myself. What makes me uncomfortable is how I would be perceived by other people." "I didn't feel dirty–I felt like a walking time bomb. It was hard not to think that I would get sick too soon. It was hard to make a selling point of being positive." Men may find that being positive forms a kind of "barrier" as they attempt to negotiate their social world. "It gets ahead of me and I start feeling guilty for being positive. It gets in the way and I don't want to go to church. It just gets in the way." There can be a sense that HIV has wrecked the progress of the gay liberation movement. "We have spent our lives trying to work ourselves out of the homophobia that is around us in the schools, churches, families, then boom! AIDS = homosexual = promiscuous sex = dirty = yech." Some men may be concerned that being positive will destroy their standing in their career. "Being successful in my career made it okay to be gay. I worry that this may wreck all of it."

There are lulls in the storm, however. Men may find that long periods of feeling better emerge, or even periods of feeling okay about themselves. "It has been a really good few months. I am almost afraid to say it but I am feeling pretty good about myself." Some men who considered themselves permanently removed from the possibility of dating and developing a relationship, find themselves feeling that they may be desirable after all. "I used to think, 'Who would want to get involved with someone with HIV?' And now it's, 'Yes, why not? I am a great catch.'"

HELPERS

Going to TPA is liberating. It's like by facing it and becoming very familiar with it the goblins will go away–or, at least I hope they will go away.

Many men will begin to form an elaborate matrix of relationships that help them negotiate the impact of testing positive. One tends to see a variety of relationships evolve that serve different functions. Physicians, psychotherapists, members of support groups, friends, and family tend to make up the matrix of people who know of the person's HIV status and respond in various ways. Some respond with technical support and information, others respond to distress, or perhaps most important, convey that they are there and available as life in the face of HIV continues to unfold.

The physician tends to be an integral person in the matrix. "Your physician tends to become your cornerstone." An idealizing relationship often develops. "He is great. He is very reassuring and I trust him a great deal." Men are often very reassured when their physician reaches out to them. "He called personally and took the time to explain all of the tests he ran. It's really important to feel that he is willing to talk to you." Many men will be highly comforted by the experience of someone looking after them in a time of distress and uncertainty. "My doctor's office would call every six months and say it was time for another appointment." The physician's response may be very different from his patient's experience of his infection. "We talked a long time. He ran some tests. I went back; he went over them, and then he said he did not want to see me for six months. I said, 'Six months!' He said, 'You are doing just fine. Your counts are high; you're in good shape. We will check your counts every six months and see what happens.' I was shocked, but then I realized that maybe I am not going to die next month after all." For some men, working with a gay physician is very important, reassuring, and can strengthen a sense of community. "We need more gay doctors. I feel it is more important than ever. Long before the whole HIV thing, I wanted a place that could be non-judgemental, and know what to look for."

Some men will engage the help of a psychotherapist in efforts to manage the impact of the infection. "I am seeing a therapist once a week." Often the therapist also becomes an integral person in the matrix. "My therapist has been very important, helping me to get it together." Just as the physician's response can have a dramatic impact, so can the therapist's. "I really thought I was going crazy . . . over the edge. He said, 'No, you're feeling crazy. A lot has happened to you; you have been very traumatized. There is a lot to be frightened about. Our job is to help you settle down, and get engaged with your life again.' After one meeting, I began to feel better." The therapist's acceptance of other aspects of his patient's life may help face the self-esteem issues often triggered by HIV infection. "I have told her a lot. Some of it is really seedy. I was reluctant to tell her but I did. She wasn't blown away. That was good for me."

For many men, joining a group of men who are HIV-positive will be an important aspect of negotiating the impact of testing positive. Men who sought out a group experience in THE TWILIGHT ZONE often find that their alliance with the group has solidified, and find themselves able to more clearly delineate what they get from their group experience.

For some men, experiencing a sense of belonging in a group will be an ironic twist. Often in the past, self-esteem issues around being gay may have impeded the the sense of belonging to a peer group. Now, membership in the group is determined by a "problem" status, and men find themselves feeling accepted. "For the first time in my life I feel as if I am a part of a group." "We felt like underdogs and we could all go there to be safe." For many men who establish a strong alliance with a group, membership provides an almost bedrock sense of belonging. "Just knowing that the group is there helps a lot." "Nothing is more supportive than someone who has been there." Again, one cannot underestimate the power of a sense of belonging in the face of the impact of testing positive. "It feels like a family. I have found people I feel comfortable with. I like that. I need that. We all share a common bond. They all understand; you do not have to explain."

Group membership is a powerful buffer against the sense of isolation. "Being around other people who are in the same shoes as me, I am not so isolated. I am not alone. The more I deal with this, the more I realize there are a lot of people involved." Membership is also a powerful buffer against the sense of being damaged. "I felt like I belonged rather than being an outcast." Men may find their own self-acceptance growing, as they feel accepted by the group. "Being with the group has helped me feel a lot more accepting of myself. And it leaves me feeling more comfortable telling others. I don't feel totally out on a limb, because I know there is a group I can go back to." "It was just so affirming. It was just what everyone would want to experience." Men may also find a sense of solidarity and strength emerging in the face of an event that left them feeling so devastated. "I feel a sense of strength with the group. Like going to a Gay Day parade. I am reminded of what a large and wonderful group of people I belong to."

Groups often provide information as well as the emotionally sustaining aspects of membership. What men often find is that there is a great deal to learn about HIV infection and its treatment. While they may have previously felt up to date on AIDS information, they soon find there is a great deal more to learn. "First you have to find out more about the disease, then you have to figure out where you are at with it." In a sense, data about HIV infection, insurance, treatments, and research results can come to take the place of fears and anxious fantasies about the disease and its potential impact. "I was overwhelmed; there was so much to learn." "I really felt kind of out of it; these guys had really been doing their homework. They had a whole room full of articles and books." One often hears of a process of the group modulating anxiety, and data or information being taken in. "I wondered how long it would take until some of the education began to sink in." "At first I did not understand a lot of it, but it helped. What I got helped." Participation in the group and the acquisition of knowledge may have a calming effect. "When I found TPA I threw myself into it. I read everything I could find on AIDS twice–until I finally found within me some acceptance."

As men find their knowledge of HIV growing, they often find their initial assumptions being challenged. "You get a sense of options and perspective." "Just reading the TPA newsletter was very stimulating and positive for me." Men may find themselves actively educating themselves about HIV. "I have learned so much at TPA and read everything I can get my hands on." "I subscribed to their newsletter and several others; there is a lot to learn." Some men begin to take a more proactive stance with their physicians. "The wonderful advantage with my doctor is that if I go in and say, 'No, I do not want to do that. I want to try this.' Or, 'I want to wait before going on AZT,' he doesn't argue with me." As knowledge is gained a shift in the experience of the infection may evolve. "Yes, I probably am going to die of this disease; it's a matter of when. Now tomorrow they may come out with something that can delay it or prolong it so I have some hope–which I did not have in the beginning." "The new studies are especially encouraging if you are asymptomatic because you realize that we now have something that can inhibit the progression and you can stay healthier longer." The range of knowledge needed in order to manage life in the face of HIV is quite vast. "A guy came in from California to talk about insurance. It was terrific. He talked for two hours, answered questions, and had a twelve-page handout. It gave me some very good ideas– possible solutions to getting some coverage." "I had no idea what kind of programs are available from the state, like free AZT, or the studies available with free monitoring and drugs, or if I was legally protected if my boss found out and fired me."

If men form a strong alliance with the group, they initially may attend as often as possible. "I was there for every meeting. For the first six months I went regularly." Initially the experience of membership and belonging are key factors for people. "I find myself going there even if the speaker is of no interest to me. I just go because we will probably end up with a group of people having dinner." If the group is an open format–that is members can come and go as they choose–men will often become highly engaged at first then gradually decline in their attendance. "The first few months I was a regular. After a while I was feeling a lot better and just did not feel the need to go as often. At first it was twice a week, now I go when the speaker or the topic interests me." Some men will find themselves focusing on other life tasks. "I got involved studying for the bar, and after I passed I didn't feel the need. When I was not going, my life was going along fine." However, men may find themselves needing to return. "I started losing my positive attitude for awhile, and it has come back since I started going to the group again."

Through the group affiliation men may form individual relationships that are important and sustaining. "I started forming relationships with other people who are positive. We call each other up and talk or 'check in' or 'go out' for dinner." Just as processes of identification described in THE GREAT DEBATE tended to influence men's assumptions regarding their antibody status, men may identify with members of the group and gain a sense of security.

Sometimes one or several people may be identified by the person. "I would always check him out. If Chris was okay, I was okay." "I tended to think, 'As long as they stay healthy, I am going to be healthy, because they were here before I was.'" Some men may find their own philosophy about dealing with being positive has emerged through these idealizing relationships. "It was so beautiful to see this guy. He looked great and his basic stance was, 'I am okay. I am feeling fine. I am enjoying life and I am going to keep it up until something happens. Then you deal with it.'"

However, in a large open group men may also encounter people who are having medical difficulties. "When you see people deteriorating and falling apart piece by piece, you think, 'God, is that going to be me?' But when you see people doing well, you think, 'Gee I hope that is me.' There is a man in the group whose T cells went from 1100 to 300 in six months." Some men may become aware of the sadness that lurks beneath the surface of the elaborate process of negotiating relationships with other positive men. "If someone's counts are lower than mine, I feel sad, but if they look good then, 'Wow! He looks fabulous–it makes me feel better . . . but also sad." The ability to form an alliance with the group seems to help modulate the anxiety and sadness inherent in encountering people who are in varying stages of the illness–some more advanced than the members, others at about the same stage, and others that are doing better. In broadening the member's perspective on the illness, knowledge can be frightening. While it may point out options that are reassuring, it also points out frightening realities. "Ever since I found out I was positive I had been going to TPA and getting to know all of these people who are positive at various degrees–it's like overload. Before, I could go blissfully along knowing I was positive and I might be worried. Now I know you can go blind, get toxoplasmosis, skin problems–the list is endless."

In the course of group membership or negotiating other relationships men may find themselves helping others in their efforts. Finding themselves helping others can be a very affirming experience. "I have led the group a few times now. I was amazed. Here I was helping someone with something I felt so helpless about." "I went out to dinner with an old friend I had run into from TPA. He was really frightened to be there. We ended up talking and talking. It turns out I was the first person he had ever talked to about the problem." Sometimes men will pass on the help, miles beyond their local community. I have a friend who lives in nowhere Michigan. They do not having anything like TPA let alone know what they are doing with AIDS. I send him newspaper clippings and the TPA bulletin, call him and check in on him." "I was down South, visiting some old friends–a couple–and one began to cry. He had just found out he was positive. It was great sharing the knowledge that I have–and the perspective I have with someone, helping someone else." In revealing their status to friends, men often encounter other men who have tested positive and may benefit from their knowledge. "I came out to a lot of my friends and found out they were positive also. I also found out that most of them had not gotten any structure for themselves, so I hauled a bunch of them down to the meetings."

Again, not all people do well in group formats. Some are not able to form connections that buffer their anxiety. "There were just too many sick people. I need to be around people that are affirming." Some may not find the format is a good match. "I felt like I was at a twelve-step meeting. I thought, 'I feel bad enough, but not bad enough to become a starry-eyed twelve-stepper.'" The general tone of the group may put others off. "I need to be around a group of HIV-positive people, but I found the group to be too down. I find a lot of the guys there are kind of down and somber." Some may devalue the group. "I thought TPA was sick–too much of a negative consciousness." Other men may find the interests of other members to be overstimulating. "I was so scared and upset, and these people kept propositioning me. I couldn't handle it, so I never went back." "It felt like going out to a bar . . . all of those 'lean and hungry looks.'"

Some men may attempt to form their own network. "The group was not working so I put an ad in the paper. I met a lot of interesting people and have become good friends with a few of them." Other men prefer their own existing friendship networks. Some may find greater comfort in being with people who are not HIV-positive. "A lot of my relationships with my lesbian friends have solidified. There is a different perspective in talking to people who are not caught up in this. There is a different response I get. I think there is some objectivity that you don't get, not as emotional, a little more practical." "I can tell them what is bothering me and I know I won't get back what is bothering them about HIV. I do not have to turn around and let them use my shoulder. Sometimes it is a terrible burden, particularly if I am struggling with something myself."

Whatever the unique constellation of the matrix for individual men, they are often highly aware of its sustaining power. "Every now and then I think about moving. I have had several job offers in other cities, and sometimes I think of living in the country. But that also means leaving all the people, my doctor, my HIV buddies that help me get through all of this." "There is just too much steadiness here. My support system keeps me here in the city."

THE GAME PLAN

I thought there must be something I can do, to take action, to deal with this. As soon as I began to feel that I was doing something, I began to let go of the anxiety.

In the course of interacting with other positive men, medical personnel, reading the literature on HIV infection, and often the popular self-help media, a Game Plan evolves. A great deal of energy, thought, time, and sometimes money can go into the components of the plan. The plan consists of relationships with individuals and groups as well as activities. Often men believe and/or hope that their actions are directly combating the virus. From a psychological standpoint, whether or not crystals or Chinese herbs or mega vitamins are as effective as antiviral treatment is not the issue. As the above quote indicates, the Game Plan can have great organizing power. A great deal of anxiety is often modulated, men feel less helpless, and believe that they are actually doing something to help themselves. In the course of implementing their plan, some men may find for the first time in their lives that they are taking care of themselves; a sense of well-being may evolve as men actively take charge of possibly self-destructive behaviors, replacing them with more affirming activities. A great deal of hope and faith can go into the plan and its implementation. It can have the flavor of a zealous mission. At this point in the experience the goal is to stay healthy, to stop the decline in T-cell counts, to keep AIDS away.

Developing and maintaining the relationship with their physician is often a key element in many men's plans. "You have to have a really good relationship with your doctor. Speak candidly back and forth–the professional and the human. I never feel rushed." A great deal of reassurance can come from feeling that the physician is an expert in managing HIV infection. "There are so many physicians that really do not understand AIDS–so you have to make sure you have one that knows." Some men need to feel that they have the best available. "I switched docs. I had to wait three months to get an initial appointment, but he is at a university hospital, and you constantly see his name in the papers as a top researcher."

Often, the first elements of the plan come from the physician. If the infection is not progressed to the point of requiring antiviral intervention, then the recommendations are fairly basic. "He said right now the best thing I can do is get plenty of rest, eat good food, and exercise." Men may become very conscious of following these basic guidelines. "I eat the way I am supposed to, exercise–common sense things–and I take extra vitamins." Periodically men may take a step back and evaluate if they are indeed following the advice. "I smoke–which I shouldn't do. I drink too much coffee. I only work three nights a week, but I am up all night and when I work I may have three or four shots. I really need to start tightening up." Some men may tackle long-standing habits. "I stopped smoking and cut out alcohol altogether." While the initial recommendations may seem "basic" for many men, it represents a fundamental shift to taking better care of themselves generally. "I made a commitment to take better care of myself the best I could. I gave up cigarettes, alcohol almost completely, and paid closer attention to my diet. Other than that I forgot about it the best I could." "For the first time in my life I am taking care of myself. I take much better care of myself than I ever did. Decreased my drinking and increased my sleeping, exercise, and watching my diet."

Many men join the numerous research studies that are available in larger cities. "The same week I found out, I signed up for the study a friend was in." "The first thing I did was join a study so I got monthly checkups and monitoring." A degree of security can often be found through participation. "It's great. Every four months you get a complete physical and lab tests and they send the results to my physician. So I am watched very closely." Participation in studies can become an integral part of men's lives. "I have been in the study for four years now. Nothing has ever happened; my counts have always been high and steady, but it is great knowing that it is there and that people are watching."

Some men find that following the basic guidelines is not enough, so they add to their plan. "I am a real control freak. I felt there had to be more I could do to take action. I got on at AIDS Alternative Health Project and get weekly massages and acupuncture. I get acupuncture for anxiety." "Going to AAHP became a ritual. I felt like I was going to take in a great deal of healing." As men interact with others, they may hear about other possible additions to their plans. "My acupuncturist told me about Chinese herbs for anxiety, so I started taking them." "I went to a lecture on vitamin therapy for HIV. He told about some very exciting results so I really got into vitamins." Some men may find themselves investing a great deal of energy, time, and money into additional elements to their plans. "We formed a buyer's group for vitamins. We can get them cheaper that way." "I started buying and reading and buying. The more I read, the more I bought. It got to the point that my whole kitchen counter and a good deal of the refrigerator were taken up with vitamin bottles." Just as interacting with others can guide men in developing their plans, encountering others can also help men decide how they do not want to develop their plans. "I have a friend who is on every chemical and vitamin in the book. When he talks about it his eyes kind of glaze over. It really scared me. I thought, 'This is exactly how I do not want to be.'"

An elaborate plan provides a great deal of structure, sense of control, and modulates a good deal of anxiety. "I tried to get everything organized so that I could feel that I had a sense of control." "It became almost ritualistic. I had my morning vitamins and supplements, my afternoon vitamins, the gym three times a week, AAHP once a week, my evening vitamins, the study, my visits to the doc." The plan and following the plan can have very high stakes—for some men, life or death. "What can get going is that if I do all these things right—vitamins, diet, drugs—*IT* will stay away. AIDS will be out there somewhere." "I was really trying to keep AIDS away. To keep Mr. Virus in check." Some men may be aware of the 'talisman' quality of their plans, but cling to them all the same. "I take liver every day. It is kind of a superstition I have. I haven't been taking it for a while, so I don't want to get a T-cell count until I have been back on it for a few weeks."

Emotional needs are often tended to as well. "I knew I needed some kind of support in addition to the study monitoring my health." Again, men may modify their plan over time. "Initially I was just so focused on my own health, but after awhile I started to realize I needed other people as well." Working with a psychotherapist can become an integral part of men's plans. "I go to individual and group therapy. There is a lot to keep on top of. It's like you are not always aware of how this chips away at your self-esteem." "My therapist has become so important, so integral. She has been there all along." Men may initiate activities that expose them to and help them feel more comfortable with the most feared aspects of the infection. "I joined the friends committee because I had no experience with death. I think it will help me be not so freaked out when my time comes."

Some men will find themselves pursuing spiritual aspects of their lives. "I really began to feel the lack of a spiritual direction–that there could be something very comforting and guiding in it." Men may return to the churches of their childhoods. "I started going back to church. Boy, has it changed since I was a kid." Some may struggle with the church's position on homosexuality. "It is hard. I get so angry sometimes. I want to be a part of my church, but then some cardinal or the Pope gets in the news calling me a sinner and I want to scream." Others may seek out churches within the gay community. "I started going to Dignity. It has been very good for me." "I got involved in MCC (Metropolitan Community Church). It was kind of cosmic. I was so discouraged, then the first time I went the sermon was on faith in the face of adversity. It helped me so much that I have become a regular." Others will seek out churches that they have heard about through support groups. "I went to Unity and saw a lot of gay people and a lot of people from the group. I was reluctant at first, but began to feel that their approach made a great deal of sense to me. It has become an important part of my life."

The plan is subject to change and alteration over time. Things that at one time seemed to be of utmost importance may lose their sustaining power. "I got tired of looking at all the bottles and taking all of the vitamins. I also added up how much I was spending. Months ago my doc has told me that all I was doing was peeing a lot of money down the toilet. I guess I was not ready to believe him then, but I do now." Some men may find themselves radically changing their approach. "After awhile I just 'AIDS out.' I just started focusing on living and being." Men who have been involved in groups over a long period of time and have seen a number of approaches come and go may develop a more mellow perspective on the game plan. "We were doing things that other people were all doing. Whether they were beneficial or not, I am not sure. Egg lecithin–everybody was doing that for awhile. I don't know what the new thing is now. People were getting some kind of aloe vera or a drug coming out of the Virgin Islands–someplace strange and tropical and expensive. But at least you heard about all of that and the studies that were going on. I was hearing firsthand from people who were directly involved. People felt so intense about their thing. Sometimes it made the choices harder. It was like there were different camps–vitamins, macrobiotic diets–even crystals. The pressure and intensity made it hard sometimes, but at least you felt like you had options."

LOOKING FOR TRACTION

I play the numbers game. When my counts are good, I am doing okay. So I am good for another year or two.

For many men, T-cell counts become an important reference point. In the midst of so much uncertainty, anxiety, and the high stakes of staying healthy or sliding into illness and death, the counts offer a seemingly concrete indicator of just where one is at. "Here we are being HIV-positive. What do we rely on other than T-cell counts? How reliable are they anyway? My doctor says he looks at the total picture. I try not to get crazed and obsessed, but bottom line it feels like the only thing to rely on." While a high count is reassuring, the possibility of the next one being discouraging tends to lurk in the background. "My counts have been fairly high and consistent–over the five hundred level for several years. But each time I go in, I wonder if this one will be it." "At first I was elated–my T cells were up two hundred. As soon as I left the doctor's office I started to come down. I thought, 'You still have to come back in March.'" Some men will keep close track. "I have kept a graph for several years." "I have them all written down at home."

For men who find out they are positive, and have counts above the 500 level, the fear becomes a decline in the numbers to the point of beginning AZT. "There was a constant progression up, then a slide down. The first one below five hundred my doctor wanted me to go on AZT. But the folks at the study said one drop was not really sufficient. They wanted to see what the next one is. They went back up and have stayed there." "I am working really hard to stay healthy. I want my counts to stay up. The idea of having to go on AZT just freaks me out. Like it is the beginning of the end."

Men may find themselves doing their best to make sure the periodic counts are "good ones." "I get them done every six months. The month or so before, I start worrying; I drink less and sleep more." A great deal of apprehension can emerge as testing approaches. "I just hate it. Every six months it's like a giant reminder of just how scary the situation is." If men have not been following their plan, then the apprehension may be increased. "I have been so stressed out at work. I haven't been eating right, been drinking too much. It's almost like the numbers will come back low and 'gotcha,' you have been bad again. First you got positive, now you're not taking care of yourself."

Men may strive to ensure their counts are accurate. "I was going to get a count but then I got the flu. I was scared that my numbers would be off, so I put off the test." "I had been sick and did not want to do it and have my numbers all screwed up. I just want to be sure of them." Men may try to balance their physician's caution regarding the count as a definitive measure with their need for a point of reference and the anxiety-modulating power that it has. "My doctor told me they vary a lot–up and down, one day to the next. I am just trying to get a reference point." "I have heard all that. A lot depends on the stress you are under and your general physical condition, and that they are variable. But when it's your count, it's your count. It's you're okay still, or you are in trouble."

Men may find themselves anticipating the results of the test. "When I had my count done the second time I had a cold. I thought, 'Well, there goes my T cells, down again.'" "I am really anxious about this one. Something tells me it is not going to be a good result." Some men will find the results different from their expectations. "I had prepared myself for a significant drop. Instead it went the other way." "I was blown away. I had been feeling great, and it was down."

When the numbers are down, the impact can be considerable. "My T cells came back the other day. They were down again. I have to work very hard at staying in a normal plane–to not get more discouraged." "I am really out of it. After being high for so long, they dropped again. I guess I am not going to get out of this after all." When the counts are high, while being reassuring, a sense of confusion may evolve. "I had not been feeling well, but my counts were up. Now I am thinking I was just imagining all of those things about being tired and achy." "For so long I thought they were a good indicator, now I am beginning to feel there are no indicators. What do you latch on to?" While a good result may be reassuring men find that they are still positive, and there is always a next time. "I shouldn't have been so elated. I was so pleased, but you never know what may happen next."

REVELATION

It's like coming out all over again, only this one is a whopper. It makes the first one look like a piece of cake.

Revelation is a process that flows throughout the experience. We all live and operate in an elaborate network of relationships. Men are faced with the need and/or desire to reveal their status within these elaborate networks. For the men in this study, by far the most complicated and often painful group to reveal to was the family, followed by friends and colleagues.

When contemplating revealing their HIV status men often confront their fears about revealing their sexuality and the constellation of meanings that has been termed "internalized homophobia." There are often many "overlaps" in the ways men feel about their homosexuality and their antibody status. This mingling of meanings tends to add to the pain, confusion, and anxiety. Just as men have learned that they have to be careful about who they reveal their sexuality to, they often sense that they have to be careful who they reveal their antibody status to. "I wouldn't go to 'Podunk,' Iowa and announce that I was gay. They'd probably lynch me on the spot. I wouldn't go to Jesse Helm's home and tell him that I am gay. He would probably shoot me on the spot." "I did tell a good number of people, but it's not something I want the world to know."

Some men feel that reluctance to reveal their status is an extension of the closet. "It's so typical–part of being gay has been living in the closet. This is just a progression of keeping things under wraps. Our whole lives are like that to a certain extent." Men may also find long-standing feelings of being different emerging. "Being homosexual is the core of our being. But also from the point we declare it we set ourselves apart from the rest of the group." Some men find themselves feeling frustrated, that they are being smothered by their prohibitions. "The crux of the issue is the taboo against sex, especially homosexuality. That is the crux of the network of lies that eventually covers you and wraps you up and makes it impossible to have any integrity."

Men may also sense the nature of the information they are revealing. "You are telling people that you could be–dead." And that they may potentially lose something by revealing. "If you did level you may get a tacit level of support, but also the risk of revelation." Men often fear being judged and the subsequent impact on the relationship. "That would shatter anyone's sense of relationship–we all fear moralistic judgements." Some men are able to identify different risks within different relationships. "It's like telling potential boyfriends that you are infected, dangerous, and not such a good catch, telling your boss that you are infectious and may be a giant liability, and telling your mother, sorry, but I am dying."

In the Workplace

Men often fear revealing their status at work. "I would like to share it with my coworkers and employer but even with the people I am close to, there is this fear of how they would react." Far too often men will witness anxiety or discrimination toward an infected or ill coworker. "At the university one of the other professors, a librarian, died of AIDS. Before he died he had lesions on his face. The students started writing letters to the school newspaper stating that he should not be handling or handing out books, citing that we do not know enough about it, that he may be endangering our health. So I had no intention of telling anyone." Homo-AIDS-phobic comments may also enhance the person's reluctance to reveal. "We had a worker who is pretty effeminate and the guys were saying, 'Don't use his phone, you may get AIDS from it.'" Sadly, some men may encounter rejection from coworkers. "I told someone in my office that I had known for years that I was gay, and HIV-positive. He chose never to speak to me after that. It cut like a knife."

Men who are self-employed feel that they also run risks. "Who would want to hire a designer, when it is at least a one-year relationship from the beginning? Who wants to hire somebody who may get sick and leave them stranded?" "My business is my livelihood, if it got out I am not sure what would happen." The fear may be heightened for men who are the central figure. "My business is essentially me and my skills. That is what people are buying. I know from past experience that if it gets out that you are positive, it quickly turns into you have AIDS and are dying. If people think that you can't function, they are not going to hire me, and the whole thing could go down the tubes."

Some men may confront the pain inherent in feeling prohibited from revealing and attempt to modulate it for a potential greater good. "I like to think that I am well thought of at work and it hurts to think that I can't tell them I am positive. Sometimes I think they would view it differently if they knew someone they like and worked closely with died of AIDS. Maybe then they would change their minds. That it wasn't some drug addict, or wild banshee–that it was a regular Joe."

Friends and the Community

Some men may choose to inform more friends than they had done in previous areas. As men become more comfortable with being positive, their perspective on informing others may shift as well. "After awhile it made no sense to me to be involved with people for twenty-five to thirty years and not to tell them for fear that it would get around." "At first it was fine. I did not want their pity; I wanted them to be what they always had been to me." Some men find that the friends that they have revealed to become closer friends and the relationships more sustaining. "I have gravitated to people who do know. I am more comfortable with them and spend more time with them." Some men may find themselves withdrawing from relationships. "I started to feel that I really did not have anything to offer except the death of another friend. But then I stopped and thought, 'I want to be with these people and I am only alienating myself.'"

Just as men may be surprised by the supportive responses of friends, and the number of men who in turn reveal their status, men may also encounter other surprises. "I told an old friend that I was HIV-positive. He told me that he heard I had AIDS and was dying." Some may find that the revelation is not all that voluntary, or planned. "I volunteered to do the coat check at a benefit, and wouldn't you know it, two old friends from L.A. showed up and asked what I was doing there. I said it was a good cause and that I was just volunteering–but I could see they were wondering, 'What's going on here?'" "I was at a benefit and ran into some friends. They asked me what I was doing there and I said, 'I am on the board of directors of TPA.' I thought, 'I just told them I am positive!'" "There was a big fund-raiser for TPA–a big formal dinner. Someone decided that all of the board members would wear red carnations. Here we were in this big room surrounded by all of these gay men, and it felt like we were marked, branded."

Men tend to sense the different status their disease potentially imparts and feel prohibitions against revealing it in the face of others revealing their diseases. "I was home for my twenty-fifth high school reunion and a friend had the old gang over for cocktails. In the middle of the conversation, one woman announced that she had just been diagnosed with lymphoma. Everyone rallied around her and said it would be okay. Then another said she had breast cancer. I thought here is my cue, but–it felt like it would be dropping a bomb in the middle of the coffee table." Again, men may sense the pain that can come to accompany the sense of prohibition. "I got a letter from an old high school friend. When I sat down to write her back I got to thinking about all of the things I wanted to tell her but couldn't. I got really sad."

As the losses of friends to AIDS mount, men may feel angry not revealing their positive status and their homosexuality. "I have just been to too many funerals where there is a big lie going on. I do not want my obituary to say I died of some innocuous disease when I died of AIDS." "It's the cover-up–the ongoing cover-up–and it is starting to get to me." Some find themselves taking a more militant stance. "If I hear an AIDS joke or a gay joke I come right out and tell them I am gay, positive, and have lost too many friends to tolerate that crap." "When I put them on the defensive, it's cathartic." Some men find themselves feeling that they really have nothing to lose. "I am fifty-nine years old, my lover died of AIDS and I am positive. What can they possibly take away from me? There is nothing left to take away, but I can gain my own integrity."

In the face of so many losses men may come to appreciate their humanity, that the prohibitions against homosexuality are no longer valid in the face of the growing very human experience of loss. "We are all upright people. I think we are a group of nice people and here we are hiding away something that is happening to us. I am no longer going to tolerate the public view that we are the riff-raff of society and that we deserve it." "I now call people on things. It may not be wise but I have little patience. I am willing to take less." Some men come to feel affronted by attempts to hide the nature of the illness that has taken a friend. "I wanted to write his mother and say, 'You don't have to pretend your son did not die of AIDS. He was a very loving and giving person. AIDS cannot take that away from anyone.'"

The Family

Revealing to parents is often a very complicated and emotionally charged process. Men may contemplate, approach, and back off from telling their parents for months if not years. At first many men decide to wait until they are actually ill. "As long as I am healthy, as long as the T-cell counts stay reasonably well, I probably won't tell them." "I will tell them I am sick when I am sick, when I have to tell them." Many feel that it will be a burden on their parents. "I am doing fine now. My mother is a worrier; why cause several years of worry?" "They do not need this now. They have just retired and for the first time in his life my father is relaxing and having fun. I do not want this to mess up their retirement."

When contemplating revealing their antibody status to their parents men often anticipate a great deal of angst. "I am afraid to tell them because it will be an emotional outburst." "I do not want an emotional scene. I can't handle it." As time goes on and men become more accustomed to knowing they are HIV-positive and become more confident in their ability to tolerate their own emotional states secondary to being positive, a longing to tell their parents may emerge. "I have been feeling more and more like I want to tell them, but I do not see a possible way." "At first I was going to wait until I got sick, but then I began to realize that if I did not tell them, there was going to be a big hole in my life if I did not begin to reconcile with them and tell them what was going on in my life." If men find themselves feeling blocked, a sense of anger and frustration may emerge. "I am angry, and I keep getting more and more so. I have never lied to my parents about anything, so now I have this big lie going on." In anticipating revealing, men tend to see themselves as acutely vulnerable and wondering what may happen. "It's the worst fear that after they find out, they won't love me." "I wonder how I am going to feel? After I tell them. I am afraid that if my mother breaks down, I will break down also. Then how am I going to feel? Are they going to say, 'I told you so, living the way you did. Now it's going to kill you.' "

Men often recall the messages regarding homosexuality as they grew up. "Growing up, we all witnessed and maybe felt directly all the stuff people said about gay people. It made the world feel pretty scary." "I remember as a kid, every now and then my gayness would creep out–or rather leap out–and immediately get slapped down, more often by my brother than my parents." "My brothers used to call me a fag, pussy, sissy." Before revealing their homosexuality, it may have been a source of oblique discussion. "I remember being around the dinner table and my aunt said, 'Oh, Chris is never going to get married. He is like my brother Ned.' My mother replied, 'That's not true! He dates lots of women.' " Men may also recall how the family dealt with other homosexual members. "I had two uncles who never married and were always referred to in ways that acknowledged they were 'different.'" "My aunt lived with a woman for thirty years and there was only one bed in their house. Though we spent a lot of time with them, 'it' was never mentioned."

For some men, being positive feels like a confirmation of all the negative messages about homosexuality that they have accumulated over the years. "It felt like, 'See, we told you so . . . if you are going to be gay this is the kind of thing that will happen to you.' You end up not just having a disease, but feeling like a bad kid." Feelings about being gay that men felt they had worked out may now make them feel that they are once again in the forefront. "I had really thought I was over all this negative gay stuff. But now I feel like that freaked-out kid in high school, wondering where the next bully will come from." "It's like someone went up into the attic of my mind, found all the old negative feelings and shook them up."

As men contemplate telling their parents, they often recall the experience of revealing their homosexuality. "I thought it was going to be traumatic when I told them I was gay, but it was okay." "When I told my parents I was gay, my mother said she was disappointed that I had not married because I would have made such a wonderful father." They may also recall how the family has dealt with their gayness over time. "My family will not deal with my being gay in any way, shape, or form. They don't want to talk about it, hear about it on any level." "I think my mother is still pissed that I am gay." When the family has not been supportive or tolerant, men sense their vulnerability in light of these past experiences. "I am coming back as the diseased son whose mother when she found out he was gay told him to go back to church." Men may also wonder what it would be like to reveal their homosexuality without the complication that HIV has imparted. "Nowadays, it might be easier to go to them and say, 'I am gay, but I don't have AIDS.'"

Disappointment and anger over the ways the family has dealt with them in the past may become intertwined as men anticipate telling their parents. "I realize that there is going to be a fight with my mother. She is a fundamentalist Christian. I have no patience for that at all. I should have more tolerance for them than they do for me, but I just want to kick something." "My mother has walked away from her kids' distress so many times. I feel like this is the final test. Here is your little boy who is dying. Are you going to take care of him?" If the family continues to be hostile and the son feels diminished, then the anger may be intense. "Now I am the family secret. I want to be more than that. It is not enough and I deserve more." "Last time I was home, my mother made a comment about the 'queer who does the exercise program.' I found myself prepared to fight, but I do not want a fight. I want it to be a good thing."

As they sort through their past and ongoing experiences with their families, men also encounter the basic sadness and sorrow of their revelation and its implications. "It's that I am probably going to get ill and that I am probably going to die, and it is probably going to happen before they do. Its topsy-turvy." "Sorry mom, but your son is not going to outlive you, you may have to watch me die." Men may also wonder what it is like from their parents' point of view. "I wonder if parents ever run through their minds that their gay son is going to come home and tell them they have AIDS." "It must be horrible to give birth to a child, watch him grow up, and then watch him die."

Some men will encounter opportunities to tell their parents that catch them off guard. They then become missed opportunities. "I had bronchitis this summer while visiting home. My mother asked me if it was AIDS. I said no." "My parents were visiting in the middle of my trying to take care of Jerry. My mother asked me why I looked so harried. I told her I was trying to help out a sick friend. She asked what he had. I said AIDS. She asked, 'Why do you have friends with AIDS? Well, I hope you don't have AIDS.' I got up and started to do the dishes." Other opportunities may not be so direct. "My parents were outlining their wills. They intended for a lot of the property that has been in the family for generations to go to me. I was sitting there thinking that all of this may be for naught, feeling that I was letting them down. That it was going to be even harder to tell them." When an opportunity is missed, regret can begin to mount. "I did feel sorry that I missed the opportunity, but I just was not ready." "I regretted not telling them. I lost an opportunity and felt that I was giving them a message right then by not responding. I just could not tell them."

Many men will begin the process of revelation to their family with their siblings, then approach their parents. Men tend to start with the family members whom they feel will be the most supportive. "The people I am gearing up to tell are my brother and sister. They are both close to the situation. They are both therapists and both counsel HIV patients." "I told my sister that I was closest to first, then the others." When the experience of revelation to the first sib or sibs is supportive, then it can fuel the process of revealing to other family members. "I told my sister and brother-in-law. It turned out to be a very loving and affirming experience." "They were so wonderful. I felt so much better afterwards it made me wonder what I had been so afraid of." Some men may enlist the help of siblings in telling other members and/or helping parents deal with the impact on them. "I was terrified, terrified. My sister would take my hand and each day we would go to the next brother's house together. It all turned out just fine, but I was terrified." "My brother and sister-in-law will be a tremendous help once I tell my mother, because when she finds out, wham!"

Men will often make a plan for telling their parents. "This visit is going to be it. I am going to tell them." "I am going home this weekend, I have decided that it is time they know." As the event approaches, men often find apprehension mingled with resolve. "It's going to be hard. The bottom line is, it hurts." "My father is the biggest bigot you can imagine. I hope he can keep in his mind that I am his son, not the people he and his friends joke about." Men may consider their parents' emotional styles. "My mother gets angry and sad in a peculiar way that can feel very attacking." "When things get intense, my father shuts down. I have really felt shut out before. The last thing I can handle around this is feeling shut out."

After much consideration and fantasizing about revealing, the event eventually happens. "We just sat around the kitchen table–the site of many family meetings–and I told them. There were no outbursts, no attacks. But it was very sad." "It was just the opposite of what I had imagined. There was no swooning, no 'Oh, my God.' They said that they were worried about just that, and wondered if that was why I had been acting the way I had been. My father is a doctor, so it ended up being discussed in a matter-of-fact, clinical way." Some men will be surprised by the lack of intense emotion and attempt to find out their parents feelings. "They did not fall apart as I had expected. I asked my mother why not and she said, 'Well, by the time you get to be my age, you have been through a lot.'" Other men will find their parents being more emotional. "I told them the night I arrived. My mother alternately would pin me down, asking some very pointed questions–who–what–when–where, then she would cry. It kind of went on all weekend. We went out to dinner one night and in the middle of that she started getting teary and asked more questions."

After revealing, men often experience a great relief. "A giant burden was lifted, it felt great." "There was a lot of pain involved, but I felt that I went through it with them." Many men will look back and wonder why it was so hard. "Three months down the line I realize it was not nearly as bad as I thought." "It turned out to be such a good experience. I wish I had done it earlier."

Some men will be faced with telling their children they are positive. "I had to gradually tell all six of my children." "I told my sixteen-year-old son about a year after I found out, after I had settled down." Just as men have to negotiate their parents' reactions to the knowledge that their son is positive, men who are fathers are called upon in a more direct way to help their children face the knowledge. "He said, 'Everything was going so well and now this' and he began to cry." "I really felt like I was letting him down, but we got through it. He is coping pretty well now." "I think it is hardest on the kids I do not see so often. Some I see weekly, others only a couple times a year. I hear the anxiety in their voices, 'How are you doing?'"

An Ongoing Process

What men find is that revelation is not so much an event as an ongoing process of bringing the knowledge of being infected into the relationship, and negotiating the relationship in the face of the knowledge. Many men feel that revealing their antibody status to people who are not positive subtly to profoundly alters the relationship. "Announcing that you are positive changes the nature of the relationship that you have with people." "It's almost as if they are organized around your death. The result is you have to work doubly hard with them in order to keep yourself looking at a future that may feel limited, but still a future." With friends, men may feel that they come to symbolize the reality of AIDS. "It shatters their fantasy. They think, 'Yeah, I am playing safe.' But when you tell them, they wonder if they really are." In the face of revelation, men are still left with the damaged sense of self that accompanies being positive. Some will find the sense of being damaged continuing in the relationship. "People tend to respond negatively, despite their best efforts to put on a brave face. It still creeps into their response. Then it creeps into their response to me." "I am surprised when friends that know come up and give me a big kiss. I wonder, 'What are you trying to do, show me how brave you are?'" Expressions of concern can come to feel like a potent reminder of the gravity of the situation. "I was at a friend's funeral. At first I had not told people because I did not want to change the way they felt about me, but eventually I told them. There I was at Keith's funeral and people kept asking me about how I was doing. I did not want to see that look of concern in their eyes."

Men must also continue to negotiate their families. Expressions of familial concern may be reassuring, but at times can enhance anxiety and feel intrusive. "My brother and sister in-law were great, but it got to the point that I had to tell them that every time we talk, we do not have to talk about how I feel." "My mother calls up periodically and asks how I am doing, am I getting enough rest, etcetera." Some parents become quite knowledgeable about HIV infection. "My father started researching and sending me articles. It's nice, but I would rather hear about his last fishing trip than the latest article on HIV he found." "My parents became very savy. They knew when it was time for my T-cell counts and would begin calling a week before, and would call when they thought the results would be in." Again men find there is a delicate balance between their anxiety and the anxiety of others. "I finally had to say, 'Look, Mom, this makes me anxious too. When you get anxious, it makes it worse.'" "Sometimes it feels like an extension of, 'Don't forget your jacket,' only this time we are not talking the flu."

Men may also find that in revealing their status to friends and family, they also 'lose control' of the information. "I ran into an old friend that I had not seen for a while. He said, 'Gee, I am sorry you tested positive.' I freaked! I asked who had told him. It turned out to be someone that I had not told. I was really pissed. It is my life, my body, and it feels like everyone knows now." "I was really shocked. I thought I had made it clear that it was told in confidence, but then I found out that they had told their friends. I found out after it had been around the block a few times." Some men may find that the information changes considerably as it travels around. "All of a sudden I hear that I am on death's door. Now I am supposedly dying when I have never felt better in my life. I do not even want that thought in the universe, let alone someone spreading around my business community that I am dying. I can't believe I did it, but I tracked down this person that I hardly knew and really put him on the spot and demanded that he correct whatever misinformation he was conveying."

SEXUAL DIALOGUES

I am not as worried about sex. I do not feel as hesitant as before.

In THE TWILIGHT ZONE sex often was viewed as an anathema. For many men sex shifted from an exciting pursuit to "the very thing that got me into this mess." During THE LONG HAUL, feelings regarding sex and a damaged self tend to modulate and many men begin once again to pursue sexual contact and relationships. For single men, revelation is often a central aspect in the pursuit of sexual contact and attempts to establish new relationships. The data indicated that revelation in the context of sexual dialogues and new relationships called for its own category.

Men who initially disavowed sex often find their interest returning. "I am starting to feel sexual again–and its nice to feel that energy." "Before it was, 'no way.' But now I find myself thinking about it a lot." Some men may encounter an opportunity long before they are ready. "He was very interested, some friends were promoting it, but I was afraid that if I had sex with him, he would go back to France and I will always be wondering if I passed anything on to him." Some men experienced little disruption in their sexual activity. "There was no way, just no way I could stop having sex. I suppose some people do, but I am having no part of it."

Whether or not men initially experience a severe disruption in their sexual fantasies or activities, when it does come to sexual contact they are faced with the knowledge that they are positive, and infectious. "At first I felt like a leper." "I have to play safe, because I am not safe. I have this condition that is a death sentence. So that makes me an unsafe person." As they return to sexual and relational pursuits, men may find themselves mourning the "good old days." "In the old days, you didn't have to worry about being safe or unsafe. The spontaneity is gone, replaced by the fear that I could kill someone."

Many men find their first sexual encounter to be an anxious one. "It was anonymous so it was easy–I suppose. I am troubled by it. We masturbated, but I think of hangnails. What if I somehow managed to infect him?" "It was pretty intense. I just kept saying relax, you are being safe, it's okay, you are not hurting anyone." Many men will choose not to tell anonymous partners about their antibody status. "I make a clear distinction between sex and dating. If it's sex, I play excruciatingly safe and that is that. If I am interested in dating someone then I put it on the table right away." "I tend not to tell them at first. If it is stretching into the third or fourth date and it feels like there may be some potential, then I will tell them." Men sense the risk of this approach. "I have heard it debated at TPA a lot. Is playing safe the issue or is honesty the issue? Should people have the option of declining having sex with someone who knows they are positive, or is it a mutually assumed risk?" "If I started going out with somebody, and then three or four months later they told me they were positive, I'd kill the son of a bitch. But then I know what it is like from the other side." Some men will encounter the risks of this approach. "One person went off on me, but it was clearly his own fears and stuff."

Some men will find the emphasis on sex shifting to an emphasis on relationships. "I have a hard time going out. Sex is not as important as an honest connection. But that means putting being positive on the table, and that is a big risk." Men who tended to use sexual activity to modulate self-esteem are faced with rethinking sexuality. Some may feel that it is no longer an option. "When I think about it I used to use my sexual frequency to bolster self-esteem. Now it isn't so frequent anymore. A voice says. 'No, I can't do that.' " "When I am not feeling good about myself I tend to lean toward sex–all of a sudden I do not have that release twice a week."

Other men will attempt to maintain the status quo of their sexual patterns. "For the longest time it was pretty much business as usual. I rarely told anybody. Sex was starting to lose its appeal. I felt like I went from being a master fucker to being afraid to tell anyone the truth." While some men will go on having sex without revealing their status, others will find that not doing so begins to feel complicated and burdensome. "I was talking with this guy in the bar the other night and it looked like we were heading for the sack. I said, 'I want you to know that I am positive.' In telling him I got in touch with my own integrity." Men are often surprised at the number of other men who will have sex with them knowing they are positive and how much better they feel about themselves in revealing their status. "He thanked me for telling him, and that it did not matter as long as we played safe. In the middle of talking about it, my self-esteem was hitting a high because I was brave enough to talk about it." "Since I started making it a point of telling people, rarely has anyone said, 'no.' It really is surprising how many men are willing to have sex with someone they know is positive." After successful encounters men may find their approach and philosophy changing considerably. "What the hell, why lie? They are going to find out anyway. If someone told me he was positive in a bar, then I would be immediately attracted to him because he was being honest." Whether they reveal their antibody status or not, the men in the study were adamant about practicing safer sex. "I read articles about the decline of safe sex. I just can't believe it–fathom it–that people would risk contracting what I am struggling with." "I see it, I hear about it and I think, 'Fools! You do not know what you are getting yourself into.' " Over the course of time, many men will handle sexual encounters and dating in all three ways. "I have done them all. Tell people up front. Not tell them, and told them after a couple of dates. None of these is any fun."

Some men whose sexual activity has tended to be in the context of anonymous encounters often resume their patterns. "I am embarrassed to admit it, but I go to the bookstores or a bar where they have a 'backroom.' Sex is almost like evil, yet so necessary." In this context men rarely disclose their antibody status. "There is so much guilt involved. I want to be able to say, 'I am HIV-positive.' But I don't." "It is hard to get away from the feeling that you are doing something wrong, no matter how safe you play." In the context of anonymous sex establishments, positive men may be shocked at what they see. "I am surprised by the level of ignorance. I would never fuck or be fucked without a rubber, but I see it going on." "Sometimes I wonder how much HIV is spread in a given week." It may also encourage them to engage in their activity of choice. "Oral sex is free and rampant. I assume everybody is aware of the risk and has made their choice. I go ahead and indulge, but it is hard to feel good about it; the doubt still lingers."

The men in the study who were primarily into anonymous sex tended to engage in activities with a level of risk they feel comfortable with. "I primarily have oral sex, giving and receiving without a rubber. The general impression seems to be that is okay." "I will do everything without condoms except fuck. That requires a rubber." Though they continue to engage in sexual activity, men may find themselves worried about transmission. "I often feel guilty, wondering if I passed it on." "They kept saying that oral sex was okay, so I kept doing it, yet I often worried about it. Then I read somewhere that it was not always safe and I felt awful."

Some men find themselves moving beyond their safer sex comfort zone. "I hate to admit it, but I have engaged in unsafe sex. I fucked a guy without a rubber, but I did not cum, and I let someone rim me once. Every now and then I look back on it and feel terrible. I was on drugs, and doing poppers and it just kept getting wilder and wilder. I did and did not want it to stop." "I kept thinking in the back of my mind, 'This is not right,' but he kept pushing things into unsafe sex. Afterwards part of me felt terrible, but then I thought he must know he is playing with fire."

Many men find that regardless of the context of their sexual activity, be it an ongoing relationship, dating, or anonymous that it is hard to feel completely good and comfortable. "It never goes away. I feel tainted and I would hate to pass it on." "I have gotten more comfortable over the years, but it is still there. Even with my partner who is positive, I worry about passing on some other virus or germ, or about passing on another strain." Yet many men will find that despite the guilt and potential worries, they continue to engage in sex. "It's weird, I'm sitting here and telling you how messy and complicated it feels, but I will not stop going out for sex either." "I know from experience with friends that you get to the point with this illness that the last thing you want to do is have sex. I want to get it while I can. Before I have to give that up as well."

Many men will find the longing for a relationship returning. "I have been thinking that I am feeling ready to go out and meet someone romantically or socially. It would be nice to have a date–to go out." While pursuing relationships may have felt complicated in the past, they often sense a greater complication. "It's never been easy when it comes to dating or lovers." The fear of rejection is often present. "I just can't risk being around people who would dump me because I am HIV-positive." Men may also struggle with their own avoidance. "There are times when I still feel, 'Keep away!' but I do not have to stay in that place." Men who pursue support groups may have an agenda. Men may also wonder if their being positive was a factor in other situations. "I do not know if it really happened, but there was this guy I used to run into. We always chatted and were very friendly. Then one day, he started shying away from me. I have always wondered if it was because someone told him I was positive." "In the back of my mind I thought I might find a boyfriend at TPA. One of the reasons I joined was the hope of finding a lover."

In thinking about relationships men often encounter the possibility of their illness. "Am I going to get involved in a relationship, get sick–then he will not be able to handle it–take off and I will really be up the creek." "I sometimes wonder what if I get tight with someone and then I get sick and they take off." In thinking about what may be ahead, men may think about the particular qualities in potential partners. "I want someone who is more sincere–who can get on my level and want to pursue a relationship. Time is of the essence." "I want someone who is strong and steady. I do not want to put myself in the position of potentially latching on to someone who can't handle it if I become ill. Then I will be in the double position of having them walk out."

Men who do not initially reveal their status and find a relationship developing are faced with eventually making their revelation. "After the fourth or fifth date when I realized that it was serious, I told him I was positive. He was very supportive. It was the first time I had ever cried with somebody in public. He was clear that he was not going to pull out–that he still wanted to proceed." Some men will find the relationship progressing significantly while they struggle with revelation. "It was going so well. In the back of my mind I knew I was HIV-positive and I did not know how to tell him. He said he thought he was and I told him I thought I was, but I just could not tell him." When men do reveal their status they often feel all of the fears that complicate new relationships: rejection, transmission, sense of being damaged. "We were practicing safe sex. But there were a few times we 'slipped' in the heat of the moment. So when I finally told him I said I was sorry. I felt even worse about that–that I may have contaminated him, that he may be so pissed he would take off. The possibility that I may have 'contaminated' him made me feel dirty all over again."

A great deal of healing can be found in a relationship. Men may find the sense of being damaged diminishing considerably. "I started to feel good about myself again. When he did not run, I stopped feeling like a leper, that I did not have to keep everybody away from me." "It was really nice to be with him–to spend time with him and to share things with him. It really started to help me heal." Men find that being with other men is still possible and highly reassuring. "He is the first person I have kissed since testing positive." "It felt like I do have a chance at love and commitment after all." Though they may have longed for it, men may be surprised when it does happen. "I wanted to date. I had no intention of having a lover again. But here was this guy who was real." Members of large groups for positive men may also observe the differences a relationship can make in a person's approach to being positive. "One of the jokes in the group is that when two people link up they have a flight into health and will not be back until they lose their lover."

Many men will encounter differences that they find hard to negotiate in dating men who are negative. "I tried dating this guy, but he refused to get tested. If he can't deal with taking the test, how in the hell is he going to deal with me?" Some men will find that they feel negative men tend to minimize the impact. "I was dating this guy–but all he would say about my being positive was that 'I love you; it does not matter.' He wouldn't hear anything else. Is that dealing with it?" "He had a hard time when I would get in a funk, and the world started closing in on me. I kept trying to explain that this was what being positive was all about. He just could not get it and I got more and more frustrated." The loss of a sense of future is often a central experience for men who test positive and they may find that it creates a strong point of difference. "It threatens to cut life short. I do not think it is unrealistic to plan ahead or have the future in mind, but that is something that I have been able to develop. Someone who is negative has not had to do that. It is a whole different perspective on living."

Others will find it very reassuring when negative men want to pursue a relationship with them. "Its very reassuring when they don't run away." "He is negative and still wants me–that feels pretty good." Some men find the sense of being damaged easing when negative men continue to pursue them. "I feel like damaged goods and who wants damaged goods? Apparently he does." Some men will find that another man more interested in the relationship than antibody status to be powerfully healing. "He is negative. He has more to fear from me than I do from him. When he went to be tested and came back negative, it was almost like he was sorry. I said, 'Please do not be sorry.'" "I am not grateful; the prevailing feeling is that it feels good." "All of a sudden I am thinking about the future again. Sure the doubts and fears about getting ill are still there, but I also am thinking about the vacation we are planning and getting a new house together."

Other men will decide to focus on relationships with other positive men. "I have decided to only date positive men. It is just less complicated that way." "I do not have to worry about infecting another guy who is positive; it feels so much more comfortable. I met him at TPA which is something I wanted. I wanted to have a friend who knew everything." Facing similar adversity together can be an important factor. "We are in the same boat. It makes a big difference." "The negative guys I dated just did not get it. He knows exactly where I am coming from." Again, many men find relationships to be healing. "One of the biggest benefits of TPA was finding Greg. I have never felt happier, never felt better about being gay." "Life really started to turn around after we got together. I find myself thinking that I should not be feeling this good with being positive and all, but I do."

Along with the relief and joy of finding a relationship evolving, the potential sorrows that the future holds may also intrude. "We were lying there. He was asleep and it felt so good, but I also found myself wondering, 'Which one of us will go first?' " "We had a big scare the past few months. Dan's T cells dropped quite a bit, but then they went up with the last count."

CALMING DOWN

Sometimes I think I am in denial because I am not at home freaking out anymore.

As THE LONG HAUL progresses, men often find themselves calming down. The knowledge of being HIV-positive and the potential for disease progression continues to exert its impact but in more subtle ways. Anxiety often becomes less dominant and men may struggle with what it means to be HIV-positive on a more existential plane. Many men are surprised when they find themselves feeling calmer after so many months of anxious torment.

Many men will look back over the period of time that has elapsed since testing positive and reflect on their initial assumption of impending death. "It's been about a year. I thought I would be dead by now." "I just remembered that it has been two years since I had my braces taken off. I tested positive four months after finally finishing with the orthodontist. At first I thought it all had been pointless. I did not think that I would be around in two years to see the result." Men who have lost partners to AIDS look back to the deaths of their partners as markers. "I never thought I would be alive six years after Ed died." "It's been five years since Stan died. I am still here, still going, and despite all my worst fears, I am still discovering new things." Men may also look back on the terror they felt. "I was just so terrified. You could have told me to go sit in front of that store and it would have helped." "It is really amazing to sit back and recall just how totally freaked out I was."

Men may also find a sense of hope growing. "I have been hearing a lot about a vaccine for infected people. This is big news. I was almost giddy when I read about it." "I do a lot of reading about HIV. It does look more and more promising." As men read and learn more about HIV and are less anxious, they are often able to assume a more accurate placement of themselves on the continuum of infection and feel comfortable with it. Articles that at one time may have been interpreted as not offering relief may now be interpreted as offering hope. "If your immune system has not gotten real trashed yet, it seems like things are more treatable. I still do not hope for twenty or thirty years down the line. But it is not hard for me to imagine five or ten years." "Every time I read a positive article I have a sense of hope; it's comforting. I do not hope to live to see sixty or seventy–but a few more." The hope for more effective treatment can become an important handle for infected men. "You gotta hang on–you just have to hang on–because something just may be around the corner."

Men are often still highly aware of being HIV-positive but struggle with its meaning and impact on a broader, almost existential plane. "Part of my struggle of day-to-day living is living with this thing of being HIV-positive. It is core to my being, to who I am right now and it is going to be until it is over with. It does not rip me apart like it used to but it is there." "It is not that dramatic anymore. I still get up and go to work, but it's there. It has kind of taken the edge off–life just is not as spontaneous and carefree anymore." As they reflect, men may encounter some sadness as they feel the loss of a less burdensome existence. "When I am up, I realize just how much I miss the way I used to be. I am never totally up. There is the reality that this is not going to go away." Some may find themselves wondering what it would be like if one day *it* went away. "I find myself daydreaming sometimes. What would it be like if one day they found a cure and all of this would be over, behind us, gone?"

As men struggle with the impact of knowing they are positive, men often encounter disease progression and death in the friendship matrix. While this can be discouraging, it can also be calming and reassuring. "Having lived through Dick's diagnosis and seeing how well he handled it, how he takes everything in stride, left me feeling that I could handle it too." "It was not a big boom like we thought a diagnosis was going to be; it was–I guess–a quiet transition." Men also may encounter the deaths of friends. Again this experience may also be reassuring. "He was the first person I knew who died very comfortably and beautifully. I think he taught me a great deal about how to face death."

Having to grapple with feelings about one's homosexuality men may find themselves at a greater level of self-acceptance. This time as they look back, they may wonder just what was going on that seemed so imperative to hide. "I am at a point where I look back on all of the years where I had to play games and it makes me sick. Part of it was me and part of it was them–the rabid homophobes and my buying into it. Why, why did it have to be that way?" "When I think back on how afraid I was, I really wonder what it was all about. I also wonder how much I may have lost out on. How much did my family lose out on? How much did the world lose out on?" As they negotiate people in the present men often find a new attitude evolving. "I look at people and think, 'What can you do to me? What can you do that would be worse than what I have to deal with now? I can be the gay person I want. I can talk about it openly with family. I would not have before because I thought it would bother them and because they would not want to hear it. No longer. I am Bob, I am a gay man, and I am HIV-positive. Accept me for all of that or get out of my life. Because I do not want to deal outside of it.'" Men may also find themselves giving up struggling with their family. "I decided okay, I can no longer fight for her acceptance. It is not worth it. She would not accept me before, she is not going to accept me now, so I do not bother anymore. I discovered that the elusive praise I wanted from my mother was over the rainbow. I can and do feel good giving up the struggle."

As the process of calming down progresses men may find themselves reporting: "I am doing very well." Men often experience and observe changes in their general state of mind. "I am able to read again. Go to the beach and read. I could not sit still all winter." "In many ways, things are a lot more focused for me than they were before." Anxious vigilance may recede as well. "After awhile, I realized that nothing bad had happened, that I did have the tools I need to deal with this." Events that may have caused a great deal of anxiety and disruption are not as distressing. "It is still upsetting to see sick guys, but I do not get as down about it." "I feel fine. I have seen people who feel fine get sick and die. But I know many people who are positive who are going along just fine. I do not feel as weird about it anymore." The sense of self as damaged may modulate as well. "The group helped me feel more normal about it. Not that I had something terrible inside me, that I was just an infected person. I think I have formed a better image." Sadness and anxiety may come to be viewed as being parts of being positive, not the totality. "There is a sadness to it, but I am doing more than I did before, and more deliberately." "In spite of the horror of this disease, there are still great times happening now."

Many men come to value their sense of calm and nurture it. Anxiety and anxious preoccupation with potential disaster is viewed differently. Anxious preoccupation comes to be viewed as a signal that it is time to calm down. "I know there are times and there will be times when I have to calm myself down or get in touch with my spirituality." "It took time to assimilate being positive and what it meant. To be able to draw on what I knew. To calm down the part of me that is scared. That I guess came out of therapy." Some men begin to realize that testing positive and learning to live with the knowledge and its impact is an ongoing process. They come to realize that getting to the point of feeling calmer was part of a larger process. "There is a hell of a lot of stuff you have to go through to get into the acceptance mode." "It was a hard road to get to this point, this place, this way of viewing it. I want to hold on to it."

Men often find their priorities changing. "I thought my Mercedes and all the other things were important. But today I realize that it is about life and experiencing life to the fullest." "I really appreciate the world and things that I normally would take for granted. There is a much greater sense of appreciation." Men may change their approach to their career and more readily dispense with people or activities that are stressful or not enjoyable. Work can be an anathema to me, which is scary because I am self-employed. I feel like I am cheating some of my clients, but I am just not willing to work twelve to fourteen hours a day any more." "I had two clients that I just had to stop working with. They were just too awful and too demanding. I felt totally justified. They were my biggest clients and brought a great deal of money into the business, but it just was not worth the stress." Men may also find that they have little patience for activities they once engaged in out a sense of obligation rather than enjoyment. "I have little time for things I do not want to do. Be it friends, benefits, clients, I used to go ahead and do it, but now I do not think about it very long. I just do not do it. I wonder why I did not do that before." "I have tended to take the approach, 'I am not fucking around with that anymore.' If I do not like something, then I ask, 'Why am I doing it?'"

As men eliminate the things they do not care for, or are too stressful, they find themselves devoting more time to activities that are calming, reassuring, and do feel important. "I want to do the things I always wanted to do. I started volunteering for things. When I am helping others, I feel that I am doing something valuable and something that means something." "In some ways the quality of my life has improved. I am more concerned about making some-thing good." Men who tended to be somewhat isolated may take more comfort in relationships. "I am more social than before." "It used to be let's go for it; let's party and not miss anything out on the bar circuit. Now it's let's make a nice meal, sit around the fire and enjoy each other." Some men find themselves more engaged with the world and what it has to offer. "I used to be content with just hanging around the house puttering. Now it's hard unless I have a wonderful book or something really good on TV. I feel some of my days are being taken away, and I want to be out enjoying life. On one hand there will be plenty of days, but some of those days I just may not be able to physically be out there."

Men may find themselves being drawn to aspects of life they may have taken for granted, finding a sense of calm and purpose. In general, the softer, calming aspects of life become more important. "We have a cute little house in Michigan. We go out and sit and look up at the stars. That makes everything worth so much." "I have become so aware of nature. We go out and just sit and look at the beauty of it. It's just awesome. I have become able to just sit and study it. The birds, the woods, the garden. It is just so incredible. I find myself wondering why I never noticed it before." "I find myself thinking a lot about love and beauty, and the things I do and can do that reflect them." Some men may renew or develop their spirituality. "I started shopping for churches. I found one that has a large gay population and is more interested in people feeling good about themselves than dogma." "I joined Dignity. It felt like I was coming home, that church could offer me something, after all." Some men find their sense of religion and spirituality changing and evolving. "I used to be very religious until I went to college. Now I am more interested in God as a God of creation. The things I see in nature. Not a God of dogma and rules and damnation. A God of purpose, and peace, and beauty."

Some men may come to appreciate HIV infection and certain aspects of its impact. "There are some benefits to this disease. It forces you to take a good, long, hard look at yourself and your life." "It has caused a great deal of grief. But I am beginning to see some good things coming out of it." Enjoyment, the lack of stress and maintaining the calm become important organizers. "I do not believe in saving. I am not as cautious with my money. I do not need a nest egg in twenty years. What the hell–I want to have a good time while I can." "I am not so worried about tomorrow. I'd rather have a nice time today, to a reasonable point." As the process continues some men find themselves better able to handle stress in general. "I am very conscious of stress. I believe it trashes my immune system so I am working on managing it better." "I am doing everything I used to but handling it better. I am much better at dealing with stressful situations, and will also eliminate things that are too stressful."

LOSS OF FUTURE

Tomorrow does not have the promise that it used to.

The loss of the sense of future continues to be a prominent aspect of men's experience. Though it may not be as dominant and anxiety provoking as in earlier areas, the disruption in the experience of self as an ongoing entity presents frustration, sadness, and challenges for men. As stated earlier, the sense of future is subject to expansion and contraction. Many men will find ways of adapting to this disruption in the experience of self, adopting shorter-term goals to help them maintain a sense of ongoing, progressive experience. "I use my plans and goals like a grappling hook. It's like I throw it out there and it is something to hold onto, it helps to anchor me."

At times a sense of despair may color the future. "There is not a really great future right now." Disruptions in dating or partner relationships may contribute to a decline in optimism. "It's feeling pretty bleak right now. I broke up with my partner of several years and I know that it is coloring things right now." Acute illnesses and deaths of friends may also contribute to a decline. "It is hard when friends get sick and die. I am there trying to help out as much as I can. It's hard not to see yourself in the same place somewhere down the road."

As the process of Calming Down continues, men often find themselves more optimistic and less anxious about what the future may hold, however, this is a fairly fragile balance. Time continues to pass. "The future is better now, though I get a little scared when I think how many years have gone by." "I just realized that I am going to see 1990. Three years ago I did not think I would be here." Looking forward often raises some anxiety. "The biggest thing about being positive is that you do not know what your future is going to hold." "You don't know when it will happen or how it will happen." As time goes by men often reflect on the sense of future, looking back on how their experience has changed and evolved. "It took me six months, actually even longer. I am still in the process of understanding–death is not imminent, it's not going to be tomorrow; it's a long process." "Things immediately feel like they are gone, another loss, then eventually it may turn out not to be true. First a shortened time frame, then all of a sudden it's two years later, then I think maybe I can push out the frame a little farther."

The prospect of illness and death often arises as men look to the future. "Whenever you say things about this illness, the specter of death rises with it." "The unknown is what's scary, and there is so much unknown in all of this." As they look ahead, men may wonder what illness and death may be like. "I spent a great deal of time wondering what it will be like." "Oh, yeah, I wonder about it, dread it, and try to avoid it. It does not make me crazy like it used to but it is there, lurking." Some men will attempt to counter this process. "I finally said, 'Look, this is pointless. You do not know how you are going to react until you're there.'" "Of course, you could be run over by a truck. But then it's a lot easier to assume you're not going to get smashed in an intersection, than to think you're not going to get AIDS."

Men are often highly aware of feeling that HIV has contracted their experience of and assumptions about life and their participation in it. "HIV narrows your vision of what you can do, personally, professionally, and for me, especially sexually." In the face of narrowed choices, men can come to feel trapped with no place to go but down. "Your choices are constantly limited and that terrible sense of feeling in a whirlpool, a narrowing at a faster and faster pace." Men may come to feel that future progress is blocked. "It kind of finalized, drew a line for a summing up. I felt frustrated that I am going to lose, or not be able to do what I want to do for as long as I can." "Sometimes it feels like a waiting game. Like treading water, not really going anywhere."

As they anticipate the future men often encounter their roles in their families and see themselves as not present. "There is a piece of property in the family that goes back for generations. I am the only one in the family that can be counted on to hold onto it until my nephew is ready. I am feeling that I am letting my parents and the whole family down. I may not be around to care for it." "There is a long history in my family of the children taking care of their parents. Now I look at my parents in their seventies and I think that I will not be able to help them." Men who have children encounter the very painful prospect of not being in their children's lives. "One son graduates high school this year, another is in college. I really feel like I am abandoning them." "I get so sad. I look at my little girl and realize that I am probably not going to see her go to the prom, or get married, or be a mother." Men who are partnered often anticipate in a similar vein. "I know it will be rough on him. I have set things up so he will not have to worry financially, but I would much rather be there with him." "We have had good times and rocky times. As crazy as things have gotten in the past, I do not want to have to leave him, to die and leave him alone."

As men negotiate relationships with people they have revealed their infection to, men often encounter other people's shaken assumptions of their future. Some men find the responses of others as confirming their fears rather than calming them. "I have a problem with people that do not quite understand the full dimension of the disease. Members of my own family and friends have this sense that death is imminent." "My birthday came around and I wondered if they were going to have another whopper party–because it may be my last." When men embark on plans and goals that will take several years to reach they may again encounter the anxiety of others. "When I told my family I was going back to school, some of them looked at me like I was crazy." When they find anxiety rather than reassurance men may find their own anxiety rise and feel resentful. "It really threw me. I wanted encouragement, but what I got was a lot of hesitation. I began to think that I was crazy for doing it after all." Other people may help them plan into the future. "My friends wanted to plan a trip to Europe for next spring. I fought and kicked, but they persisted. It really made me anxious. But somehow their confidence that I would still be here helped win me over. It is turning out to be something to look forward to." "I finally realized that my closest friends assume that I will be here for quite awhile. It made me sit down and think. To be less anxious about looking ahead. That yes, I probably will get sick and eventually die, but there is an awful lot I could be doing in the meantime."

Men often find long-term career plans blocked. "It short circuits your mental planning. The things you planned on doing with your life. That you have envisioned for yourself." "Before I was going to close down the business and open an interiors-oriented gift shop. I love to travel so that would be how I would stock the place. But now I say, 'No way.' I just cannot take that kind of risk." Men may encounter a sense of bitter disappointment. "I used to operate on the assumption that I was going to live a long time and was going to be a certain type of gay male. Now I am struggling with the contrast that being positive brings to the picture. At times it really gets to me, like it's all down the drain." "I have tended to view myself along a path, and tended to look to the future with a great deal of optimism, hope, and joy. It's an affront to now have to deal with life this way."

Many men eventually come to terms with the narrowed view of life and plan within that framework. "I finally stopped fighting it, stopped railing against it. I realized that it was also a release to say that I might not see 1993." "When I graduated, I did not think about a long-term career. I did not have to worry about getting into a big law firm, where I would have to work sixty hours a week for seven years to maybe make partner." "I began to think more short-term. I extended my student loans over twenty-five years, did not worry about coming up with a down payment on a place to live, and charged more on my credit cards." Some men may find a sense of permission to not delay the good things in life. "In a way it gave me permission to live now, to go out, do and see things now, stop worrying about scrimping and saving for the future. The future is now." "I realized that I can't take it with me so I started traveling. I went everywhere, spent lots of money, but I am glad I did it. Now I am more interested in hanging around home and enjoying the garden."

The process of Calming Down is integrally related to the activities, experiences, and encounters of the Game Plan. In tending to the impact of testing positive, men are also tending aspects of their psychological lives that may have been problematic in the past. The experience of individual psychotherapy and/or group membership often entails a reworking of past traumas and pain. Tending to current and past trauma leads to the process of Calming Down and becoming increasingly comfortable with one's self in the face of HIV infection.

A dramatic example of this is seen in men who have struggled with addictions for years and in the course of negotiating HIV, find the courage to seek and maintain sobriety. "I was out of control, mainlining cocaine. I thought sure my counts were down and I would be dead soon, but they came back a hundred points higher than the last. I thought, 'I am going to live after all.' I have to get off of this stuff." "I realized I was in more danger of the drugs killing me than the HIV. I realized that I wanted to live after all, and the only way to do that was to get out of my addictions."

PLANNING AHEAD

You have to plan ahead. It makes you plan.

Men who know they are positive find themselves planning for the future in radically different ways than they were previously accustomed. Rather than planning for dream vacations, new homes, careers, or other goals, they often find themselves planning more in the direction of adequate insurance, and to be able to live in a reasonable manner in the face of AIDS. Maintaining and/or obtaining medical, disability, and life insurance become major concerns. Some men will find career moves blocked by the threat of losing their insurance benefits and the fear of facing AIDS without medical coverage. Considerable anger, resentment, and fear can become organized and expressed around medical insurance and the threat of its loss.

The tendency in our country to view health coverage as a commodity and therefore subject to the profit motive can arouse considerable stress and anger. "The only thing I get angry about in this whole thing is insurance." Accounts of insurance company practices often filter down into the community. "A friend of mine works for an insurance company. I get furious when she tells me what they are doing. They have blacklisted my zip code. They even have a list of doctors in Chicago–if you are one of their patients, they will refuse you." "It's really fucked. Being sick or potentially sick is grounds for losing your health insurance."

Considerable fear can be generated that can at times intrude into the patient-physician relationship. "I even get paranoid with my doctor. Wondering what he was writing down–and what if some insurance company got ahold of it." "Finding out was a revelation–but there is not as much fear about getting sick now. I worry about insurance, that is what I am afraid of." If men need to approach their insurance company around HIV-related questions considerable fear may be generated. "My T cells were on the borderline. I called my insurance company to find out about AZT. She asked, 'What's your name, sir?' I freaked."

Pre-existing condition clauses can cause men to have to plan carefully and incur additional expense should they make a job or career change. Again insurance raises considerable uncertainty. "It's real scary around insurances. Since I left my old job, I have been paying for all of my tests for fear that my new insurance would not cover me at all." "It took elaborate planning and expense. I did a COBRA on my old policy, and paid for all of my tests until I met the pre-existing period for the new one." Some may feel trapped. "I really would like to get another job. But then I would lose my benefits. Then I would really be in trouble. Not only would my salary be cut in half, but I would lose my benefits and with half as much money I could not afford to COBRA."

Some men may find out they are positive at a time when they have no insurance. "I do not have insurance. I am not working now–that really worries me." "Right after I found out I was positive my company went bankrupt. There was no COBRA and the conversion that they offered was outrageous. Especially if you are trying to live off unemployment." For men who are without insurance, obtaining it can be tricky. "I am not being treated now. So I am trying to sneak in. I found out that companies base it on whether you are being treated." Some men will find themselves feeling that they are being dishonest. "I know I am cheating. I guess I kind of lied to them. They asked if I was being treated for AIDS. Technically I am not. I am not taking AZT, so I am not being treated. It feels like a fine line. I would like to be straight about it, but there is no alternative. I am doing what I can do."

For men who do obtain insurance in the face of HIV, the pre-existing time period is an important marker. "In September I will be halfway there. The pre-existing limitation is two years." "I get furious. I do not worry about holding out until I can get to Europe or my fortieth birthday. I worry about holding out until my pre-existing is met." Men in this position may come to resent the money spent on future coverage. "I cannot do anything with it. All this money so two years from now I will have coverage. I cannot put anything on it, not the important stuff like my T cells. If I get hit by a truck or break my arm I am okay." Paying for insurance out of pocket can be very expensive. "I had to take another job just to pay for my insurance. It was coming down to having food or having insurance."

Men who have health coverage often find themselves attempting to expand their coverage in anticipation of future problems. "I have already started making plans. I increased my disability coverage short-term and long-term. I got mortgage insurance so my partner will not have to leave his home." Uncertainty can invade even the most well-laid plans. "I checked on all my policies at work. I have a great disability plan, but if I lose my job, it all goes." Sadness and anger are often present. "It really is fucked. Here I am planning for my illness and death–not my retirement. It's like this disease takes everything, even your retirement."

Men also find themselves planning for their illness in different ways. "I told my doctor that when I have had enough, I have had enough. My father died of cancer. The last month he had enough but the docs kept poking at him. That is not going to happen to me." "I made out my living will and medical power of attorney. I do not want to prolong things, be miserable and suffering." Men find themselves planning out their wills. "It was spooky reading it and signing it. It sounds good in the lawyer's office but when you read it. . . ." "A will is not a testament to the fact that you have been financially successful and have a ton of money to leave around. It's a testament to the fact that you have to get your life in order because you are going to be dead in two years." Again, the sadness is often present as men plan for their future. "The whole poignancy of the two of us sitting down when we should have all of life ahead of us and planning out our funerals. It is really bizarre."

LOSSES

It feels like you are in the middle of a group of people in a field and they are shooting bullets. As people start to fall, the bullets are getting closer.

As men negotiate their own HIV infection they often encounter the illness and death of friends to the same disease. Some men will witness the gradual destruction of friendship matrixes that have evolved over several decades. Many men will be integral participants in their friends' illnesses, helping out as much as they can. Many men will say goodbye to friends they have known for many years.

The pain and sadness is often quite evident as men describe their encounters with friends. "Frank, what a sweet man. First he had a mild case of pneumocystus, then he got KS lesions all through his lungs and he has had hiccups for eight months." "I went out to see Bob. After I saw him I just cried. He looked so pitiful." As men negotiate the illness of friends the sadness for their friends' plight is often mingled with fear for themselves. "It's real difficult not to think about when you have friends. This summer I had two friends come out to visit. One was the minister for my partner's funeral. He is now ill with AIDS. The other is covered in KS lesions." Friends may serve as stark reminders of what may come. "One night it really upset me. He opened up his shirt and was covered in KS lesions. They were everywhere. We were both just devastated and depressed." Encounters with friends also remind men of the unpredictable nature of the disease. "I did not think I would see him again. But he bounced back one more time." "I expected him to die a year ago."

For many men the most difficult aspect of negotiating life in the face of HIV is the continued decline and loss of friends. Often men find the terror and uncertainty returning. "The hardest thing is to cope with my friends. A lot of them have been dying. I have had friends that I knew were positive and they are getting sick now. It's scary because you do not know when it might happen to you." "That's one of the problems seeing people in other stages. I saw my partner go though his getting ill and all that he went through. I am scared to death. I do not think I could go through it all." The continued deaths can have a powerful impact on men's sense of self. "It's hard to say goodbye to a friend without also saying goodbye to my hope, to my future."

For many men the death toll of friends, acquaintances, and partners continues to mount as time progresses. "Since the last time we met, I have lost many acquaintances." "He died last week. I was getting sick with a cold and was exhausted. I felt like I was hurting myself but also that I should be there for him." Many men will find in the wake of mounting losses that there are still more friends to tend to and often, far too often, to say goodbye to. "I have to fly out West to say goodbye to a friend I have known for ten years. He is near death. I just have to see him, though I dread the thought of going there." As painful as the process is, many men find themselves needing to say goodbye, to attempt to put closure on the relationship and its meaning. "I am so bonded to him; we have done so many wonderful things together." "We went out to LA to see my ex-lover–he is near death. We got off the plane and there was my old boss standing there talking to what looked like a little old man. I walked by and someone called my name. I recognized the voice.

The 'little old man' was my ex-lover." The loss of a partner often becomes a sad and powerful memory, many times a powerful reminder of what they may face as well. "I watched him. But as the days progressed I saw him change a great deal. Each day became an entity in itself. You do not think of life as being months or years, you look at it as being day to day. I think he finally accepted the fact that he was going to die. He used to look at me and break into tears and say, 'Joe, I am going to die.'"

Despair and confusion can emerge and a sense of incomprehensible enormity come to dominate men's experience as the losses continue to mount. "Initially I knew friends that all their friends had gotten wiped out. Then all of *my* friends got wiped out. It really hit home." "I do not know. I am losing all of my friends here in Chicago." A sense of sadness may come to color one's experience. "The whole community is less gay. We are dealing with a disaster of magnitude." A profound sense of vulnerability and aloneness may emerge. "I have felt the most vulnerable by being involved with friends during their illness. Right on the precipice of the process. I know for me that is a problem. I feel that I am caught up personally. I see myself in the future and it's very difficult." "I am getting closer to being alone again. I moved back here, worked hard at developing a support network and boom! there goes another one."

Men who developed an extensive network of other positive friends may come to find the relationships that were so helpful for them being whittled away. "I get invested in people and they get invested in me. Then they get sick and die and it all gets ripped away. It's like a part of you dies each time." "When I joined TPA a year and a half ago there was a whole bunch of people who have since died. Now there are a whole bunch of new faces." The very relationships that helped reassure, calm, and comfort may now become stark reminders. "I am seeing flocks of people drop. I can't turn away from it. It's hard to think I will have another five years. All of the people that were healthy when I joined are now dying or dead." "My biggest fear of belonging to the group is continuing to watch their disintegration–and then have to watch my own." Some men may find it increasingly difficult to keep engaged with people and to establish new relationships. "There are times I think it would just be easier to isolate, to be a hermit and not to have to constantly say goodbye." "Some of it is the fear of the pain to come. Getting to know and getting involved with people also brings the potential pain of losing them in the future."

As people continue to die men may find themselves wondering, at times feeling guilty, that they are still alive. "When people you love die, you do wonder why them and not me. Patrick, Chuck, both of them have been dead for five years now and I am still living." "I get a guilt complex around people who are so much younger, being on AZT, this and that. I am an old lady, and here are all of these young guys getting sick and dying." At times it cannot be comprehended; men find themselves feeling acutely alone–that the warp and weave of life has come unraveled. "I look about my apartment and there are group photographs. Everyone in them is dead, or dying, except me."

BALANCING

I can balance the fear I had earlier with the hope of making it through another year.

As time progresses men come to realize the sometimes delicate "balancing act" they are engaged in, trying to hold on to the sense of calm and hope that they have gradually achieved in the face of events that threaten to prompt despair. "Sometimes it feels like I am on a sidewalk. Then other times the sidewalk gradually narrows and it feels like a tightrope."

Men consciously or unconsciously look back to their initial response, and their gradual calming down and decide that they want to maintain the calm. "I made the decision that I was not going to let this change my life. I did not want it to. I wanted to go on living and enjoying life the best I could and what was going to happen was going to happen." "It did not do me any good, sitting there and wringing my hands. I used to think about it every day. But now I just go on."

Activities that buffer the damaged sense of self and are reassuring become emphasized. "When I am at work my life is pretty normal. It never enters my mind." "The business has probably been a godsend. It is something that I can really focus on and it will be able to support me and take care of me." "My career is giving me a wonderful outlook. It gets tense and crazy but it does not allow me to dwell on the other things. When a job is finished and looks great. I say, 'Yes, you still have it, you're still getting better, you're still living."

A sense of acceptance of a limited future often emerges. "At least now I know there is a future. Whether it is three or four years, it is not an endless amount of time, but it is time." "I do not look at myself as dying anymore. I look at myself as living and doing my damndest to enjoy it." As men come to feel more balanced, hope and joy may once again emerge and men are able to accept it as real and valid, a powerful buffer against the despair. "Sometimes I pretend that they have found a cure and I let that fantasy spin out. The energy I get from it is a real boost." Men who begin dating in this area find that the relationship is a powerful buffer and adds to the balance. "I spent the night with a guy I had been dating. I woke up the next morning and thought, 'This is great!' In the midst of all of this coming apart it still is possible to come together. It felt good to be with someone and have playful contact. It was a moment, a small place in time to forget what has happened."

Many men find that a good deal of effort will go into maintaining the sense of balance. "It really can be a burden just trying to keep your act together." "It's real hard sometimes to keep your mind centered on having a positive approach to this. It's all these little shock waves." Anxiety, doubt, and hopelessness invariably creep in at times. "Despite feeling on top of this disease there are still those moments of self-doubt, the job, disability, insurance. It all threatens to fly out the window."

Men often find themselves learning to tend to their emotional states, rather than be swallowed up by them. "I get in these, 'I want to be alone' moods. Then half an hour later I really want to be with somebody. I finally learned to pick up the phone. There are plenty of people who enjoy being with me; all I have to do is access them. I realize that sometimes I am keeping myself down, and that I can get myself back up." Men may become familiar with their emotional patterns and go with them, rather than fighting against, or being overcome. "Some days I find myself in a depression and lay in bed. I know it will pass. I don't feel like I am giving up; I feel like I am giving to me." "I go through cycles of being real paranoid about what is going on with me and being real positive and hopeful. It's a cycle–I guess it's just part of living with this. I am not as afraid that the way I feel one day will be the way I feel forever."

Time continues to pass and can again be reassuring and disconcerting. "I thought I would be dead with PCP by now. I have known I was positive for seven years. I wonder how much longer I have to go. On one hand I am amazed and hopeful, on the other, am I just another year closer?" The unexpected often happens. "The other day at work a friend called at 8:30, totally distraught that he was going blind. It took me all morning to pull myself back together." "It was a beautiful day. I was feeling great, looking forward to a good day, then the call came. Dean had died in California."

The Game Plan tends to buffer a great deal of anxiety and for many may replace worrying and preoccupation. "The preoccupation with AIDS is there but it's in the background. I am spending such a greater portion of my time taking care of myself. Basically it is because of HIV, but you know, I never really took care of myself until now, and it feels great." Some men will come to view anxiety as a sign that they need to engage in their plan. "I know the more I can hold on to this feeling the better. The minute I start slipping I need to do something. Go to the health club, work on an exciting project, whatever." Some men who go into psychotherapy use the process to help maintain their balance. "I resisted going to counseling at first but it makes a big difference. It really helps to keep me steady and I have learned different ways to keep myself steady." "There are so many things that can rock the boat. My therapist is real good at helping me see them, and to trust my feelings rather than run from them." Men who are able to observe their emotional processes are often able to apply them as they continue on their journey. "When everything is fine, there is nothing to assimilate. But then when something happens–your T cells go down, a friend dies–you have to assimilate it. At those times I get scared and I cannot make sense of it. I have to take care of the scared part before I can process it and understand it."

MELTDOWN

*I used to think that over time you reach some accommodation.
But you do, then something happens and it starts all over
again.*

Meltdowns are often painful and discouraging times. As the
quote indicates men reach a point of feeling calmer, less terrified
and more optimistic, then an event or series of events triggers the
all-too-familiar anxiety, sadness, and despair so prevalent in the
earlier areas of the experience. The events that tend to trigger Meltdowns– personal illness, the illness and/or deaths of friends–are
often discouraging in their own right. However, part of the profound sense of discouragement so prevalent in this area appears to
stem from the feeling of lost ground, the return of the intense
vulnerability of earlier areas. The ongoing effort to find a balance
has failed and men are plunged into despair. Meltdowns vary in
degree, intensity, and duration. Some may last a few moments,
others days and weeks.

Men often encounter times when feelings of intense sadness and
vulnerability intrude into their consciousness. "I have these moments where all of a sudden my strength has fled and I just start to
cry. A particular song or movie or something said triggers it." "I
have no symptomatology but I go through swings–probably more in
relation to friends and people who get sick. I do it right when I am
waiting to go to sleep. 'Gee, I wish I were dead–I do not want to go
through this shit anymore–I do not want anyone to have to bother
with me.'" Some men are able to reflect on their experience and
realize that these feelings do not come out of the blue, rather they
gain dominance. "It never really goes away; I can feel it turning
around in the back of my mind. It's just that sometimes it's right
there in my face." "When it hits it hits, it just takes over, then after
a while quietly recedes somewhere, only to come back again."

When Meltdowns are intense and protracted a profound sense of
discouragement is often evident. "At times the whole vulnerability
of life takes over." "Sometimes I just want to throw up my hands
and say, 'I have had it with this! I can't hear about it, read about it
anymore, or help anyone with it!'" Men may become confused and
frustrated wondering just what the problem is. "I think I am trying

to cope with coping. I have to operate on a level that I do not want to be operating on." "I really am very tired. I don't know if I am tired of waiting for something to happen and scared to death if it does happen. I am just scared to death of this thing." Preoccupation with body integrity and possible signs and symptoms may emerge as well. "I imagine pains here and there, suddenly I realize that I am driving myself crazy." "I found myself checking, checking, checking. Just like I was doing months ago. When I realized what I was doing I just broke down and cried. I thought all of that was behind me."

The future and hope for being taken care of often looks incredibly bleak. "I get really frightened when I read a study that said medical facilities are not gearing up and in ten years there will be a crisis. What if I get sick then and there is no place for me to go?" "I am beginning to think some of the people who died from this disease in the beginning are luckier than the people who will die in the future. The hospitals and insurance companies could handle it, but times have changed. I think of the black plague with people dying in the streets. The future does not look good."

Men may find themselves thinking about giving up. "I am afraid to say this but I am tired and I want to give up. I wish it would all be over with." "I used to get angry at my friends with AIDS who I felt were giving up and dying. But then I found myself feeling that way and I am not even on AZT. I realized that I needed to view it from their standpoint." In the midst of a Meltdown, death again feels imminent. "It's like a slide. All of a sudden you start moving faster, you pick up momentum, there is no way to stop, you keep heading toward the impact–death." A sense of misery, sadness, and lack of hope can come to dominate. "I am not very happy and it seems to be getting worse." "I have been at this for the last six years. I am so tired, I just want to go into a corner and cry."

Men may question themselves when they find themselves thinking about giving up, and may feel that they are doing something wrong. "I get confused about my attitudes. Is it smart or stupid to think this way? Is it true what some people say that if you think you are going to die you will?" "I went to TPA to learn how to be a positive person. Either I didn't get it, or it's all a bunch of nonsense. Was the way I was feeling just a facade? Or is there more to it than

'Chin up, keep plugging away'?" Men who are struggling with despair and confusion may find themselves isolating from sustaining relationships. "I am keeping to myself a lot." "My ability to relate has gone downhill. I just keep to myself a lot. I do not go out very often. Especially TPA and the after-meeting dinner groups." Some may feel that their feeling state will not be responded to in a helpful manner. "Everyone talks about fighting it, but when do you give up?" "I am afraid to tell my friends about the way I am feeling. Even though they know exactly what I am talking about they would say, 'get over it.'" When they find themselves thinking and feeling contrary to the "party line" a sense of failure may emerge. "I can't ask for help. No one talks about this. They all talk about fighting, and living positively and hope and courage." "I guess I am just not cut out to be a positively positive person." Some men may feel a sense of anger growing. "Sometimes when I hear people doing their up and positive about being positive number, I want to say, 'God damn it! Let me wallow in my own self-pity!'"

One of the triggers for Meltdowns is personal illness. "I got a cold, then I thought, 'This is it. I am going to be in big trouble.'" "I came down with a sinus infection and got so upset and depressed. I started seeing the rest of my life as one illness after another, of day in and day out of feeling lousy. Then I thought if I can't handle a sinus infection, how am I going to handle it when it really hits?" Some men may encounter the illness of a friend and a personal illness at the same time. "I got the flu, then Bart went into the hospital. I thought, 'This is it–I am dying.'"

Anniversaries can also trigger the emergence of the sadness and deep despair. "I am in my dying mode again. It has been two years this month that I tested positive. Everything is fine medically, but I do not feel hopeful at all. All of a sudden the bottom fell out. I was going along fine and then bam! My therapist pointed out that I had first come to her about this time last year, right after I tested positive." For seropositive surviving partners the anniversaries of their partners' illnesses and death often trigger similar reactions. "It's that time of year–the fall, the light is fading. This is the time of year Steve started to go downhill. Everything starts looking bleak this ᵗme of year. Including any hope for me." "It was as if somebody ᵗᵉ in and wiped out any and all of my hope. I was doing so well.

Then I realized it was the time of year when we first realized that Greg was not going to make it."

The illness and deaths of friends can also trigger a Meltdown. "So many people are ill now, I really get discouraged. I do not think I have felt really happy, or well, in months." "So I wonder when is my stroke coming, when are my KS lesions going to appear? My best friend had lesions all over his body." The deaths of friends can be profoundly discouraging, eroding into hope and confidence. Men are faced with not only mourning the loss of the relationship, but with mourning the loss of their optimism. "It's scary because I feel like it's getting closer to me and I feel more vulnerable." "It seems that every time someone dies it brings me that much closer. Even though my labs are fine and I am asymptomatic, I start feeling like I am dying."

As the losses of friends continue to mount, men often find their grief and sense of isolation mounting as well. "If your mother dies it lessens over time. But this just seems to get worse every day. I have buried three people in the last month. I read about this disease every day and its effects before you die." Some men can enter a state of continuous mourning. "My perspective is that I am in a state of constant grief and bereavement. I am losing all of my friends, all of my past history. Every picture I look at there are five guys and me. The rest of them are dead, but me." Men may stop and wonder if there is any way to find a sense of comfort and well-being in the face of the constant loss of friends to the same disease. "How do you go on 'living' when you are in a state of constant bereavement?" "I did not realize how hard it was going to be. I finally get back on my feet, the people started dying, so many friends are now gone, all to AIDS. Here I am doing fine, at least medically so, but I have not felt good in months. I really want my hope back and I wonder if it will ever return." In the face of the sadness the world come to look very bleak. "These are unhappy times. I am mentally and physically tired. So tired of trying to keep going. My last T-cell count was great–higher than last year–but I am so tired."

If a relationship that was formed shortly after testing positive was an integral factor in men feeling better and more optimistic, then a disruption in the relationship may trigger a flood of previous concerns. "After we met it all seemed to go away. Now we are fighting all of the time and he is threatening to leave. I am starting to get worried about my health, and feeling dirty and icky. I am freaked out about him and our relationship and freaked out about me." The breakup of a relationship, especially if it appears to be over HIV concerns, can trigger an intense Meltdown. "I thought it was going well; we were spending a lot of time together. He decided to get tested. I thought sure he would be positive. He turned up negative and shortly after that said he did not want to see me anymore. He would not say so, but I am sure he all of a sudden was afraid I would infect him." Some men may encounter a series of events, and find themselves in a long protracted Meltdown that shades into a considerable depressive episode. "I think I am in shell shock. I had a flu that lasted for several months, my T cells dropped, Ken died, and Jeff dropped me. I really got scared when I found myself wanting to die, to get it over with."

The human mind is often a maze of contradictions. Despite the profound sadness and discouragement there often remains a kernel of hope. "Yet at the same time I am saying my prayers and saying, 'Thank you for what I have, and please give me a few more years.' It's crazy; it's all at the same time."

TRANSITION TO AZT

I am a month overdue for my count. I figured this one would be it for AZT. I did not want to deal with it over the holidays.

Men tend to view beginning treatment with AZT as a central milestone in their experience of being positive. For those men who have known they were positive for a number of years with counts above the 500 level, approaching the point of beginning AZT often becomes a feared event. An indicator of how medical knowledge and approaches to the disease have evolved is indicated in the many men in this study who began AZT when 200 was the level most often used for initiating treatment, while currently, 500 is the range considered appropriate for beginning treatment. Men who were engaged in the process of rebuilding their sense of selves and becoming more comfortable with being positive often find their confidence shaken, and disappointed with the re-emergence of anxiety and fear. Once again being positive and its frightening implication intrudes and demands attention.

Men often become anxious as the time for their count approaches. As illustrated in previous properties, T-cell counts often become highly meaningful markers for positive men. A symbol of whether one is doing fine, or declining toward a diagnosis and death. As counts approach the 500 level some men may have a harder time going to be tested for fear of what it may symbolize. "I am due back for another count. I am balking at it. I am scared, afraid to go back. The fact in my mind is that it is not just a count–it means so much more." "I am very anxious because my doctor is one who believes that once you go under 500 you should start on AZT. I do not want to do that. I think I would have to admit that I am chronically ill. It was 520 last time."

Some men who have reached a more hopeful stance toward being positive may find themselves feeling shaken once more and resist the anticipated return to a more anxious state of mind. "I hope I do not have to go on AZT for another year–to give me more time to think and reflect on it. I have been feeling pretty settled lately after so many months of feeling awful. If I viewed it as a transition to a more hopeful stage it would be easier. But I am seeing it as the beginning of the end." Others view AZT as the beginning of a process of decline. "I am delaying going in for my count. The last time it was 540. I am sure this time my doc will say it is AZT time. I should just go in and get treated but I haven't. I feel like I am losing my life."

Some men will attempt to minimize the significance of the count. "The T-cell count is still in the primitive stage. You want to look for viral activity." Others will have developed a plan. "I will not go on AZT. I really do not think it does any good. I do not care what my doc says." "I am going to wait till my count goes lower. I am in the camp that says 500 is just too early." Other men will view AZT as a rather minor step. "I think I will go on AZT until something else comes along and then I will go on that until something else comes along. That is how I avoid the point of death." "For me it is a matter of what point do I decide to go on it. I hope I can wait long enough until something better is there and just keep moving to better things. It's just a matter of when to get started."

Some men will find their counts hovering around the 500 level for several years. "On one hand it is a relief. For four years they have been around 500. Some days I am thankful, but then every time I go in for a new count I wonder if this one will be it. There are times I wish they would just drop so I could stop sitting on pins and needles." "Every four months I wonder if this one will be it."

For some men the approach of AZT represents the enormity of what life has brought them. "I feel like I have been cheated and robbed. Life should be a little more laid back. Not so intense." "It is such a roller coaster. I get settled down and then something stirs it all up." Some men may find themselves confusing the work they have done to settle down emotionally with the progression of the illness. "It just does not seem fair. I have worked so hard to come to terms with this–groups, psychotherapy, exercise, relaxation–and they still drop." Many men sense that they are approaching another milestone of the illness. "I sense it's coming–AZT that is. I feel like I am being pushed forward. Forward into a place I do not want to go."

Chapter 8

It's Time

The study called me up first thing in the morning to say my T-cells had dropped below the magic number.

For many men, beginning antiviral therapy is a highly traumatic event. It often comes to symbolize disease progression, another step on the road toward illness and death. Many will find the turbulence of THE TWILIGHT ZONE returning. Concerns and fears that quietly receded into the background often once again dominate experience. Some men who did not experience the massive loss of coherence described in THE TWILIGHT ZONE after they tested positive, may experience the massive disruption in the wake of going on AZT. Just as in other categories, there is often a gradual calming and settling back into life's routines. While the fear of life being over may again dominate, gradually men find that life continues to unfold. For many men, the biggest challenge will be to feel that they are engaged in and able to keep pace with the opportunities that continue to be presented.

The properties of IT'S TIME are:

- *It's Real*–the sense of a higher degree of realization about being positive;
- *Poison or Helper?*–fears about toxicity versus confidence that the drug or drugs will help;
- *Meltdown*–the profound discouragement, disorganization, and often dramatic decline in functioning as encountered in THE LONG HAUL;
- *Doing Something*–a sense of relief that there is now something that can be done;

- *Losses*–the reminder of how many relationships have been lost to AIDS;
- *Established Dialogues*–the effects of the transition on established relationships;
- *The Game Plan*–efforts at combating the disease, and
- *Balancing*–regaining and attempting to maintain a sense of equilibrium.

IT'S REAL

Before I had to begin taking AZT, it was not all that real. But now that I am on AZT, it's real, real.

For many men one of the most difficult aspects of knowing they are positive, but asymptomatic, is the combination of knowledge of infection but the lack of symptoms to organize their experience around. While they possess knowledge of their infection that is extremely frightening, men often feel they are only left with an array of confusing, at times intense, feelings. The only marker for many men up to this point has been their T-cell counts. In the case of HIV infection, doing something in terms of medical intervention also means a decline in counts or disease progression. The need to begin antiviral therapies imparts a new degree of reality to the situation. A reality that must be reconciled. Many men will go for years knowing they are positive and gradually making accommodations to this knowledge. AZT treatment often triggers a need to reconcile the fears of disease progression.

Many men will experience a return of the feeling that death is imminent. "That's the thing, when you start taking it, it's like God. You are almost on the verge of getting sick and dying." "The day I began AZT I went out and did my will." Men who struggled to regain a sense of future and to modulate their fear that death was around the corner now find the fear returning. "It was so discouraging. I was doing so well emotionally. Year after year my counts kept staying up and then wham!" "You know, I think I had almost convinced myself that I was just going to be fine. Now I really feel that I was just fooling myself."

For many men, beginning AZT is an important milestone in their experience. "It's a scary marker. One that I have been dreading for several years. I know a lot of people that AZT seemed to work for one and a half to two years, then it doesn't." "It's here. I have been dreading this. It feels like another corner that I am turning and I cannot go back." Men often find the balance that they have achieved slipping away. "For me it's a fine line between feeling contaminated and feeling that I am going to die. Ever since I began AZT I have shifted to the 'I am dying' side." "Since going on AZT, I do not think I have had a session with my shrink when I have not been talking about death."

POISON OR HELPER?

I was terrified of AZT at first. I had read so many horror stories.

Some men will find themselves being frightened of the drug. Many positive men remember the effect on friends when doses were much higher and the drug was only available to men in the later stages of the illness. "I kept thinking about how sick Tom got. I really think the AZT killed him, not AIDS." "Fred was in and out for transfusions all of the time, always nauseous. I did not want to be that way." Others who have read about the drug in a variety of sources will rely on that data. "I read a couple of articles on AZT that made it sound like poison. They kept saying the long-term survivors did not take the drug at all." "Alternative therapies always talked about how AZT was poison to the body and it would work for awhile and then if you take it for a year or two its stops functioning."

Some men will opt not to take the drug at all. "I am just not going to take it. I am going to focus on spirituality, a vegetarian diet, and Chinese herbs." "No way am I going to take it. I think I freaked out my doc, but I will stick to my alternative approaches."

Others will turn to men who have had experience with the drug. "I started talking to people and got a lot of good feedback. It seemed like people who had problems with these lower doses are in the minority. A couple of people even said they felt better after taking it for awhile." "I figured out whose beepers were going off at meetings and then would talk to them about how they were doing with it. Most people said, 'Just fine.'" Physicians often help to soothe fears. "My doc really eased me into it. He took a lot of time to listen to my fears, and responded very gently with a lot of facts and his observations." "I think my doctor knew this was going to be rough for me. It still was, but his preparing me for it for over a year before I began really helped."

Men often find their fears of the drug subsiding over time. "At first my hands trembled every time I went to take it." "I was terrified at first, but gradually, that beeper became very reassuring. It is the closest thing I have to a magic bullet." However, the knowledge that AZT is no magic bullet often is present as well. "I know it's not a cure. In the back of my mind I wonder when is it going to stop being effective. How much time will it really buy me?"

MELTDOWN

I really lost it after having to go on AZT. I couldn't sleep and was anxious all of the time. I ended up having to go on anti-depressants.

Beginning antiviral treatment can and often does trigger a Meltdown. "At the point my counts went to 500, I went on AZT. That was monumental." "Starting AZT really freaked me out; I was just terrified." The sense that one is moving closer to being ill and death often triggers a great deal of anxiety and often depression. "Everything just started spinning." "All that stuff about being ill, diseased, untouchable, just got thrown up into my face again." Some men will experience such intense anxiety and depression that they will require medical intervention. "I couldn't sleep, concentrate. I lost my appetite and was anxious all of the time. I was in therapy and my therapist pushed me to go on antidepressants." "I really went over the edge. I needed to take medication just to function." Some men will feel their experience of beginning AZT as the most traumatic event in their life. "I do not think I have ever been this freaked out, upset, disturbed. I thought Vietnam was bad, but this is it."

Men may feel profoundly discouraged. "It's just so difficult now, being well for so long and now this. For two years my counts stayed high. I was taking care of myself and having a good time. Now it feels like the beginning of the end." Some men will become preoccupied with feeling ill. "I keep thinking to myself, 'You are now chronically ill.'" "It just reminded me of who I am–a person who is infected, and is probably going to get ill."

Some men will experience nausea when they first begin taking AZT. This often compounds the anxiety associated with beginning antivirals and their implications. "I took my first pill and by midday I was feeling awful, like I was going to vomit at any minute." "I was constantly feeling like I was going to throw up, or actually throwing up." Initial difficulty with the medication often compounds the discouragement. "Is this what my life is going to be like from now on? Driving to work and having to barf by the side of the road?" "I was so sick and freaked out. I had to push myself to take the pills because I just knew I would get sick thirty minutes later." "After a week I just broke down and cried. It really felt like this was now going to be my life." While men often experience degrees of interference and intrusion into their lives by their emotional reactions, when they find their lives intruded upon by physical reactions as well, discouragement is often magnified. "I picked up the AZT on the way to the airport. Here I was on vacation with this wonderful man, beginning AZT, just feeling awful. I was just going through the motions." "How am I supposed to function. How can I make my sales calls when I keep thinking I am going to throw up?"

In contrast some men will experience few symptoms. "I was surprised. I took it and kept waiting for a 'big bang,' but nothing happened." "It was really quite painless. No nausea, no nothing." These men will find their experience reassuring. "I kept thinking that when I hit AZT it was going to be traumatic, but it did not amount to much at all. It was really no big deal."

Some men will find fears and preoccupation with illness coming to dominate their lives. "I am in danger of losing my home. It's all taken care of, but the fear is there." "I am really afraid of getting wasting syndrome and Kaposi's." Men may also anticipate the trials of illness and hospitals. "I work in a hospital and I know what goes on." "I just keep thinking about all the diseases and wondering who will take care of me."

Some may find themselves feeling angry. "I am really angry that

I have to see doctors, that I have to take AZT that is probably killing me at the same time it is helping me." "It really pisses me off sometimes. I am forty, my career is taking off, and all of this is just sending me down the tubes."

Some will find a resurgence of the constellation of feelings previously described as Damaged Goods. "This disease makes me experience every bit of shame and guilt that I have experienced in my entire life." "It's sick, but sometimes I find myself thinking that I am getting what I deserved, as if this disease is some sort of penance." Fears of rejection may once again emerge. "Another fear is rejection. The place I work, people are so ignorant that they probably would not sit with me. I am so cautious about hiding my pills and sneaking my noon dose." "Who is going to want to date someone on AZT?"

Some men will find out they are positive, and that they need to begin AZT at the same time. "It just hit me like a rock. I found out I was positive, my counts were down and that I had to go on AZT in the course of a week." "It all came down at once. Positive, AZT." These men will often experience the turbulence of THE TWILIGHT ZONE and the need to begin the process of integrating being positive as described in THE LONG HAUL in addition to beginning AZT treatment. "I knew I had to do something when I ran a stop sign and almost got into an accident." "It was just too much at once–positive–pills. I ran to TPA, and to a shrink."

Some men do not experience the intense disorganization of THE TWILIGHT ZONE upon testing positive. However, the need to begin AZT often triggers the emotional constellation described in that area, as well as the need to seek out help and support. "It really did not bother me. My counts were up. I was sad for a few weeks but I was really fine. But when I started AZT it all fell apart. It reminded me of just who I was, and what I was dealing with." "I kept hearing about people freaking out after they tested positive and wondered what the big deal was. Well, when my doctor said I needed to begin AZT right after I buried my best friend, the world just fell apart." Men who previously did not feel the need to join groups or seek help now may decide these activities are necessary. "After I went on AZT, I felt the need to be around other positive men. I started going to TPA and have been going regularly since. It really helped." "I always balked at going to groups. I am a bit of a loner and a 'pull yourself up by your own bootstraps guy,' but after I began AZT, I realized this is like nothing I have ever experienced."

DOING SOMETHING

In a way it was a relief, that now there was something I could do.

In sharp contrast to men who find themselves feeling discouraged and disorganized by the need to go on AZT, some will find beginning antivral treatment reassuring. While some men view AZT as a sign of approaching the end, others view it as a sign of hope. "I watched my T-cells go down for several years. It was like sliding closer to the edge. AZT felt like at last there was something I could do." "When I first tested positive, things were pretty dismal. Then they came up with AZT, and I told myself to slow down, there is hope after all." Rather than view it as a poison, some view antivirals quite differently. "I viewed AZT as a lifesaver." "All along it felt like I had something to pull out of my pocket to deal with this disease."

Some men will view and embrace antiviral medication with a more proactive stance. "When AZT became available I started paying attention to my T cells and when they hit a certain point I asked my doctor." "I was kind of looking forward to going on AZT. I was really getting jealous of all those people at TPA with their beepers. They at least were doing something. Every time their beepers went off I thought, 'They are at least taking drugs to go after this thing.' When I went on it, I immediately went out and got a beeper."

LOSSES

For so long I thought I was one of the few. It never dawned on me that so many of my friends could be positive. Now they are dying and I am going on AZT.

In the face of their shaken hope, as they begin AZT, many men will find themselves being reminded of the relationships they have lost. "I have lost so many friends to this damn disease." "When you have got people dying all around you, or in various phases, it does not take much to feel that I am dying, versus asymptomatic and on AZT." Some will feel that they are now a part of that very process of life and long-term relationships slipping away. "Every time I pick up the paper there is someone else. I should be enjoying my friends that I have had for twenty years, not going to their funerals." "I see my friends dying very quickly and very fast. Not as fast as they used to–maybe because of AZT–but they are still dying."

Men who have a long history with the disease may find themselves pondering how things have changed. "Patrick and Chuck died before AZT. It was just coming out as Patrick was getting sicker. It was so sad to see him dying because he could not get it." "Sometimes it feels just like when Stan was dying, then sometimes it feels so different. There was no AZT then. It just does not seem fair that there was so little that could be done for him, but now there are all of these things that they can do for me."

The loss of integral people may come from other illnesses as well. "Right after I began taking AZT, my sister came down with lymphoma. She and I were very close. It felt like my world was just falling apart." "My father died shortly after I began taking AZT. On one hand it felt like he was being spared my death, on the other it felt like there was one less person to be there for me."

Some men may be more consciously aware of their tendency to identify with certain people. "It's complicated. Who do you look to–the people who are dying or dead, or the people who are on AZT and doing well? I try to keep looking at the guys that keep hanging in there and whose counts are going up, but it is so hard to keep being hopeful." "There are good days and bad days. Sometimes I am low and I think about how we all seem to be slipping away. Others I see that I am holding my own, and that there are so many others who are holding their own or doing a lot better."

Men may also feel the loss of relationships that they do not form. "It's not just the loss of people you know, but relationships never made because you hesitate to get involved." "I notice myself being much more insular. So many old friends are gone now, or going. Sure, they cannot be replaced, but I also find myself not making new friends. It's almost as if I wonder if I will just lose them too, or if they will have to feel what I have felt these past years when I get sick and die." Some men may find themselves hesitating to get involved with other positive men. "I hate to admit it, but I just do not want to make friends who are positive and might get sick. Sometimes I feel that I just cannot take one more person dying on me." "I do not get close to people anymore because I do not want to watch them die."

ESTABLISHED DIALOGUES

We are trying to talk about our fears about this, but it is hard.

When men are in established relationships, the advent of AZT is often disorganizing in the context of the relationship as well. If the partner who is beginning AZT is disorganized and discouraged then the other partners will be faced with his partner's diminished state of mind. Each man will be faced with his own fears about the medication and what it represents as well as the other partner's response to his state of mind and what that represents. Some couples may feel themselves distancing from each other, and consequently fears about the relationship intrude and make the situation all the more tenuous and complicated. The challenge for couples is to find a way to talk about their fears together and attempt to reestablish the balance of the relationship in the face of fears that threaten to disrupt their dialogue even further.

Partners often react to the state of mind of their spouse. "I have been very depressed ever since I started AZT. It is really starting to wear on our relationship." "I know I have not been very available and I have been leaning on him a lot lately." If a man feels his partner is distancing from him, then his anxiety may be enhanced. "He was great at first, but lately he has really pulled back." "I really feel him pulling away. I know I have not been much fun lately. I really have not felt well physically since going on AZT, not wanting to go out. It's all I can do to make it through work."

In the wake of their partner's distancing, many fears may come into play. "I think he is angry with me for being positive." "I think he still wants to remain in a relationship with me. It's there in the background, 'Does he not want to deal with this? Is he going to leave?'" Difficulties in the dialogue of established relationships can compound the distress of positive men. "When we get out of touch with each other then it feels like we are just swimming in all of this shit, not going anywhere, just in it." "It's just one more thing to be angry about, 'This disease is even fucking up my relationship.'"

In the wake of a disrupted dialogue, concerns for the future are often evoked. "It will be hard enough to maintain our relationship if I get ill. If we can't handle this, how are we going to handle my getting really sick?" "I kept thinking that this is what our life is going to be like from now on." Some men may feel that they have failed. "I guess I really have tried to protect him from all of this, but I just have not been able to lately." "I feel like I have been doing something wrong. I know I have been a mess." In trying to sort out what is happening in the relationship, some men may feel that their partner is not appreciating just how hard they have been trying. "I realized that I have been trying to protect him from this. Right now I just don't have the energy to protect him anymore." The sexual dialogue of the relationship may be affected as well. "He wasn't touching me. We have practiced safe sex all along. I was afraid that all of a sudden he was afraid of getting infected." In positive/negative couples the increased focus on the disease secondary to AZT may indeed stir up transmission fears that may be played out. "He had some surgery on his feet. We were in the hot tub together. He jumped and took his foot out of the tub as if he could get AIDS from me." "It seems to me that ever since I went on AZT he doesn't want to have sex and when he does he is extra careful, if not sanitary about it." Some negative partners may convince themselves that they have seroconverted. "I just had this feeling that I had been infected by him and was all prepared for it. I was tested again, but I am still negative."

Couples often have trouble responding to each other's stress and acute vulnerability. The seeming disappearance of a positive, fighting attitude is often frightening for both men. "I was getting scared. Periodically I would get flooded, break down and start to cry. He just would stand there and look helpless." "He is very good with sympathy but not empathy. He goes, 'There you are sitting on the pity pot,' or he gets analytical and says, 'You are acting like you are dying.' I was getting more and more angry until our therapist pinned him down and he 'fessed up' to being afraid that I was losing my fighting spirit and that he was trying to push me to get it back." Couples who have a hard time tolerating or talking about their feeling states may have a harder time given the apparent high stakes of the situation. "We have been trying to find a way to talk about this, but it has been very hard. It kind of feels like picking our way through a mine field." "I was getting really angry with him. For three months he didn't say anything. Finally he said, 'I notice you have been depressed.'"

When couples find a way to talk about their mutual distress the relief is often considerable. "One night we were able to talk. We had a long talk about all of this. His feeling abandoned, my feeling abandoned." "I found out he wasn't mad at me for being positive. He was reacting to my being so depressed because it stirred up his father being depressed and unavailable so much of the time." "It got so bad we went to a therapist. It took awhile but he finally got us talking about what was going on rather than bouncing off each other." Often times both men are feeling abandoned. "I was depressed and unavailable and started shutting off. He did the same thing too." "It was like I was in left field and he was in right, but after we talked it felt like we were back with each other. Things are still pretty scary when I look down the road but I am more confident that we can make it."

THE GAME PLAN

My goal now is just to keep myself healthy.

Similar to the process observed in THE LONG HAUL, men often develop a Game Plan. Earlier in their experience the goal may have been to prolong high T-cell counts and avoid going on AZT. After beginning antiviral therapies, the goal tends to increase or maintain T-cell counts, thus avoiding an AIDS diagnosis. Again the plan often involves tending to one's physical, emotional, and often spiritual needs. As observed in the earlier areas of the experience, many men will find themselves engaged in a process of tending to themselves in ways they have never done before.

Men who previously did not feel the need to develop a plan may now find themselves needing to do so in the wake of AZT and its implications. "I had just kind of gone with it, it did not really bother me. But, after going on AZT, I really felt I needed to do something." "After going on AZT, I really wanted to be with other people who were in the same boat. I also wanted more information on treatment and alternative therapies." Men who previously were engaged in plans may now alter or step up their efforts. "After I went on AZT I read an article that indicated that men who smoke tend to progress faster to an AIDS diagnosis, so I took the plunge and stopped smoking. I also started eating better, and cut way back on alcohol." "I added more vitamins and less running around to my routine."

Some men may take on major changes in their approach to life. "I had made some monumental changes in my life but I wanted more. I started investigating facilities around the country that detoxified the body–putting it through a cleansing mode. The one I chose was a very rigorous three-week program of cleansing, exercise, re-education regarding diets, having to learn to cook vegetarian, and it was a very warm friendly environment." From a psychological standpoint, feeling tended to and/or tending to oneself is highly reassuring and often helps to heal the often deep feeling of being damaged. "I wanted to feel all of the wonderful things they were doing for me." "I have never spent so much time taking care of myself. That is what it is all about, taking care of ourselves."

Some men will encounter evidence that their plan is indeed working. "Before I started the program I went off AZT. After six months of the vegetarian diet, and no AZT, my counts went up. My doctor was amazed." "I have been at it for a year now. Exercise, watching what I eat, no alcohol. My counts have kept going up. I do not know what it is–AZT, my program or what–but I am keeping it all going."

As described in THE LONG HAUL, psychotherapy, groups, organizations for seropositive men, the relationships with the physician and friendships will also be elements of men's Game Plans. Reassurance, confidence, and a sense of belonging come from relationships with others who are experienced as understanding and tolerating the impact of HIV infection and the efforts needed to maintain one's self in its wake. Also as described in THE LONG HAUL, the need to reveal one's status continues to be an ongoing aspect of HIV infection. Men may now choose to inform more people and face many of the dynamics detailed earlier.

BALANCING

I realized that I was feeling like an AIDS diagnosis, not just going on AZT.

Men often find their sense of balance gradually returning as they become accustomed to their new status. Efforts at the Game Plan appear to be integral in helping men feel that they are again back on track, and that life does not feel as tenuous or threatening as it may have felt in the wake of their response to beginning antiviral therapies. "Going on AZT gave me a scare and shook me up. But nothing bad happened." Considerable time often passes after beginning treatments and men find their perspectives shifting as well. "I have been taking the drug for twenty-two months now. All the fears are kind of fading away. I do not think about it much anymore." "It was scary at first, but it turned out to be a positive marker for me."

As time passes, and life continues, many men will find themselves taking on new pursuits. Life continues to unfold and present its possibilities. "Time seems real strange to me. A year ago I was ready to give up and die. Now I am on AZT, and starting a new relationship. Sometimes it doesn't make sense. Except that maybe I let go of whatever was telling me that I could not form a relationship." Career opportunities evolve as well. "They gave me a new department to be in charge of. It was the last thing I wanted, but it eventually gave me a new focus."

As observed in THE LONG HAUL, the balance is not always easy to maintain. While men may be very engaged with their lives, reminders tend to surface. "It's all too scary sometimes, too hard to keep yourself balanced. In the back of my mind is always this fear. I saw a friend who used to be an Adonis. His hair was falling out, his face all puffy from the medication. When I see that I lose my focus. All the fear floods in." Some men do their best to resist identifying with others in more advanced stages of the illness. "I consciously fight not to go with indicators I see in other people and look to myself, my own situation." Men often face the illnesses and deaths of friends who have helped them keep their balance and hopefulness. "It's been a real hard few months. Jim, who became my HIV buddy, went downhill and died. We really kept each other going. On one hand going through that with him helped me with my own fear about getting sick–on the other I feel kind of lost without him." "We have lost so many of the old gang these past few months. It just feels overwhelming sometimes."

Some men will adopt a rather stubborn stance. "I refuse to allow myself to feel that I have one foot in the grave. Sometimes it's hard not to drift into that way of thinking, but I find that I catch myself earlier and remind myself that if you think that way, that is just what is going to happen." Others take a more gentle stance with themselves. "Sure it gets rough, but I remind myself that I am doing all that I can. I am praying, or I am visualizing, or doing something to try to boost my T cells. Most important I am trying to keep a positive attitude about it. I am alive today and that is what matters." "So much of it has to do with how you are psychologically thinking about the disease–how you think about yourself and the disease. That is where I am putting my energy–in feeling good about me."

Chapter 9

Moving On

*Here I am. I have been on AZT for two years now. I am doing
fine physically, I have a new job, and a new boyfriend. I did
not think it would turn out this way.*

Despite their worst fears, for many men life continues to move on
and unfold. As men stabilize psychologically after beginning AZT
and what it may represent, they often find that they continue to be
engaged with their lives, and opportunities are presented to them.
Many men will experience a number of years of relatively symptom-free life following initiation of antivirals. The use of prophylactic medications to prevent opportunistic infections often further
extends the period of not having to negotiate acute illness.

Many of the basic properties continue on though this area, in fact
the entire experience of being positive can be viewed as a series of
psychological disruptions and the gradual restoration of a sense of
balance and being engaged with life. In the wake of losses or medical challenges, Meltdowns periodically occur and the loss of the
sense of future and deep sadness come to the forefront of positive
men's experience. Revelation and negotiation of relationships continues to be an aspect of the experience. In general the experiences
of men who remain asymptomatic during the early parts of this area
are highly similar to those of THE LONG HAUL.

However, most infected men eventually experience physical decline and/or the emergence of bothersome symptoms. While some
men may not experience mild to moderate symptomatology, they
may watch their T cells gradually decline and experience the
vulnerability inherent in that knowledge. While the stakes may feel
higher in this area, one often observes a growing calm and contentment in men who have negotiated HIV for a number of years.

A reflection of the changing nature of how HIV infection is

conceptualized and treated, many men will find themselves being diagnosed with AIDS not due to long-feared defining opportunistic infections, but because of changes in diagnostic criteria. Thus men who have feared being diagnosed for so long in the wake of a severe illness find themselves being diagnosed via laboratory indicators. Men also continue to face the loss of a partner, close friend, or friends to AIDS.

Many properties addressed in earlier chapters continue to be an aspect of the experience of being infected with HIV. This chapter will focus on those unique to this area of the experience, when people begin to feel the effects of the decline of T-cell counts and health in general, losses and their effects, and the sense that they are moving on, and often moving closer to major illness.

The properties to be addressed in this chapter are:

- *Hanging in There*–life continuing on in the absence of symptoms;
- *Declining*–the emergence of mild to moderate symptoms,
- *Disrupted Dialogues*–acute illness and deaths of partners and friends,
- *The Big Bang*–anticipating the first defining infection; and
- *Balancing*–the accommodations men reach in face of the progression of the disease.

HANGING IN THERE

I am doing great–knock on wood.

Many men will experience a considerable length of time of being relatively symptom-free after beginning AZT. The lack of illness, and sense of renewed body integrity is often very reassuring. "I did not even have a cold over the winter." "I have not been sick since July." The sense that one's body is continuing to function is a powerful buffer against the fear of chronic illness and death. As the opening quote indicates, men are often highly aware that this feeling is subject to change. "Right now I feel fine, my head is in a good spot, no physical problems, but I know that can change." "I am feeling great, and right now it feels like I am walking on a sidewalk, but I have felt it narrow to a tightrope in the past."

Some men may take on new pursuits, deciding that it is better to risk taking on a lifelong dream in the face of uncertainty rather than not to "go for it." "It was a complicated decision–it was scary–but I went over my finances, quit my job in banking, and went back to get my masters in social work." "It was a big decision. This new company wanted me, I wanted to work for them, to take on something new. I laid it all out for them, we worked out a way to maintain my insurance and disability coverage and away I went." When men find ways to obtain aspects of life that they thought were permanently blocked from them, the experience is often exhilarating. "This disease puts up so many roadblocks–some of them are solely in your head, others aren't. I hate hearing 'No' and I hate feeling 'No.' I have not found a way out of being positive, but I have found ways to get around some of the problems–some of the blocks." "Going back to school was the best thing I could have done. It's hard work, but it has been so exciting."

When men feel opportunities are blocked either by health considerations, maintaining insurance or basic anxiety, a sense of discouragement often results. "I just could not do it. It was just too risky to change jobs and move across the country. It would mean new doctors, losing my support base. It was just too much." "It feels like one more thing this disease has taken from me." When contemplating new challenges, men often encounter a sense of vulnerability. "Things I used to take for granted–changing jobs, an exotic trip to a third world country, now seem very formidable." "I find myself daydreaming about a new job, a safari, something adventuresome and outrageous, then I freak and think, 'No, you had better stay put.'"

Some men may find themselves developing relationships. "We have been seeing each other for a few months now. We are both positive, he lost a lover, but it's happening. The HIV thing, one or both of us getting sick, was talked about a lot, but we both felt we have lost so much, why waste an opportunity?" "We are moving in together. I feel I may be giving him a bum rap with his being negative, but he said, 'A few good years is better than none,' so I said okay." Some positive men struggle with entering a relationship feeling that death is in the near future. "It feels nice, but I think in two years I may be dead." "I backed out, there are just too many questions, too many uncertainties."

ESTABLISHED DIALOGUES

We always assumed that when one of us converted from HIV to AIDS we would have two to three years left.

Men in established relationships where one or both of the men are positive find themselves anticipating the future without each other. "We are both at that stage where the counts, and just general physical problems, make things feel pretty tenuous." Some men may feel the toll of years of worrying. "We have been together for six years now. He came along at a time when I assumed that I would be dead soon. It's been six good years in some ways, but this disease has taken so much in that time, that I keep waiting for it to take me, or him." Some couples may find themselves struggling with the sense of future in terms of the relationship. "We are trying to look for a future. Bob is trying to look to a future without me." "We both assume I will go first." The other night he freaked out and said, "If you die, I will be totally on my own. I will have to rebuild my life from scratch." Worry about the partner's future may be a concern. "If something happens to me, what about Bob? Our health insurance is through my business. He thinks of this city as his home, but his family is back East." "I know what I went through when Sam died. It breaks my heart to think that he will go through that also, but at the same time be sick as well." When men have already lost many relationships to AIDS, the thought of their partner becoming ill as well may be overwhelming. "I just can't face him getting sick. Yet I could and I would."

Men in established relationships where one or both of the men are positive may face the illness and death of their partner. "Things were going along fine, then he started slurring his speech, then to have trouble writing, now he can't button his shirt. There isn't much they can do for PML (Progressive Multifocal Leukoencephalopathy)." "They found lymphoma. With chemotherapy, they gave him six to eight months." These couples find their plans, dreams, and accommodations made within the context of being positive being dashed. "It wasn't supposed to be this way. Our hope was that life would just slow down and we would have a couple of years left." "I always thought he was the younger one–and that he would take care of me."

As in previous areas, the biggest challenge for couples is often in responding to and tolerating each other's often intense feeling states. "He is so reflective on death and dying–he gets so depressed. I get depressed too, but when I express my depression he gets more depressed." "We really had it out the other night. He had a bad day, and kept telling me I did not get it, he was the one that was dying, he had it the worst. Finally I lost it. Eventually I was able to tell him what I did feel, what I was struggling with and that my life was no picnic either." Great relief is often found when the two men can share their grief together. "We were crying in separate rooms. I thought 'Enough of this.' We ended up crying together." "After that big fight it all changed. We both realized that we were losing each other."

Positive men who lose their partners are faced with the complicated task of mourning the loss and facing their infection alone. "I feel so lost without him. I did not realize just how much the relationship changed things. Sure we knew we would get sick. We planned our funerals and all of that but somehow when he was here it all did not seem to matter as much, or hurt as much." "I want to be at home, but I also hate it. Every time I shut that front door, I feel alone. The place is empty." If the dynamics of the relationship were such that one man tended to focus on his partner's infection and illness more than his, now he may find himself grappling with his own sense of illness and impending death. "Pete had a way of keeping the focus on him. I may have bought into it so I would not have to worry about me. Now I am left with me. In some ways it feels like I am facing being positive for the first time."

Men may also face the acute illness and deaths of their friends. "Michael is not doing very well. He has been my HIV buddy for years. I really think we are going to lose him this time." "He is not long for this world. I miss our lunches. Now it's hit or miss, some days are good and we can talk, others he just is not there." Some men will actively participate in the deaths of their friends. "We snuck his dog up to his hospital room. He looked so content with that animal, I knew it would be over soon when I saw that peaceful look as the dog curled up beside him." "He had a real good day on Sunday. He was alert, funny, and stayed right with the conversations. I was glad we had that time together, after that afternoon he went downhill."

While the losses of these central relationships may trigger a Meltdown, especially for men in this area of the experience, seeing a friend go through the process of acute illness and/or death may also be reassuring. "We kept in close contact all through his hospitalization. It did not freak me out at all. I wanted to know what it was like. Somehow I am less afraid." "Going through Michael's death was very important. I am not so afraid of it anymore. It was so quiet and peaceful. I used to snicker when people talked about death as a 'transition,' but now I know what they mean."

DECLINING

I have had sinus infections all of my life, but this time they are almost impossible to clear up. It scares me. Things are not working the way they are supposed to.

As time progresses, many men will become aware of physical changes or symptoms. "I have felt the last six months a lack of energy. I used to work out three or four times a week–not any more. I am hoping it's just age." "I just do not have the muscle tone I used to." Other people may notice the changes as well. "About six months ago people at work started asking, 'Are you losing weight?'" "I can't get rid of this rash on my hands. People notice it, then I see the look in their faces and I feel like a leper" Physical changes and symptoms often bring discouragement. "I look in the mirror and I do not like what I see. My face used to be round, now it looks gaunt." "It really hurts sometimes. It's these little things. Not enough to really wreck things, but they poke at me, remind me." When men encounter the reactions of others the effects are often profound. "The look in my mother's eyes when she commented on my weight just ripped my heart out." "Someone at work said my pants were baggy in back. I started really getting self-conscious." Some men will identify medications as the culprit. "It's the AZT. It feels like my muscles are atrophying." "I went to my doctor and said, 'I am losing my butt. What is going on?'" "We have dubbed it 'the AZT butt syndrome.' It makes you lose your ass." Some men will notice changes, then attempt to fight them. "I have to slow down. I get tired then I push myself. I think I am trying to reassure myself that I am just fine. I guess I have to give in and listen to my body." "I realized that the issue is taking care of myself, not fighting to make things all right, because they aren't."

Physical changes and bothersome symptoms can greatly erode confidence. "I had a couple of bouts of not feeling good. That and everything else combined I started getting paranoid. Double checking to make sure everything was okay." "Every now and then I get thrush. So I take my pills and lozenges. It really gets discouraging sometimes. 'Oh, you are back again.'" As one's confidence becomes shaky, men may turn to the experiences of others. "Joe was on AZT for two years, then he got KS, PCP, and boom–he was gone. I have not been feeling well; now I think I only have a year left." Men may also observe in others an accommodation to the changes. "I guess as you get farther along in the disease process, you learn to cope with the disease–the changes in your appearance. I guess you learn to accept it."

Many men will not experience bothersome symptoms of infections, but will watch their T-cell counts and ratios gradually or suddenly decline. Considerable fear and disorganization often accompanies a lower count. "Welcome to T-cell hell. One hundred twenty-four! So many feelings are going through my head; I am trying to decide which one to latch onto. Anger, sadness, totally freaked out–it keeps shifting around." "It was a great week until the study called and told me I had dropped again." When counts decline, a great sense of vulnerability often emerges. "For so long they were consistently in the three hundred range. Then I felt like I had a buffer. Now my buffer has disappeared and there is hardly anything between me and getting sick and dying." "It really is not going to go away. I really am not going to get better. It feels like getting sick and dying is just around the corner."

Men who are otherwise in good health may struggle with the discrepancy between the way they appear and generally feel, and their counts. "I look in the mirror and I do not see a sick person. I feel great; I go to the gym every day and I look better than I ever have. Then my counts go down, and I see that I am in bad shape." "It just does not make sense; if I at least felt bad, then it would." In the face of declining counts men may contemplate their options. "I bought *Final Exit*. I just cannot face falling apart, wasting away,

purple spots all over my face." "I want to do something extrava-
gant, either a new stereo or a long trip to Europe." The question of
retirement may also surface. "I am beginning to think it is time to
go on disability. With these counts, at least I qualify. I am beginning
to change my mind about disability–it is more like retirement. I
have been juggling so much for so many years. It is time to rest, and
enjoy what I have left."

As bothersome symptoms emerge and medical bills begin to
mount, men who may have avoided using their medical insurance
for fear of rising rates or cancellation may decide to submit claims.
For many men this is an enormous step. "I finally submitted my
first claim. That was a big one. I keep waiting for alarms to go off."
"I kept seeing some claims adjuster in Kansas going, 'Aha, another
diseased fag! Can we drop him?'"

Other men may decide that now is the time to reveal their status
to parents or other family. "When I started having the skin problems and the thrush and my counts dropped, I felt it was time to tell
them. I always planned on waiting till things started happening. I
wanted to tell them before I get hit with something big." Again
many men face the complicated meanings surrounding revelation as
described in THE LONG HAUL.

As anxiety provoking as new symptoms may be initially, men
often find that they adapt or get used to them as well. "The first
time I had thrush I freaked out. But now, it's more like, 'Oh, it's
back. Well, take the lozenges or the other thrush medicine and it
will go away.'" "It stops being a freakout issue, and becomes an
annoyance. The thrush, the rashes, the this, the that, can all pretty
much be managed. It just can be time consuming and expensive to
manage it."

THE BIG BANG

*You keep waiting for it, looking for it, wondering if this is
it–the big bang.*

Since the time they first find out they are positive, men often live
in fear of the first opportunistic infection. As detailed in previous
chapters, men often go to great lengths to keep their T-cell counts

up, watch their general health, and take care of themselves emotionally and physically. All this is done in an effort to stave off that first defining condition, one that takes them from just being positive, to having AIDS. "I have dreaded it–being diagnosed–ever since I tested positive." "It is something I have lived in fear of for years now." Men have often felt The Big Bang was near only to have it be a false alarm. "It just makes you nuts. You get a cold or the flu, and you think 'This is it–I am going down,' then the doc says, 'Relax, you have just got the flu like everyone else.'" "It's almost like a reflex. I start getting sick with something and I start feeling like this is the big one–this time it is it."

Some men may experience a major illness that is not necessarily HIV related, but may come to experience it as a defining condition. "I came down with hepatitis. I have never been so sick in my life. I kept thinking that Joe died of hepatitis and his T cells were a lot higher than mine. It feels like a real turning point. I am thinking of myself as having AIDS now." Partners may have similar reactions. "Jim had viral pneumonia. We were both freaked out. He was so sick and helpless. Things have just not been the same since then." Men may find that they in subtle to profound ways redefine themselves as now having AIDS. "Things feel a lot more tenuous now. I guess I feel like I have crossed that line into AIDS."

When men recover from significant illnesses that are not necessarily HIV related, but were experienced as such, they often begin to realize just how terrified they were, and the extent to which they viewed themselves as having AIDS. "I am beginning to get my confidence back–it really shook me up. It broke through that denial–that belief that this is not going to get me, that I am going to survive." "I am just now realizing just how scared I was, just how much I was thinking that this was the beginning of the end. I was really acting as if I had been diagnosed with AIDS."

Just as the way in which individual men experience being positive is ongoing, dynamic, and evolving, the manner in which the disease is conceptualized and treated is dynamic and evolving. Previous to January 1993, AIDS was defined by a person experiencing an opportunistic infection. Now it can also be defined on the basis of T-cell counts. Thus, many men found themselves being "diagnosed" not by a long-feared opportunistic infection, but by a change in diagnostic criteria. "Well, I guess I have AIDS now. Overnight I was diagnosed." "So much for the big bang." Some men may feel the need to inform others of their change in status. "I need to tell my niece and nephew I do have AIDS. Last fall they asked and I told them I was only positive. I want to be honest with them." "It's time to tell my parents now."

The lack of a much-anticipated and feared infection to organize around may leave some men feeling confused. "It's really weird. For so long I have fantasized that I would come down with something big–it would be a marker, something to hang on to. Now I am technically diagnosed, but I feel like I am still left hanging just like I was when I was positive." For some men the changes in diagnostic criteria may symbolize many of their struggles with the disease. "This whole thing is just one mind fuck after another. For so long I thought of a series of markers. First you test positive, then your T cells drop and you go on AZT, then you get a big opportunistic infection, then you go downhill and are diagnosed–then you die. Instead here I am–diagnosed–and I feel just fine. What the hell do you use for markers? As time goes on, it feels like there is less to hold on to, not more."

For some men, waiting for The Big Bang may come to define their sense of future. "The longer I go on, the more I think the hardest part of this disease is how it destroys the future. The future? What future? What do you do? If I had invested all the money I spent because I thought I was going to die soon, I would be a rich man. I never thought I would be alive today. Now that money would come in handy." When men step back and realize just how much the future is defined by the prospect of illness and death, considerable anger may come to the fore. "I got so angry. We are planning a trip next spring and I found myself worrying that I might not be well enough to go." "I thought, 'I can't even plan a trip anymore and look forward to it. It's more like, can I make it until then?'" "Sometimes I just get plain old pissed. Take, take, take–that is all this disease does is take. It even takes looking forward to next year." "People keep referring to this as The Plague. Hell, at least the Great Plague in Europe was efficient. This takes forever."

BALANCING

It's an interesting place to be. Things do not throw me the way they used to. If I get thrush, I take my thrush pills. If I have a day when I just do not feel good, I stay home. This is my reality. I never thought I would say it, but things feel balanced for me.

Men in this area of the experience oftentimes do reach an accommodation to their medical and psychological reality. There is a great deal to keep balanced. "There is a lot to try and keep straight–the pills, what is going on in research, listening to my body." "My world does feel a little smaller now, but it also feels manageable. Friends or family who do not know what HIV is all about get overwhelmed and it's puzzling. I guess it is just my world and I have learned to live in it without being freaked out all of the time."

Some men may take great comfort in their peer group which may be dominated by men who are in similar medical situations. "I met up with some old friends at the Quilt display in Washington. On one hand it was kind of sad that we are all on these drugs, but then it also felt really comfortable. We ended up trading 'war' stories about drugs and side effects, and tricks for managing it all." "I just feel more comfortable with guys that are in the same boat. You do not have to explain things or worry about freaking someone out."

When men are faced with declining counts, adding other antivirals and prophylactic medications to their regimes, planning ahead often comes to include consideration of retiring or going on disability. "I have been going over all of my disability policies, looking at when I could quit working." Retiring or going on disability can come to be a highly charged area. "A lot of guys view it as giving up, resigning that you are going to die. Chuck said, 'Enough,' decided to go on disability and enjoy life while he still could. A lot of people gave him grief, said he was giving in." "I struggle with it. It is not a sign of giving up, it's facing the facts and that I want to have some semblance of retirement. It's my money. I should be able to use it."

Given the way disability programs work, deciding to retire is often a complicated decision. "When do you do it? I looked everything over. If I went on disability I would have sixty percent of my salary, but I could COBRA my health insurance for only twenty-nine months. What if I live longer than that–what do I do then? I do not want to work until I am too sick to do so, but then I do not want to be without insurance either." "I am in school. I really want to be able to work in the field for awhile first, but I also want some quality time." The hope for a cure in the near future may surface as well. "What if I retire, keep on going, use up all of my money and then they find a cure? I would have to start all over again, but, hey, gladly."

As economic pressures cause large companies to lay off their employees, positive men may find themselves especially worried. "They are talking lay-offs. There would go my insurance, my disability, everything out the window." "I have been counting on my benefits to see me through all of this. If they lay me off, I don't know if there is enough time for pre-existings and a new disability policy." When faced with the possibility of benefit loss the fear is often immense. "When I think about it it just shakes me to the core. I see myself homeless on Public Aid." "Those benefits are what kept me there all of these years. I get totally freaked out at the idea of not having anything to fall back on."

As observed in earlier areas, men come to value feeling calm and peaceful, and engage in activities that enhance these feelings. "I really have become a homebody. It's quiet, it's my space. Running around all weekend, out 'looking' just doesn't do it for me anymore." "I have really gotten involved in church again." Men find themselves appreciating different qualities in people and their world. "I tend to avoid the party crowd I used to hang around with. I want to be around quiet, sane people." "The garden is so peaceful, that is where I am spending my time. I no longer see the beach as cruising and being seen. It's more taking in the beauty of the lake, and the sky, and the dunes."

After focusing on T-cell counts for so many years, men may decide that the numbers are no longer relevant. "After awhile, the importance of each count diminishes. It loses its power over the way I feel." "They went down to almost one hundred, and the study wanted to change my medications. I got freaked out and was all ready to make the change, then they went back up to almost two hundred. It's too much. I told my doctor I did not want to know anymore. I do not need that roller coaster in my life." "I got tired of freaking out and obsessing about it. I asked my doctor if at this point it made much of a difference. He said, 'Not really,' so I told him to just do what needed to be done."

Men often continue to have a Game Plan, but that too may shift. "It's not such an intense focus anymore. It keeps changing in content and my investment in it." "After so many years of doing this and that, I now find that people–my various friendships and maintaining them–are now the main part of my plan. Sure the medications and all that are part of it, but the central part is my friendships."

Men may also come to feel vastly more comfortable with themselves. "I am beginning to understand those AIDS meditation books that talk about HIV as a blessing. I feel like I have really grown up the past few years." "It's really strange. I am not complaining mind you, but here I am, on all of these meds–I probably am not going to live to see forty–and bottom line, I feel better about myself than ever." "The sadness is there, but so is the contentment. I have not felt a great deal of contentment in my life. On one hand, it makes me sad to think that this is what it took to find it, but I am doing my best to hold onto it and to nurture it."

Chapter 10

The Big Bang

It finally happened. I started feeling worse and worse. When I could not climb the stairs I called my doctor. In the hospital we all kind of knew before the tests came back that it was pneumocystus.

The first major opportunistic infection is a often a watershed. Men who have known they were positive for years have long dreaded the event, anticipating it as the final beginning of the end. However, many men who have anticipated and fought against a diagnosis for so long, often find the experience considerably less dramatic than they feared. Several men in the study found out they were infected at the time of diagnosis. For these men, the diagnosis was more of an upheaval as they faced the mental processes similar to those who had known for a much longer period, in the context of being diagnosed with AIDS.

This chapter will describe only the earlier experiences of men who are diagnosed with AIDS. Since the study concerns the experience of testing positive, only the initial upheaval and process of reorganization will be addressed.

The properties of *THE BIG BANG* are:

- *It's Here!*–the confirmation of a major opportunistic infection;
- *Time to Reflect*–initial efforts at coming to terms with the diagnosis and its implications;
- *Revelation*–revealing the diagnosis to family, friends, employers, and colleagues;
- *Lingering Pain*–the deep sense of hurt that accompanies HIV;
- *Making Sense*–efforts at trying to to make sense of the diagnosis and its implications,

- *The Game Plan*–the plan that emerges for combating or dealing with the disease,
- *Calming Down*–regaining a sense of optimism and direction;
- *Meltdown*–periods of acute sadness and discouragement, and
- *Looking Ahead.*

IT'S HERE!

It's here now. It happened.

Men find themselves being diagnosed in a number of ways. For some it was not anticipated. "I thought I had a hemorrhoid. My doctor sent me to another doctor and before I knew it, I was in the hospital, having surgery. It turned out to be cancer and I was diagnosed." "I was doing just fine, then one day my vision in my left eye was cloudy. I called my doc, the next thing I knew I was in the hospital hooked up to an IV." Other men will experience a more protracted period of not feeling well. "I just started dragging. I did not feel well for months, but they could not find anything wrong. Finally my temperature shot up, they took an X ray, and there it was." "I don't think they ever really figured out what it was, but I landed in the hospital being pumped full of drugs."

While some men may have feared the first hospitalization, in the midst of acute illness, they are often quite relieved to be there. "It's weird. I dreaded going into the hospital for so long, but when the nurse told me to go there I was so relieved." "I felt so awful, as soon as I got inside the doors, I knew that is where I wanted to be." Some men may find themselves very surprised by their experience of the actual event versus their anticipation. "Granted, I was really out of it, but I kept thinking, 'Is this all there is to it? Where is the sturm and drang?'" "I was amazed. I had nightmares about this for so long, but, I just loved the attention, it was so gentle. It turned out to be the big bang that wasn't."

Several men in the study found out they were infected at the time of the actual diagnosis. "I was feeling well. I had none of the known symptoms of AIDS. I was in a swimming accident and bruised my lungs. I got an infection and was admitted to the hospital and told I was HIV-positive and had AIDS." "It happened all at once. I never wanted to be tested. I started feeling awful, ended up in the hospital with pneumocystus and there it was, 'You're positive. You have AIDS.'"

Many of these men who had not been tested reported that they had a strong feeling that they were coming down with an AIDS-related illness. "I kind of felt that I had AIDS. I must have. I did not go to see my regular doctor who is straight and not in the AIDS loop. I went to a doctor that I knew was on staff at a hospital with a good AIDS unit." "I really thought that was it. It was like, 'Well, Jim, you probably have AIDS. No time to panic, just get to a doctor that knows what he is doing.'" While men who did not know they were positive may have lived in terror of the possibility of contracting AIDS, here again there is often an absence of panic as the actual defining moments approach. "In all that time I wasn't scared. I just knew I had AIDS and pneumonia. I knew once I got to the hospital, everything would be just fine." "I knew what was happening. I actually knew several days before, but I was resisting as long as possible. I was trying to settle into my mind that this is what I have. I have AIDS."

TIME TO REFLECT

It turned out to be a real watershed for me. I got rid of a lot of emotional garbage.

If they are not too ill, many men find themselves with considerable time to reflect on the impact of the diagnosis while they are in the hospital. If the staff and surroundings are supportive and reassuring the process is enhanced in a positive direction. "Everybody was wonderful. I was in the St. Joseph's AIDS ward. If you have to get sick, that is a good place to be." "It was such a nurtured, supportive place. My roommate was great, plenty of people to talk to when I needed to talk; they left me alone when I needed to be alone." If the facility is not supportive then the experience can be quite traumatic. "It was horrible. I was on a general floor with signs that looked like radiation hazard warnings posted on my door. They left my food at the door; everyone came and went as fast as possible. I felt like a leper and that they could not wait to get rid of me."

Some men reported initially feeling numb after the confirmation of the diagnosis. "There is not much I can recall that first week . . . I was so numb–not depressed–just blank." "Initially I was kind of lost in space. I was never frightened. I knew enough about the disease to know it was not an immediate death sentence. But I knew something very important and profound was happening to me." For some men the experience may have a surreal quality. "It's very bizarre. It is like you're in a movie, like a wide-angle lens. All of these people come and lean down on you on the bed. Everything is magnified. The words, the sounds, your whole condition." If men are acutely ill, then they may not have the capacity for philosophical musings. "I was just honed in on staying alive. All the philosophical musings go out the window. All the thoughts about wanting to end it before it got this bad evaporate. All you want to do is live."

Some men find themselves facing the question: Are they up to going through the process of illness? "It puts all of the questions in your mind of, what am I going to go through? Is it going to be that bad? Do I really want to go through it?" "That day and night after I was told it was AIDS, was very hard for me. But I woke up the next day and found that this was something I could deal with. I was not crushed. It gave me incentive to clean up some old stuff in my head and to take a better direction in my life." While in the hospital, often elements of *The Game Plan* for dealing with the illness begin to emerge. "I had so many friends, coworkers, business associates test positive, come down with ARC and AIDS. I found that when I was in the hospital I could not mourn for myself because I had mourned for so many people already. I did not know who I would be angry at, so I just went straight forward. That is the way I have dealt with having AIDS ever since. Straight forward, eye on the ball of staying healthy."

The initial hospitalization is often a watershed event in a variety of ways. For men who have known they were positive for a number of years, and lived in terror of THE BIG BANG, going through the first hospitalization may actually feel freeing. "It was not at all what I expected. I always imagined it being a harsh, terrible event, but it wasn't. It all felt very gentle." "It freed up a lot. I realized that I do not have anything to worry about anymore. I no longer have to be terrified of being diagnosed with AIDS. It really feels like I can move on now." Feeling nurtured by hospital staff cuts into the anticipated harshness. "I felt so reassured. I came out feeling rested and optimistic, not devastated." "The nursing staff seemed to really want to be there, really wanted to help me. It was hard to feel pathetic and like a leper in that environment." Some men may feel that a giant burden has finally been lifted. "For six years I felt like there was this giant Sword of Damocles hanging over my head. It's gone now. It's weird. For so long I lived in terror of crossing over into AIDS. Now that it has happened, I feel that I can relax."

Men whose entry into the realm of HIV was at diagnosis often have different aspects to work out. While in the hospital, some may reveal their infection and their homosexuality to their family. "I called the family down. My parents are dead, so it was just my brothers and sisters. They were all great. They were so supportive." In the context of a supportive environment and responses from family members, men find themselves releasing other long-standing painful feelings. "It released a lot of shame and negative beliefs about my father, myself, and our relationship." "I went through a lot of mental housecleaning when I was in the hospital, a lot of issues came up for me, and a lot got laid to rest." Some men may find their spiritual beliefs coming to the fore. "My spirituality helped a great deal. Throughout the whole experience I felt that I had come very close to God. Closer than I had ever come before."

For men who have kept their families updated on their medical condition, the first hospitalization often feels like another step with their family. "We all knew this was going to happen someday, and it finally did." "My sister is a nurse and we both knew things were just not going well. I called her before I went into the hospital and said, 'It's happening.'" Family members often find ways of conveying the depth of their concern over the past years of anxious waiting and hoping. "My mother told me that she had said two hundred and twenty-seven Rosaries since I told them I was positive."

Many men are quite ready to leave the hospital environment as they feel stronger. "It was great while I was so ill, but the stronger I got, the more it started to get on my nerves." "Toward the end it was *get me out of here!*" However, men are often faced with a sense of vulnerability as they leave after a defining illness. "When I was ready to leave the hospital I felt bad because it is such a safe environment." "On the hospital unit you are safe. The place is set up for you, but the world outside is different. I wanted to leave to get back to work and to my life, but I felt vulnerable in a different way. I was going out of the hospital as someone with AIDS."

REVELATION

My family found out that I was gay and had AIDS at the same time. They were wonderful about it.

Some men may face a double revelation to their families–that they have AIDS and that they are gay. When men are acutely ill, often fears of revelation are diminished. "It was kind of strange. All of these years I have hid the issue. But when I was that sick, I just wanted my mom and dad there to hold my hand." "Maybe I thought it was safer, that they would not kick me while I was down." If the encounter with the family goes well, the effects are often highly reassuring, if not healing. "I was so impressed by how my family responded. They were great." "There was a lot of tears about the diagnosis but that felt right."

Many men find that now that the secret is out in the open they feel closer to their family of origin. "It brought me, my brothers, and their families closer together. It's been good for me. We were really never close." "My sisters and I were very close except for that aspect of my life." A supportive response from the family often leaves men wondering what the big deal was about in the first place. "I actually felt kind of ashamed. I had assumed they would reject me. I guess I did not give them enough credit." "It really seems strange now. We were close in every way accept for my being gay, which I hid from them for fear they would reject me. We talked about how we all danced around it for so many years. I was denying myself and them an important part of my life." Men may also be touched by efforts of relatives to understand what is happening. "I had one sister-in-law who went to the library and looked up everything on AIDS she could get her hands on. My sister became the family expert, kind of an 'AIDS Information Clearinghouse' for the rest of the family."

Some men whose parents live out of town may decide to reveal the diagnosis after they are out of the hospital and feeling more stable. "I wanted to tell them when I was feeling better. About two weeks out of the hospital I went out and told them." "I am going to fly home in a couple of weeks and lay it all out to them. They know something is up, but I do not want to tell them on the phone. I want to spend some time with them." Some men may feel they are setting things in motion for the future. "I figure if I tell them now, they will be more available to me when I get sicker."

Again, when the response is supportive, the effect is highly reassuring. "My father who has been distant at best throughout my life softened up and said, 'Don't worry about anything. We will take care of you if you need us to.' That was comforting." Family dynamics come into play as the diagnosis is revealed, and men often encounter problematic aspects of their family style. Some men take them in stride. "My mother did her usual guilt trip of, 'Oh, I just knew this was going to happen to me.' I said, 'It isn't happening to you; it's happening to me.'"

Men are often amazed at the amount of support they receive. "After I got sick, all of these people came out of the woodwork and I discovered all of this love that was available to me but that I have been denying." Some men may be a bit anxious by the response of their friends. "My friends have rallied, though it is somewhat frightening. I want to say, 'Wait a minute.' I do not need all of that support yet. It is comforting to know that if and when I need it, it will be there." As discussed in previous chapters, revelation is also an ongoing process of negotiating relationships in light of the knowledge that at this point in the experience, one has AIDS. "Once people find out you have AIDS, they think, 'Oh, my God.' It is a bit much at times. Sometimes I get annoyed and want to say, 'Calm down, I am not dying yet.'"

As men recover from their initial illness, many return to work and other daily routines. As they re-enter their lives, the process of revelation continues. In returning to work after a long absence men often need to explain what happened, or is some cases, pass a return-to-work physical. "I told my supervisor. He was great. He told me that he had family members who do volunteer work with AIDS, and that there were a number of employees who were also diagnosed, and working." "In order for me to return to work, I had to clear a company doctor. They wanted my discharge records. I went to the medical department, and had to wait while the doctor reviewed my records. I started trembling. The nurse asked me if I wanted to talk. I lost it and told her what was going on. She said they had already figured it out, and that they just needed to be sure that I was strong enough to go back to work. The doctor just asked about my stamina, and if I felt ready. He then went into a big lecture about how important support groups were, watching my energy, not getting overly tired, and taking care of myself. I walked out of there feeling ten feet tall. I keep expecting something awful to happen to me, like I hear about on the news, but it hasn't."

LINGERING PAIN

It's like a big hurt. It's like one of those wounds that does not want to close real easy.

Men who knew they were positive for a number of years often have become accustomed to the lingering hurt and pain that goes with the experience. Many find it shifting somewhat after a defining illness. "In some ways it does not hurt as much, in others it does. In one sense I feel there is nothing else to lose. In another, I feel closer to having to say goodbye to this world." "I find myself feeling sad in that I feel one more step further removed from the world of those around me." Men who find out they are positive at diagnosis face the task of feeling the pain in the midst of the upheaval of life changing so radically in a short period of time. "Lately, there have been times when I pull over, stop the car, and I sob for ten minutes." "Sometimes I just stop whatever I am doing and go have a good cry for ten minutes, then I pull it together and get right back on track."

Some men may find the sadness dominating at unexpected times. "I was at an aerobics class a few weeks after being out of the hospital. My instructor is one of these positive mental attitude people. She was doing her spiel about positive attitude and I just broke down and started to sob. She held me and said, 'Let it out.' I told her what I had just been through while she held me. It was comforting to know that someone was not afraid to touch me."

Some men are aware of how basic experiences of self have changed. "I have always had a *joi de vivre*, but I find that since I have been ill, it's diminishing." "I am feeling pretty old these days. Like my age has been accelerated. I just feel so much older." Men often find their body image changing as well. "They had to help me in and out of the car. I felt like my grandmother. I just wanted to cry. I am thirty-seven and feeble." "I no longer feel like a sexy individual. I actually feel dirty on some occasions." The fear of contagion may also emerge at unexpected times. "My friend is going to have a baby in three more weeks. My instant reaction was 'keep her away from me!' But then I thought that was kind of stupid because I know how it is spread."

Some men may find themselves having trouble engaging with life and its events. "Christmas was hard this year. I had no involvement with it this year. I am usually into parties and celebrating. This year it wasn't there, nothing special about it." "A lot of times I find myself feeling on the outside looking in. I just have trouble really getting into holidays and celebrations. I keep wondering if this will be my last." A strong sense of being different, of being changed may dominate at times. "It is like there is this gap between me and the rest of the world." "I kind of feel a couple steps removed from other people, especially when they are negative."

MAKING SENSE

There is a lot to make sense of. Everything seems up in the air.

Following a diagnosis, men often grapple with just what the diagnosis means. Men who find out that they are infected may face a more profound experience similar to THE TWILIGHT ZONE described in previous areas. "It turns you around, upside down, inside out. It makes a big difference in the way I think about anything." "I look in the mirror, I see the same old me, but somehow I see a stranger. Even though I no longer look sick, I feel so different inside. Where everything was on track, now there are big question marks everywhere I look."

Men often struggle to make sense of the diagnosis in terms of their previous experience of self and life. "I feel like I have been dealt a big blow. My life has been very easy. I never really had any hardships. I always maintained a grip." Men may feel that they cannot approach the diagnosis as they have other aspects of their life. "If I wanted something, I worked hard and I got it. Now I have got something I did not want. And no matter how hard I work, it feels like there is no way out." "All of my close friends are negative. It's sad that they will go on and live their lives out together, where I am going to be stopped. That I have to leave behind so many people I love."

Life often feels highly tenuous. "I am questioning how long I am going to live. What will the quality of my life be like?" "I have never felt this vulnerable before." Men often anticipate horrible problems ahead. "My biggest fear is financial. I have always been afraid of being a poor old queen." "I see guys who are not financially capable of taking care of themselves. I am determined that is not going to happen to me, but the fear is still there." A fear of a horrible death is often present. "I do not want to be a vegetable." "It is not the dying part that frightens me. It's getting there."

Men often find themselves contemplating an afterlife. "I really wonder if there is something after this, and if so, what is it?" "I wonder about reincarnation. What will I become? Where am I going after this?" "The actual dying part is not difficult. The part that is difficult is what is beyond it. I cannot see it, examine it; it's frightening." Men who have lost their partners may view death as a reunion. "If there is something after this, then I will get to see Jim again." "I used to think the stories about heaven and seeing loved ones again were silly. But I do find myself daydreaming that at least I will be with Mark."

As discussed in previous chapters, the collapse of the sense of future brings with it sadness, often depression. "It's hard to imagine forty happening. I know I am not going to die tomorrow. But for some reason, I just cannot see myself going on forever; it's depressing." Men who have known they were positive for a number of years may recognize these feelings. "It's back again, the sidewalk shrunk to a tightrope–again. It's hard to describe the trapped, sad, scary, place that it is." Some men will find that the diagnosis takes a tremendous psychological toll. "For several weeks–maybe months– I was severely depressed. My therapist has been helping me work through it." "I was so devastated. I just felt like I had been beaten with a two-by-four."

Eventually the turmoil subsides, the questions and fear lose some of their urgency. "Technically I passed the halfway mark in life. At least I got something. Some of these guys are only nineteen or twenty years old. Jesus, they haven't even started to live." The process of calming down and the sense of order re-emerging is often helped by supportive relationships. "This has been a horrible thing, but it has been a gift as well. My parents are more attentive. My dad is friendlier; he has made a complete three-sixty. I am finding out there are some positive things that happen." "It is hard to reconcile sometimes. On one hand I am faced with this horrible illness, on the other I am feeling more settled, and more connected with my family and friends than ever before." Gradually the press to answer so many questions evolves. "I realized that I do not need to sort it all out right now. Things are starting to fall into place. I realized that some things you cannot force." "Living your life one day at a time isn't as bad as I thought. It takes a big load off."

Men who have known they were positive for a long period of time may find that there is more of a sense of freedom and relief. "It is a big burden off my shoulders; it is actually freeing. The fear of getting sick is gone. For the first time in a long, long, time, I feel free to move on with my life." "I find myself wondering what the big deal was. I was so scared of this for so long, but it was so gentle. I realized that I have nothing to lose. I feel free to decide what I want to do with the rest of my life."

THE GAME PLAN

I have my own little treatment regime which consists of three factors. I trust in Western medicine, I am taking Yoga classes— some Eastern beliefs and some spirituality. All three combined have changed my life.

As described in earlier chapters a Game Plan often evolves following the diagnosis. Men who found out they were infected following diagnosis tend to proceed with a similar intensity as men who knew they were positive did in earlier areas of the experience.

Men who have known about the infection may alter their Game Plans in light of disease progression. For these men there is often less zeal and anxiety associated with the plan–more of a quiet adjustment than determined effort.

For some newly diagnosed men, their plan may have a zealous quality. "I have completely turned my life around. I have incorporated Silva, Louise Hayes. The church I go to has a lot of New Age thoughts and teachings which I have found to be very meaningful." "I have set up a very rigorous exercise regime–vitamins–and I am researching going to a vegetarian diet." Some men will radically change their approach to life. "I have come to believe that we are totally responsible for our lives and our reality. That includes illness and wellness." "I am doing a lot of mental work and spiritual work, growth going on at all levels. I am finally ridding myself of a lot of shame."

Some men may opt for alternative approaches to health and treatment. "I went off AZT. I ran across studies that showed rats developed cancer and the people who live longest seem to do alternatives–no AZT." "I have read about people who are working with alternatives that are now negative. That is the direction I am going to take; that is my goal." Some men may take a slightly different approach to alternative therapies. "I am firmly rooted in Western medicine. But I have found that what some people refer to as alternatives, just plain make me feel better. The massages are great. I do feel energized after acupuncture, and the meditation stuff really helps calm me down."

As in earlier areas some men make it a point to gather information. "I have discovered an HIV/AIDS data base, a BBS balloon board. I have learned a lot from it." "I am amazed at how much I have learned in the few months since I was diagnosed. I needed to find out as much as possible. It's like going into a dark room with a monster. I need a light; I needed to know what he looked like." Men may also seek out support groups. "I need a support group. I started going to TPA. It was very important for me to be with other HIV people, too see how they view it. It is a battle, but I am not sure if we are survivors, or surviving." "I went to TPA in hopes that it would help me feel better. Just being around other diagnosed people and seeing that they have a life was the best part."

Men who have known about their infection for a longer period of time may take a somewhat different approach. "I see all of these newly diagnosed men at TPA and they are taking a real fighting approach. I guess I am just more accepting–not giving in–but willing to go along with the flow. I have been through the fighting stage." "I really want to retire. I made some good plans a few years ago. The money is there, the insurance is there. I do not want to work until I drop, or until I am so sick that I cannot enjoy life." The previously described sense of relief that these men report often enables them to do things they have held back on. "I have been cautious for so long, saving my pennies. Worried that I would get sick, be diagnosed. Well, I am diagnosed now. I do not like to admit it sometimes, but this may well be the last good year I have. I have a bunch of frequent flier miles; I am going to use them."

Some men may look back over the years and reflect on how their Game Plan has changed. "Looking back it feels like a bunch of plans or phases or maybe even fads. The vitamin phase, the egg lecithin phase, the visualization phase. Finally I learned that the important thing was feeling content, doing things that make me feel good. So right now my plan is to maintain feeling content."

CALMING DOWN

There is a real strong thing in me–joi de vivre. *It is part of my make-up. I am a live-er and a do-er. I thought it was gone forever after I was diagnosed, but it is back.*

The psychological experience of AIDS is strongly influenced by the disease course. Many men will experience periods of feeling well and healthy after the initial illness. "It has been a fairly quiet year health-wise–no colds, or flu. Sometimes I forget I am sick, then my medication beeper goes off, or its pentamadine time. It used to throw me, but now I just keep plugging away." When this is the case, they often find their optimism and sense of well-being returning. "Things are pretty much back to normal. I am back to work, working out at the gym, in bed by eleven. Just doing the things they always said you were supposed to do, but I never paid any attention to." "I felt so lousy for so long after I was diagnosed.

I was making plans to retire and go on disability, now I am having second thoughts. I get too much out of my job."

Men may find their sense of future expanding once more. "It's a few months away, but I am looking forward to digging in the garden again this year." "The urgency to get everything done, go on my dream trips, line everything up in case I get sick, is waning somewhat. It will get done, Europe will happen. I am planning for this fall." Men may also take on new pursuits. "I am starting a new business. I am doing landscaping with a friend of mine." "I am going to take the Silva training course to become an instructor." "I am looking forward to spring, summer, and fall."

Men find reassurance from a number of sources. "When I am working, moving around rootballs or cutting trees I do not feel sick." "I was out working on the garage in ninety degree weather. Working hard and sweating. I felt very good. I felt alive. I did not feel like I was sick or that I was even supposed to be sick." In sharp contrast to the way they initially felt after the diagnosis, men may find themselves feeling even better about themselves. "My life has changed so much; I am not the same person who went into the hospital. I feel much better about myself than I did back then." "I feel so connected to my family. My parents have changed a lot at a quick rate. My father is softening up. I gave him a watch for Father's Day and he actually got out of his chair, came across the room and gave me a kiss on the cheek. I had to take the dog out for a walk because I could not stop crying. It's sad that it took something like this for my parents to soften up."

Though they may feel optimistic, and basically well, the knowledge of being ill with AIDS never goes away. "I feel real good about my life. It feels strange sometimes that I have AIDS. Sometimes it really throws me when I tell people and I see that look in their eyes." "It never completely goes away, the AIDS thing. But all in all, I think I am doing a swell job of handling my potentially deadly disease."

When men's health is stable, and as the process of Calming Down continues, thoughts often turn to relationships, and/or sex. On some level, men grapple with their often damaged self-image and the possibility of transmission. Initially, the idea of a sexual encounter or relationship may feel too anxiety provoking. "I have not slept with anyone since my diagnosis–hand holding is all. I have never taken my clothes off and gone to bed with somebody. There is a part of me that feels defective now." "I do not know where I got this, but I do not want to give it to anyone else." Some men may resume their usual patterns of seeking sexual contact. "I go out cruising now and then. I always make a point of telling them." "If I say I am positive and they still want to go ahead and do it, 'Okay, if you want to play with fire.'" Diagnosed men are often surprised at the number of HIV-negative men willing to have sex with them. "It really surprises me that I met a number of individuals who were not positive, but made attempts at pursuing a relationship."

Though men may yearn for a relationship, they often find themselves wondering what they have to offer in the long term. "It is one thing to go out and find someone to have sex with. It is another to find someone that you want to be intimate with." "I can get a lot of dates, but it is hard to imagine them turning into long-term romances." "When you can't imagine a long-term, it's hard to imagine a long-term relationship." "Sometimes I wonder, 'What is the matter with you? Are you just setting yourself up for a no-win situation?' How many of us will be around in five years?"

Other men will opt out of pursuing relationships or sex. "I am just not interested in sex anymore. It seems pointless and a lot of work. In retrospect, it is a lot of work to go out and meet someone for a thirty-minute roll in the hay. I'd rather have a quiet dinner with friends and be in bed early." "I need to socialize, but cruising for sex is just not in me anymore. I do not go out to the bars anymore. I go to country western dancing. It's more of a social thing. It is not cruisy. You do not go there to pick up people."

MELTDOWN

Sunday I was an emotional wreck. I just went down the tubes.

As in previous categories, after diagnosis men experience Meltdowns, times when confidence and hope are shaken, despair emerges and life feels very tenuous. "When my confidence gets shaken, I feel trapped. I feel like I got on a short path and I cannot get off it. Then I think there is no tomorrow, and no hope." "I feel like I am on that tightrope that I could fall off of at any moment–again." Meltdown may be triggered by a variety of events–illness and death of friends, or the anniversary of the diagnosis. "It's really frightening when I think about several friends. How so many things with HIV can happen so explosively, or seem to happen explosively." "I went out to dinner the other night with a friend who has been diagnosed for two years. He was always an optimist and a fighter. Last night he said he was tired of fighting. He wanted it to be over with. He wanted to die."

Sometimes men are aware that something is building up. "There has just been too much bad news. I am being wound up like a golf ball." "I am not sure what it is, but something is stirring the embers a bit." With others, the Meltdown may slowly take over and dominate experience. "I was feeling kind of sick and run down. I took a few days off to take it easy, and the next thing I knew I was in bed for two weeks. I wasn't calling anyone or returning calls–I just withdrew. I got pretty depressed before I realized what was going on–wondering if this was it, thinking about the hospital, if this is what it would be like from now on. I finally realized that this was about the same time last year as when I was diagnosed."

As time goes on, men may learn to recognize and manage their Meltdowns. "If I sense something coming on, I will just sit back and meditate or visualize." "Sure there are rough days, but I have found that if I just go with it, and try and figure out what is gnawing at me, look it square in the face, and cry if I need to, that it is over and done with." Men may also find their experience of Meltdowns changing over time. "It does not last as long anymore. An afternoon maybe. It just kind of rushes through."

BALANCING

It's been quite a year. A great summer. Things are special now. The crickets. They are fascinating. I can just lie back and listen to them for hours.

Again as in previous areas, men often find themselves reaching a point of feeling balanced. "I am finding that it is easier for me to talk about this as time goes on. It is easier for me to say, 'I have

AIDS.' There was a time when it was very difficult." "I am not as scared as I used to be. I do not know if I knew how really freaked out I really was." The diagnosis may be viewed in a broader perspective, rather than a death sentence. "This has been a real educating experience. I really have gotten to know myself, gotten rid of a lot of baggage, and realized that there is so much more to life than worrying about dying." "Things are going well. But they are going well because I have good support, I am not carrying around a lot of excess baggage. Work, exercise–it all fits in whereas it did not fit three months ago."

Men often come to strongly value the sense of being calm and enchanted. "Things that I like have suddenly become more important. They are priorities, not just treats. I like beaches, big bodies of water, the coast of Florida. I would just sit there and spend two or three hours on a beach or looking at a lake, just absorbing it, because it feels good." "We used to be party and travel animals. Now we are into the garden. It is a lot of work, but evenings hanging out in it, enjoying the smells, how it has come together, the sounds–all make it worth it. It's those times of feeling incredibly connected that are so important now."

"Men may also find themselves being able to look back on their life and contemplate without a sharp, painful sense of loss. At first I used to reflect on my life as a series of lost opportunities and failures. Of things I can no longer correct or alter. Now I can think and daydream and think, 'Yes, it may have been better that way, but it was not. Let's see what we can do now.'" "Sometimes I find myself wondering, if I had done anything differently, I would have joined the Air Force. I have always wanted to learn how to fly a jet plane."

LOOKING AHEAD

It's a hard decision. Do I retire now, and take my disability benefits, travel and enjoy myself, or try to get another year in?

Diagnosed men find themselves Looking Ahead, making plans in the context of the diagnosis and its implications. "I am trying to lay down some plans so I have a sense of a path to follow. I do not think that I am being negative and a victim by wanting to make sure I get some quality time in before things start to go downhill." "From now on the emphasis is going to be on quality of life. I have a list of places to go and things to do. I am going to start doing them."

Deciding what direction to take career-wise is often part of Looking Ahead. "I have known too many people that worked until they dropped. I am not ill or debilitated, but I do have AIDS. I want some semblance of retirement." "What to do with work is a hard one. I do not think I could just lay around all day, and I do not want to travel alone. I get a lot out of my job so I think I am going to cut a deal where I work a few days a week."

Some men may find their plans changing. "I was all ready to retire. I was accepted for disability, but I kept feeling better and better, and more and more bored. I think I am going to keep working a while longer. It just does not feel like the right time yet." "At first it was full steam ahead, back to work, no problem. But then I felt, 'Why are you doing this? What are you trying to prove? You have the money, the travel benefits–relax and enjoy yourself.' Besides I found that the job was taking more out of me than I anticipated." Some men may find themselves working through issues that have kept them moving at a frantic pace most of their lives. "I realized that I have been trying to prove something or the other all my life. I finally realized there was nothing left to prove–get over it and have fun. I want my tombstone to say that I lived life to the fullest, not worked my ass of in pursuit of something I really did not understand." "This is a time to be rebellious, to take time off and be a little crazy. I do not know how much time is left."

Chapter 11

Clinical Intervention

Considerable literature has accumulated on the various aspects of clinical intervention with people diagnosed with AIDS. In contrast, little research and clinical writings are devoted to people who have tested HIV-positive yet are asymptomatic, have not developed a defining opportunistic infection, or whose immune functioning has not declined to levels that are now considered AIDS defining. The results of this study clearly demonstrate the enormous psychological consequences of testing positive for the HIV virus, as well as ongoing efforts to manage the impact and psychological growth in the face of HIV.

People who have tested positive but have not developed AIDS represent the vast majority of people directly affected by the epidemic, yet appear to be the least investigated and understood (Borden, 1991). In summarizing the research and descriptive clinical literature on the initial reactions to notification of seropositivity, Borden (1991) cited, "Disorganization of self, particularly in the initial weeks after notification of results, episodic periods of anxiety, depression, demoralization, psychosomatic symptoms, low self-esteem, exacerbation of premorbid relational conflicts, and social withdrawal in the months following discovery as consistently reported and observed psychological reactions" (p. 438).

Research efforts to assess psychological symptomatology in infected men at different points in disease progression has yielded interesting results. The findings of Hays et al. (1990); Ostrow et al. (1989); and Perry et al. (1990) suggest that gay men who are HIV-positive are not more psychologically distressed than gay men who are HIV-negative. Moving farther down the disease continuum, Hays et al. (1992) found that depression is likely when HIV-positive men begin to experience physical symptoms of HIV illness. Wu (1990) found that men who are experiencing symptoms but not yet diagnosed exhibited higher rates of depression than men diagnosed with AIDS.

In thinking about this study in light of the above findings two issues are evident. First, this study is not about psychological symptomatology. It is about the experience of, or meaning of, testing positive and how that meaning often transforms over time. Second, epidemiological studies are difficult to apply to the individual. As clinicians we are aware that people can present as considerably depressed, confused, and disorganized on one day but not several days later. In a similar vein, people can be considerably disorganized, anxious, and depressed as they work through, or attempt to understand distressing events, yet not exhibit clinical signs of symptomatology.

The often long period of knowing that one is positive, but the infection has not advanced to the point of an AIDS diagnosis, taxes the resiliency of the self in many ways. Cohen and Abramowitz (1990) state: "The lack of clear-cut symptoms and the multiplicity of affected organ systems can leave the PWA [Person With AIDS] without a well-defined physical locus around which to organize his or her sense of self in relation to the illness" (p. 161). While the authors refer to people who are actually diagnosed with AIDS, a recurrent theme in the results of this study is the process of attempting to place one's self in relation to the illness. The results of this study serve to begin to fill this gap in our knowledge of the complex, dynamic, and evolving experience of testing positive. The narrative presented in previous chapters illustrates these aspects of the experience and offers us as clinicians a general framework with which to listen to the unique experiences of our individual clients.

In the clinical practice setting people who are positive may well make up the majority of people presenting with HIV-related problems. This chapter will attempt to provide a dynamic clinical framework for understanding and intervening with clients primarily in the earlier phases of HIV infection. The Self-Psychological theoretical framework will guide the understanding and clinical approaches to the difficulties that our clients present.

THE CONTINUUM OF HIV INFECTION

In Shelby (1992) I conceptualized a biological continuum of HIV infection and a parallel continuum of the person's emotional response to the knowledge of, and eventually physiological effects of

HIV infection. In establishing a framework for clinical intervention the conceptualization of a continuum needs to be elaborated further. We must take into account the presence and response of the selfobject matrix, and in the context of clinical intervention the continuum of the transference. (See Figure 1.)

The biological continuum refers to the initial HIV infection, often lengthy period of of non-apparent symptomatology (save perhaps laboratory indicators), emergence of symptoms, introduction of antivral and prophylactic medications, and the body's response to them, development of opportunistic infections, decline in physical and often emotional status, and finally death. Parallel is the person's experience of the biological continuum, which was the focus of this study: the decision to be tested, initial psychological response to the knowledge of infection, and the ongoing psychological experience of the infection and its progression. As the study indicates, the person's experience of the infection may be radically different than biological indicators, and the experience of the infection is dynamic and evolving. People often experience numerous fragmentations as they reach different points on the medical continuum and gradually reintegrate as they progress through the stages of HIV infection.

Parallel to the person's experience is the continuum of the selfobject matrix. HIV infection does not occur in a vaccum; we all live in and are sustained by a matrix of human relationships. The matrix includes partners, friends, family members, physicians, other medical personnel, support group members, and the therapist. The people of the matrix respond to the HIV infection and the person's experience of HIV infection, and the infected person responds to the response of individuals in the matrix. The matrix can have considerable sustaining and organizing power. It can also have considerable destabilizing and disorganizing power. Selfobject failures, a lack of attunement to affects and self states of the infected person, the loss of members of the matrix through disease progression, or outright rejection of the infected person can lead to severe fragmentations and profoundly affect the person's experience of HIV infection and the experience of self. The term selfobject matrix is used rather than "supportive relationships" or "social support" in that these conceptualizations imply older formulations that funda-

FIGURE 1. Parallel Continua of HIV infection

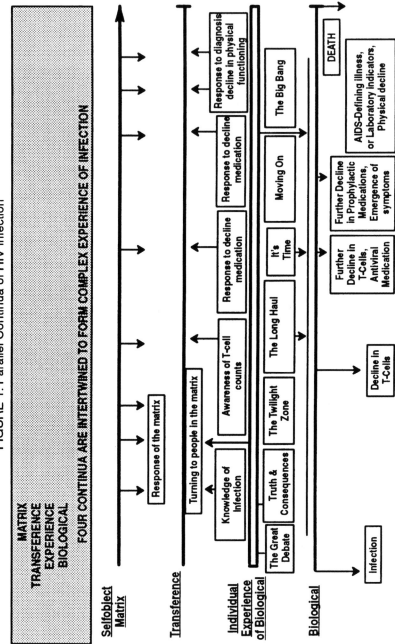

mentally pertain to the support of defenses rather than the integral role selfobjects play in the sustenance of the self.

When the person is engaged in psychotherapy, we must also consider the continuum of the transference. This line of experience lies between the person's experience of the infection and his experience of the matrix. The primary conceptualization of the transference employed in this model is the selfobject transference. The transference is a reflection of the person's selfobject deficits, their need to establish relationships that help them stabilize in the throes of a fragmentation, the ongoing narcissistic stress of being positive and/or reflects a thwarted need to grow.

The conceptualization of four parallel continuums is useful in that it helps us sort out the data that clients present to us as they seek our help in managing the psychological impact of their infection. It also helps us to determine the appropriate intervention, i.e., individual, couple, or family intervention may be called for at different points in the person's experience. The four parallel lines are for illustrative puposes only. In reality they are interwoven and together combine to form the complex experience of HIV infection.

THE PSYCHOLOGY OF THE SELF

Self-psychology holds that psychopathology in adulthood is ultimately derived from deficits in the overall structure of the self or from distortions of the self (Muslin, 1985). As stated earlier, adult selves exist in varying degrees of coherence, vitality, and harmony. Consequently, selves vary in their degree of vulnerability to narcissistic injury or the loss or failure in a self-selfobject relationship and the consequent fragmentation of the self that occurs. Fragmentation is the experience of the breakdown of the self. Fragmentation states can be either ubiquitous, of minor degree and short duration, or chronic, protracted, and intense. Going back to our continuum and thinking about our patients we often observe multiple fragmentations of varying degrees and intensity throughout the experience of HIV. Some may be triggered by disease progression, and others triggered by selfobject failure in the matrix. As people come to HIV and us as clinicians with varying self-deficits, we are always working in the realm of the patient's experience of HIV and its unique meanings. We never work just with HIV, we work with what HIV means to the patient and what the matrix's response means to the patient. Saari (1986, 1991) has described the self as a meaning system. Meanings tend to be highly interrelated, hence the experience of HIV infection is bound to trigger past, often highly volatile, experiences, and their related affects.

A person with HIV infection or anyone else in acute distress often needs and seeks out more archaic selfobject encounters to maintain the self's cohesion. In the face of the trauma of HIV infection, when we are able to respond to our patients, to help contain and modulate anxiety and other affects, we are likely to see a selfobject transference emerge rather rapidly. The transference is an entity unto itself that determines the kind of relationship we have with the client as the psychological impact of HIV is addressed in the treatment. The transference reflects how the person organizes his experience of life and its personal meanings in accord with the self's strengths and deficits.

In tending to the psychological impact of HIV we are invariably tending to previous self-deficits and injuries. As people enter a therapeutic relationship, join support groups, or enlist other helping relationships in their efforts to tend to the psychological impact of the infection, they tend to form relationships that have a modulating effect. Consequently previous trauma encountered with peers as a child may be reworked as the person joins a support group and finds himself welcomed, rather than excluded. In individual work, the clinician's attunement to affect states and empathic efforts to comprehend with the client the depth and personal meaning of his distress often re-awakens the hope that people can and will be able to help in times of need as well as times when central selfobjects failed to sustain.

The primary conception of the transference in a self-psychological framework is that it is a thwarted need to grow. In this framework it is not the inappropriateness and distortion of transference reactions that is seen as primarily important. What is regarded as primary is the need of the client to establish a tie with the helping person which will allow for the remobilization of developmental needs that were inadequately responded to by the person's original caretakers. In this context the patient who uses alienating defenses or is hostile is warding off the fear of traumatic disappointment which would occur if the therapist were to misunderstand or reject his remobilized appropriate developmental needs. In this conceptualization, the patient's potentially healthy wishes to re-establish object ties that might forward his development are interfered with by noisy defenses which are meant to protect him from a repetition of past selfobject failures (Faigen, 1988). The selfobject transference is the dominant "flavor" of our relationship with individual patients, reflecting their dominant selfobject functions or needs. As the transference relationship solidifies and emerges, these ways of being come to dominate. Baker and Baker (1987) describe the three selfobject functions and consequent transferences:

1. Idealizing . . . our need to merge with, or be close to someone who we believe will make us safe, comfortable and calm . . . An external object serves an internal function–calming and comforting– and so functions as a selfobject for the child. . . . Initially there is a wish to merge with the idealized parental imago; then there is the wish to be very near a source of such power; eventually the mature person is satisfied knowing that friends and family are available during times of distress. (p. 4)
2. Mirroring . . . The delighted response of the parents to the child–the gleam in the mother's eye–is essential to the child's development. This response mirrors back to the child a sense of self-worth and value, creating internal self-respect. . . . In the context of a generally responsive environment, the intensity of the grandiose self is diminished, but not destroyed. (p. 3)
3. Twinship/alter ego . . . the need to feel a degree of alikeness with other people. The small boy may stand by his father when he shaves; the son also "shaves" using a bladeless razor. These sort of experiences lead to a feeling of being like others, of being a part of and connected to the human community. . . . The third pole [talents and skills] develops from twinship/alter ego needs and experiences. (pp. 4,5)

In thinking about the often volatile and intense affects that accompany HIV infection it is important to consider the sustaining and organizing power of an idealizing transference with the clinician. Palombo (1988) elucidates on the idealizing selfobject function:

1. The experience of safety that results from the faith in the strength and omnipotence of another who is seen as a protector. The sharing in that strength and protectiveness results in the function of feeling powerful and effective as a human being.
2. The experience of having one's excitement and overstimulating affects modulated by another who provides regulation. These experiences result in the functions of self-control, self-discipline and self-regulation.
3. The experience of being soothed, comforted, and calmed by another who provides solace and succorance as well as joyous vitality. These experiences result in the capacity for enthusiasm and equanimity.

AIDS AND THE SELF

Cohen and Abramowitz in Goldberg (1990) discuss the psychological impact of AIDS in a self-psychological framework. Though they tend to focus their discussion on people who have been diagnosed with AIDS, their descriptions of the disruptions in the body self and selfobject bonds are highly applicable to understanding the experience of people across the spectrum of HIV infection. As one reads their discussion in light of the findings of this study, it is clear that one does not have to be diagnosed with AIDS, and to have experienced acute opportunistic infections, to experience these disruptions. Being informed that one is positive for the HIV virus is enough to trigger these massive disruptions in the self. The authors describe the following disruptions in the experience of self.[1]

Disruption of the Body Self

The body self according to Kohut (1971) is the original vehicle for our exhibitionistic needs. Correspondingly, the integ-

---

1. Quoted material from *The Realities of Transference: Progress in Self-Psychology*, Volume 6, 1990, A. Goldberg, editor. Reprinted by permission of The Analytic Press.

rity, smooth functioning, and compliance of the physical body is a key component of body self-cohesiveness. In addition, self-esteem derives in part from the body's structural integrity, physical and sexual attractiveness, and athletic prowess. Conversely, a subjective experience of physical defectiveness through disfigurement or malfunctioning of the body is destabilizing to the self-organization. (p. 159)

Disruptions of Selfobject Bonds

The dimensions of loss caused by AIDS are staggering. Losses range from the concrete–job, income, social role, physical health, and attractiveness–to the abstract–basic security, predictability, self-determination, being in control, and other means for the expression of healthy grandiosity, ambition, and ideals. The diagnosis of a terminal illness, especially for someone in young adulthood, is a direct blow to normal grandiosity, to the common, if illusory, sense of invulnerability and immortality. . . . The very lovers and friends of a PWA need to serve sustaining selfobject functions are often themselves dead or dying. Thus while mourning his personal losses, a PWA may feel anticipatory grief for his ill and dying loved ones, while simultaneously acutely grieving the recent deaths of others. Tragically at a time of heightened selfobject need, the PWA often must mourn an ever-shrinking selfobject milieu. (pp. 160-161)

Disruption of Mirroring Selfobject Bonds

AIDS profoundly disrupts bonds with whoever or whatever provides mirroring selfobject functions. For example, sexuality provides support and validation, a confirmation of worth. With AIDS this important avenue for meeting mirroring needs can be closed off or at least more problematic. Many PWAs no longer feel sexual after diagnosis because of physical debilitation, fear of infecting others, fear of their own further exposures to infection, or perhaps a disenchantment with sex itself since it can be a route of HIV exposure. The stigma of AIDS also leads many PWAs to reject needed support. As one's need for self-affirmation through mirroring increases, one can become more shame prone when those needs are left unmet. Since the self-cohesion of PWAs is threatened by a stigmatized catastrophic illness, their intensified need for attuned mirroring leaves them very vulnerable to feeling shame. . . .

Unfortunately, when PWAs come from families or communities where AIDS and its association to homosexuality and intravenuous drug use is usually highly stigmatized, these PWAs understandably expect that their support systems will view them disparingly. This expectation can cause them to feel deep humiliation about their diagnosis, leading them to withdraw protectively from potential caregivers, just when they most need reaffirming mirroring. Rejection by family and community is unfortunately often a harsh reality; but it is equally unfortunate that many PWAs avoid family and communities that, if given the chance, might have been quite supportive (p. 162-163).

Disruption of Alter Ego Selfobject Bonds

AIDS deeply undermines the alter ego stabilization some PWAs experience as part of a community of others like themselves. For example, gay men whose self-esteem has been stabilized and validated by their "coming out" and openly identifying with the gay community must, as a growing segment of that community becomes ill and dies, deal with traumatic loss of those who provided alter ego selfobject needs. Differences in health status may cause splits in a formerly cohesive community: splits between those who have AIDS or ARC, are asymptomatic antibody positive, or are antibody negative, and those who remain untested for AIDS. People in each category may feel ostracized by those in the next healthier groups. Alternatively, estrangement from the community may be self-imposed. For instance, the diagnosis of AIDS may stir up self-blame, self-hatred, and internalized homophobia in certain gay or bisexual men. Aroused conflicts about being homosexual may lead the PWA to seek emotional distance from the previously stabilizing alter ego community. (p. 163)

Disruption of Idealized Selfobject Bonds

The seriously ill person yearns, like a vulnerable child, for omniscient and omnipotent figures to merge with; thus, physicians, nurses, therapists, and other caregivers are sought to fulfill idealized selfobject functions. Such caregivers, the PWA hopes, will know what to do, will have all the answers and will care for and cure. For this new and complex disease, however, the doctors and other caregivers do not have all the answers. Thus, for some PWAs, physicians and other caregivers fail to provide the idealizing selfobject function of the caregiving parent with whom one can merge and experience safety, calmness, and healing. The resulting disappointment undermines the cohesiveness of the self.

. . . Medications and other treatments, like caregivers, may serve idealized selfobject functions; they can be yearned-for powerful agents that calm, soothe, and cure. The stabilization experienced by ingesting, and thus merging with, these idealized treatments may underlie the powerful "placebo effect." However, here, too, selfobject needs are often traumatically frustrated. There is no magical cure, only a plethora of more or less experimental treatments and little hard data. Even relatively established treatments like AZT have potentially devastating effects. (p. 164)

The results of the study illustrate the disruptions in the various aspects of the self and efforts on the part of HIV-postive men to modulate their impact. We see men seeking out and forming a wide variety of relationships that ultimately have a modulating effect on the disorganized and damaged self. In Shelby (1992) I asserted that selfobject relationships have a tremendous impact on how a person experiences AIDS and HIV infection. Selfobject relationships provide a sustaining, affirming, modulating, and reassuring force in the wake of the massive narcissistic trauma that accompanies HIV infection.

In describing the nature of selfobjects Goldberg (1990) states:

Selfobjects are not experiences. They are not distinct and separate beings. These two ideas insist on the boundary between what is internal in opposition to what is external. Selfobjects are the others that allow one to achieve and maintain an individual integrity. They are what makes us what we are, our very composition. But the individual is not reduced to these selfobjects, since there is an "owness" inherent in the individual (Cahoone 1988, p. 239) that goes beyond and is logically distinct from, these relations. Individual integrity and internal relatedness are not incompatible. They are joined together to form the self. Therefore we never become free of our selfobjects, nor should we, because they are our constituents. (p. 126)

Individuals tend to form an elaborate matrix of selfobject relationships that help sustain them through their experience of HIV infection. In the context of the treatment setting, the clinician becomes a member of the sustaining selfobject matrix. The nature of the treatment relationship mobilizes a more focused selfobject transference which also reawakens developmental needs and traumas. The transference also contains and modulates affect so that the traumas can be addressed in treatment by either bringing them into consciousness and/or by sustaining affect during their recall, or by reawakening the hope that tasks, activities, or encounters that seemed beyond reach are obtainable. A central tenet of self-psychology is that from birth onward we strive for cohesion and order. Previous styles and behavior patterns, though seemingly maladaptive, also reflect the patient's attempt to modulate anxiety and negotiate his world in accordance with the self's ability. In treatment we ultimately expand the person's capacity to negotiate a wider range of experience with self and other. A study participant referred to HIV infection as being like a "burner on low" that keeps things heated up just enough to be constantly aware of, then periodically is turned up full blast. Essentially, the psychological effects of HIV infection may enhance self-esteem deficits through the ongoing experience of feeling damaged, diminished, and frightened. One often observes an ongoing erosive effect on the self as the individual continues his efforts of remaining engaged with life while he may feel it is slowly slipping away.

HOPE IN THE FACE OF ADVERSITY

As the transference emerges and development is rekindled, the treatment may address increasingly the need to grow, to rework old relationships, and to keep expanding self-esteem and confidence. Thus the transference may be a potent buffer against the feeling that life is over and meaningless. HIV infection and its threat to the body's integrity taxes the most resilient self. As we work with our patients and address old traumas and self-deficits we often see their capacity to negotiate HIV increase markedly, as well as their capacity to negotiate other relationships, take on new tasks and challenges in life, and to feel more content and calm.

Thus we often observe tremendous psychological growth in our clients as we work with their unique experience of the infection. Borden (1991) in a smaller scale study of men who had tested positive found that:

> The experience appears to have led to increased reflection, reappraisal of priorities, and consolidation in self and identity for a number of the men. In some instances persons revised their life outlook and found more meaningful ways of living in view of actual circumstances and realistic prospects. That the men believed they had experienced enduring change since discovery of HIV seropositivity is itself an indication of psychological growth in the face of misfortune and adversity. (p. 445)

This seeming paradox of tremendous psycholgical growth in the face of considerable narcissistic trauma and potential or actual physical decline and eventual death provides infected individuals with hope to keep on living. The basic processes of finding meaning and order in life have not come to a stop. Life and the individual can and often do continue to unfold and evolve. It also provides clinicians with reassurance that some good can be found in the midst of the devastation that HIV and AIDS has brought to the communities we work in. Thus both client and clinician find that the ongoing process of seeking coherence by making sense of our experience of life; is not brought to a halt by HIV; rather it can continue, often in remarkable ways despite the devastation.

CLINICAL INTERVENTION

In assessing a new client presenting with HIV-related problems or in ongoing work with a client we must consider many dimensions: the point that medical testing and observation indicates the client is at on the biological continuum of infection; the individual's experience of where they are at on the biological continuum; the disruptions in selfobject bonds and the individual's unique constellation of deficits and strengths; the particular symptomatic problems being presented and their severity (i.e., anxiety, depression, rage, confusion, disorganization, panic); the response of the selfobject matrix to the individual's distress and his response to the matrix; and in ongoing treatment, the dimension of the transference. Our empathic attunement to the client in light of the above factors enables us to come closer to understanding the unique meaning of their current distress, dilemma, or triumph.

The results of the study indicate that there is a general range of experience that men who test HIV-positive encounter. In the context of individual treatment, the results serve as a general frame as we listen to our individual client's experience of the infection. Ultimately, the personal meaning for each individual, with its particular nuance, is the focus of treatment. We cannot intervene in the realm of HIV without intervening in the context of the individual self. As we come to understand and address aspects of the infection and its disruption of selfobject bonds that recapitulate previous injuries, and the selfobject transference is mobilized, the transformational aspects of the transference often result in altering the client's experience of HIV infection.

When working with clients who present with HIV-related problems we are working with people at various points on the biological continuum. Often we will develop relationships that endure as the client crosses several key points in the progression of infection. The cases and discussion will begin with the decision to be tested and proceed across the span of HIV infection. The central effort of this chapter is to place the theoretical understanding of HIV in a more dynamic context. To emphasize how the disruptions in the various aspects of the self as described by Cohen and Abramowitz (1990) are played out with others in the selfobject matrix and with the therapist. As the authors point out: "As selfobject ties are disrupted, destabilizing the self, the PWA may experience his or her current situation as a recapitulation of an early, inadequate, unempathic selfobject milieu. Stated in another way, the person's feelings, fears, and vulnerabilities about AIDS are often diagnostic of the deficits of the early developmental environment." (p. 166)

In the context of intensive psychotherapy with HIV-related problems, the ongoing erosion of self-esteem and the intensity of the selfobject transferences tend to bring the recapitulation of the early selfobject environment to the fore. Thus we often have a rich and fertile context for helping our clients make sense of their experience. The experience of feeling understood, of pain being tended to, of anxiety being modulated, is a powerful buffer against the feelings of damage, of life being over, of joy and equanimity slipping away. The hope that arises from the treatment relationship often spreads to the broader experience of life in the face of HIV.

CASE ILLUSTRATIONS

The following cases present the treatment of men at various points in the experience of HIV infection. Clinicians who work with HIV-related problems often encounter people with a wide range of presenting difficulties and self-organizations. To some degree, the needs of individuals will vary depending on the stage of the infection. However, the unique meaning for the individual clients, the dynamic nature personal meaning imparts to HIV infection, and how the therapist intervened will be consistent themes throughout the case presentations.

The Great Debate

Mr. B

As the first two chapters illustrated, the decision to be tested for HIV is often highly complex, filled with anxiety and uncertainty. Many men in the study debated for years whether or not to be tested. People will often go to great lengths to avoid narcissistic injury, and we see the same defensive process employed around decisions to be tested. Some people will be able to just go ahead and do it, for some it will be a complicated and highly anxiety-provoking process, for others it will become an annual event. In the context of individual psychotherapy, a client may engage our help in making the decision and following through on it. Again the central issue is helping the client understand the meaning of being tested, his anticipated fears and fantasies of what a positive test result would mean, and the reassurance that the treatment relationship will sustain them in the face of the results.

When Mr. B sought treatment there were a number of stressors in his life. His presenting complaints included feeling confused, increasingly unhappy in his relationship, and generally feeling "lost." Substantial difficulties were emerging in his relationship of one and a half years. Mr. B's partner was seropositive and had been on AZT for approximately one year. Though his T cells had made a substantial rebound, the emotional effects of seropositivity were being seen in his need to keep his lover as close as possible, becoming disorganized if he was late, and feeling quite threatened in response to Mr. B's efforts at a more autonomous existence.

Mr. B was approaching 30 and finding his career to be less fulfilling. He had moved from a smaller city, obtained a job tending bar and subsequently became a popular bartender. While he got a great deal of mirroring out of his job as a bartender, he was beginning to sense that he needed more career wise. He did not feel that he was taken seriously, yet, something about the job felt too precious to give up. Several old sexual partners had died, and he was being pressured to get tested by his partner. While Mr. B was increasingly worried and beginning to feel the need to know, he also found himself angrily resisting the idea of being tested in response to his partner's pressure. A further problem in the relationship concerned Mr. B's dependency on his partner, who generally ran the household finances, and who Mr. B relied upon for a basic sense of security and structure. As his partner presented increasingly vulnerable both physically and emotionally, Mr. B was becoming increasingly anxious and frightened.

Several weeks into treatment he returned for a visit to his home town. Several more old friends had died, and several others were sick. Shortly after he returned home, he developed a mild case of shingles. His physician suggested being tested. Mr. B's partner became acutely anxious and stepped up the pressure for him to go through with taking the test. During one of his sessions, we discussed the various events and pressures he was feeling. In a rather matter-of-fact manner he announced that his plan was to be tested the following week so he could time getting his results with the day of his session. As soon as he announced his plan he began to panic. He was convinced he was positive, was worried about being able to afford AZT, anticipating being disabled, unable to function in his current job, and wondering what it would be like to die.

I worked at getting him to slow down, pointing out that he was way ahead of himself–sure, all of the thoughts and fantasies he was having were reasonable ones, but he was only getting flooded. Let's take it a step at a time. By the end of the hour he was calmer, still frightened about testing positive, but was approaching finding out about his antibody status in a less overwhelmed state.

The following week he did not show for his appointment. It took some effort to contact him, with many messages left back and forth. When I finally reached him in person, it was clear that he had not been tested, was feeling ashamed that he had not followed through with his plan, and was "hiding" from me. He appeared at his next session looking very guilty and ashamed on one hand and ready for a fight on the other. I suggested that perhaps he was not ready to get tested yet and that he needed to talk some more about it.

Mr. B was immediately relieved, and in the session we discussed what being tested meant to him. I had seen him in action as a bartender which provided me with confirmation of ideas I had formulated in the context of his individual sessions.* What emerged was a 30-year-old man whose main source of esteem was the admiration of the bar patrons. Clearly he was an expert at tending bar, efficient at the task of keeping up with the high volume of service, and flirting just enough to make people feel good, but not enough for someone to be disappointed. Mr. B was in heaven behind the

---

*The ultimate issue in encountering a client in a social setting outside the treatment hour invariably is the meaning for the client. Mr. B related that while seeing me in his bar was initially unsettling, it was also reassuring that I could appreciate and understand a central part of his life, rather than devalue it.

bar. He projected the image of an eight-year-old in a 30-year-old body, with an eroticized component that was quickly eclipsed by an eight-year-old longing for mirroring of his maleness and basic worth. It took very careful maneuvering, but I began working along the lines of "clearly you get something very important from your work and the attention of your patrons." Eventually he asked, "Is it possible to be a closet exhibitionist?" I pointed out that, perhaps, he feared that if he tested positive he would no longer have anything to exhibit, that he would be crushed, that he would be brokering damaged goods, instead of the image he is used to. At this point he looked very sad, on the verge of tears, and said, "Sometimes, I think it is the only thing I have." He went on to relate a childhood very different from the life he had found in the city. He was lonely, overweight, made fun of by his peers, and painfully unsure of himself. As he began to explore the gay community in his hometown he was surprised by the interest other men had in him. In sharp contrast to the ridicule he felt from his peers as a child, as a young man he found other gay men highly attracted to him, and who were flattering if not actively pursuing his company. Soon he found himself tending bar, then obtaining a job in a bar in Chicago. For the first time in his life he felt admired and accepted. He felt tired of the "bar life," but the admiration of his customers felt too precious to give up, and he feared that there was little else he could do career wise. Testing positive, he feared, would leave him feeling like the "fucked up little kid" again, and he could not imagine his customers admiring him if he were positive, let alone sick.

In a very real sense, Mr. B was correct in anticipating a disruption if not a shattering of of his exhibitionism, if he tested positive. In his case, the primary self-deficits lay in the mirroring sphere with subsequent problems in the idealizing sphere. Here we see a young man who was painfully unsure of himself, yet highly exhibitionistic and hungry for the admiration of others. Deficits in the idealizing sphere are seen in his reliance on the idealization of his partner for a basic sense of security and grounding. His partner's emotional distress secondary to his own HIV infection was disrupting Mr. B's idealization and causing him further distress, confusion, a desire to flee the relationship, yet fear of being without an idealized selfobject.

In the context of clinical intervention the task is to identify self-deficits, observe how they are coloring the client's experience of the infection, and perhaps most important, how the deficits and attempts to manage the distress are being played out in relationships with others. While Mr. B obtained considerable reassurance from the admiration of others, he privately felt rather transparent. He himself experienced his own vulnerability given his experience in childhood, along with the assumption that others could see the deficits he felt so painfully.

While this was a painful and complicated constellation for Mr. B, it was able to be managed in the treatment relationship. I pointed out that he was probably right, he would feel that he had lost something important, and that it might be rough going for awhile, but that if he stuck with it, we could work on managing it. We worked on the area of his "exhibitionism," or need for constant mirroring, for several more sessions until I felt this area of his self was a well-established area of the treatment alliance. Mr. B related that he felt like a "fake," while the eroticized admiration of other men was highly seductive and gratifying for him, he himself lived in fear of being found either lacking or being attacked for his exhibitionistic needs and fantasies. There was considerable relief as we were able to discuss this highy complex and painful aspect of his self in the treatment.

After several sessions, he was tested. As we all anticipated, he was positive and began antiviral therapy. He was shaken by the confirmation of his assumption that he was infected, but not to the extent that he feared. To his surprise, he found life at his job tending bar pretty much unchanged. He was not as transparent as he thought. He did find himself, to his delight, flirting less with his patrons and listening more to the stories and problems they presented to him. At one point he reflected, "They say bartenders are like shrinks. I am feeling less like a 'boy toy' and more like a real bartender."

The Twilight Zone and The Long Haul

Mr. J

When he entered treatment, Mr. J was in his early thirties. Intelligent, creative, highly successful in his career, he had a highly exhibitionistic flair about him that was tempered somewhat by his charm, wit, and ability to engage with people in a such a way that he presented as highly entertaining, yet also tended to prevent him from conveying his distress in a way that people took seriously. He was referred by his physician after several weeks of intense anxiety, insomnia, disorganization, and intense somatic preoccupation following being informed that he had tested positive. He had been calling the physician's office several times a day (and often in the middle of the night) with somatic complaints and symptoms (intense, persistent headaches, nausea, a fear that he was contracting various illnesses) and questions, due to his fear of addiction, regarding the dosage of the anti-anxiety drug that had been prescribed.

During the initial interview, he was extremely anxious, sweated profusely, and chain-smoked, literally chewing the filters on his cigarettes. He related the above experiences of anxiety, somatic preoccupation, and intense headaches but added that while he knew he was "out of control" he could not stop worrying that he was sick with something, actually had AIDS, or would not be able to find someone who could help him with his anxiety. Exploration revealed that he had terminated his previous treatment several weeks earlier (prior to obtaining his antibody results) because the therapist was "only frightening me." Mr. J reported that the previous therapist had a very strict interpretation of safer sex practices which he experienced being conveyed in a very "strict and pressured" manner. Mr. J's physician recommended less restrictive practices leaving Mr. J feeling torn between his physician and therapist. He found it increasingly difficult to relate his sexual experiences and growing anxiety to his therapist, and when he did, he experienced the therapist's response as lecturing and anxiety provoking. In the final session, Mr. J stated that he had screamed, "Don't you understand? You are only frightening me!" In the throes of his disappointment in the therapist and disruption of the treatment alliance, Mr. J learned of his antibody results.

As Mr. J was very anxious, I maintained a very active, yet calm stance, encouraging him to relate his experience, while empathizing with his distress, and interjecting the reality that he was HIV positive and did not have AIDS when I sensed that this would provide relief, rather than be experienced as an empathic break. As the hour progressed, Mr. J's anxiety markedly decreased. Concurrently, his associations revealed a lessening of his somatic preoccupation, and the ability to discuss and allow me to empathize with his affects which were predominately intense fear, panic, and sadness. A dramatic decrease in anxiety occurred when I pointed out that I felt he was experiencing himself as infected and ill due to his test results, and the subsequent knowledge of the virus being in his body, yet there were no medical indications that he was ill. However, his experience was of being sick and infected. A further decrease in anxiety occurred when I related that I thought he was looking for someone who could help him feel less frightened.

Mr. J enthusiastically agreed, relating that he experienced his previous therapist as scaring him, and that he was trying to feel better by talking to his physician so often. However, his physician was also experienced as potentially being the bearer of "more bad news." I pointed out that people often are highly upset when learning of positive antibody status, and experience being angry, sad, scared, and preoccupied with being sick, but that over time people pick up their lives and go on. Our work together would concentrate on helping him to experience the feelings in a way that he could tolerate so that he could get on with his life. Mr. J paused and replied, "I have been assuming my life is over, but it isn't . . . now I have a sense of what I need to do."

By the end of the hour, Mr. J was considerably less anxious and an appointment was made for several days later. On the day of the appointment he called from his hospital bed to say that his physician had hospitalized him for more thorough tests. Mr. J went on to say that he felt considerably better after our meeting but that he "just couldn't hold onto it." The day after our first appointment had been a holiday weekend. After finishing work Saturday afternoon, his anxiety increased, as did his somatic preoccupation. His calls to his physician resulted in his being hospitalized for more extensive testing. Mr. J went on to describe all the attention he was receiving from the hospital staff, friends and family, flowers, that he was feeling considerably less anxious and wanted to make another appointment as he was being discharged the following day. The tests indicated no medical problems other than a severe sinus infection which may have contributed to his headaches.

In sharp contrast to his initial fears that his life was over, the treatment relationships continued over a period of several years. As the treatment alliance developed, Mr. J's anxiety and somatic preoccupation gradually decreased, with periodic increases secondary to the illnesses or deaths of friends, news reports, or finding out that several friend's test results were negative. Further work revealed serious self-pathology: a history of drug abuse (treated successfully), a long history of periodic acute anxiety, depression and somatic preoccupation, and highly masochistic relationships with men who Mr. J experienced as intensely attractive by virtue of their muscular bodies, yet were distant, highly narcissistic, and emotionally abusive, and consequently, consistently frustrating. Mr. J's eroticized need to be in a selfobject relationship with a highly idealized, hyper-masculine man in the hope that he would feel adequate and loveable by another man and the self-deficits it represents have subsequently become the focus of treatment.

Gradually, the fragmentations in response to the illnesses of friends, news accounts, and disappointments in his T-cell counts became less protracted and severe. A year and a half into treatment he was presented with the opportunity to open his own business. This represented a number of things to him: the stress of the venture; his own health; his own ability to create the business; and ultimately, would he live long enough to see the venture to its fruition? Mr. J went ahead, the business opened, and several sessions were spent contrasting his sense of satisfaction with his long-standing feelings of incompetence and the sharp contrast with his experience of himself after testing positive.

Mr. J illustrates a number of aspects of working with an individual whose self is highly vulnerable and experiencing acute fragmentation secondary to the narcissistic injuries of seropositivity and an empathic failure in a selfobject relationship. On referral, Mr. J was experiencing a state of acute fragmentation–disintegration anxiety, feeling acutely disorganized and "out of control." Self-esteem was profoundly shaken and somatic preoccupation was dominant. He was also frantically seeking out an archaic self-selfobject encounter with someone who could serve primarily idealizing functions. The previous therapist's inability to correctly identify and respond to Mr. J's distress resulted in an empathic failure which disrupted the selfobject relationship and left Mr. J experiencing himself as bad, disappointed with the therapist, and feeling that no one could help him with his growing distress.

Mr. J's increasing anxiety prior to being tested had to do with a beginning fragmentation secondary to being overstimulated by the illnesses of several friends. His increasing distress and concern that he too may have AIDS was probably the nature of his communication around safe sex practices, along with the hope that finding out his antibody status may provide relief. Following the break with the therapist, Mr. J took the test, obtained a positive result and experienced further fragmentation. Mr. J subsequently attempted to engage in an idealizing encounter with his physician, but, as he was able to say, the physician also represented for him a potential source of confirmation of his somatic fears. Most likely, the physician's attempt to ascertain clinically significant pathology, from somatic concerns also impeded his ability to perform idealizing functions.

The first task for a therapist with a patient such as Mr. J is to attempt to establish themselves as a selfobject performing idealizing functions. Baker and Baker (1987) describe idealizing needs or functions as "our need to merge with or be close to someone who we believe will make us feel safe, comfortable and calm." Being able to allow merger experiences with a patient such as Mr. J, calls for the therapist to be comfortable with allowing acutely anxious patients to experience the merger, to have mastered to a reasonable degree their own AIDS anxiety, and to place the patient's experience of fragmentation secondary to the AIDS-related problem at the center of attention. Empathic relating to the patient's experience facilitates the merger and the sense of the therapist being able to help contain the anxiety and provides mirroring functions that help restore the shaken grandiose self.

In reviewing the initial session with Mr. J we see a gradual decrease in anxiety as the therapist conveyed his willingness to serve as an idealized object, mirrored his experience of distress and acknowledged the reality elements of his distress which also served to facilitate the merger. Empathic attuneness with a patient will help the therapist determine when reality testing will be experienced as useful and reassuring versus an empathic break. Describing the therapeutic task–essentially, to integrate the experience of the knowledge of seropositivity–by helping the patient experience affects in the context of a selfobject encounter provides twinship/alter ego functions. The therapist and the patient have a task to perform together. If the patient is feeling cut off from the rest of the world by virtue of his antibody status, then the conveyance of the therapeutic task provides a sense of belonging to a human endeavor.

While the initial session provided some relief, it was only one self-selfobject encounter with an acutely fragmented self, and Mr. J was not able to sustain the tenuous cohesion he experienced as a result. The subsequent hospitalization resulted in a considerable amount of selfobject gratification and functions as family and friends visited and a great deal of attention was given by hospital personnel in the course of the various testing procedures and care taking. This massive "infusion" of selfobject functions helped to further restore the self's cohesion. Often one observes individuals being able to begin to obtain selfobject experiences from existing social and family systems after they are able to experience the therapist as a selfobject capable of tolerating and empathizing with their acute distress. (Mr. J initially did this in a very dramatic manner highly consistent with his previous style of negotiating the world). Mr. J obviously found the initial session helpful, contacted the therapist and arranged to continue treatment.

Over the next few months Mr. J's level of anxiety and somatic concerns gradually diminished with periodic peaks but nowhere near the intensity as upon referral. In encounters with patients such as Mr. J, an increase in anxiety or somatic concerns may represent fragmentation secondary to an empathic break in the treatment relationship or it may reflect the self's response to the news of the illness or deaths of a friend from AIDS, an empathic failure in another relationship, a news report on AIDS, or the experience of affects associated with the self's gradual integration of the reality of seropositive status. Clinical experience and the study results indicate that after being informed of their antibody status, patients often experience fragmentation in varying degrees, in the resulting disequilibrium they experience to varying degrees anger, sadness, feeling diseased, that they are now different, and that life is now limited. Gradually, as the self integrates the knowlege of seropositivity, concerns over health and longevity become less predominant and there is a sense of continuing on with life although there is a reality-based degree of uncertainty. Concerns may be periodically reactivated if the individual enters into a selfobject relationship with sexual components. The self must then integrate the reality of antibody status in the context of the relationship.

Some patients may end treatment as soon as they experience cohesion and a sense of integration of seropositivity. In Mr. J's case, treatment gradually became focused on the self's vulnerability secondary to its preexisting lack of cohesion. As described earlier, the self-pathology centered around the eroticized need for a relationship with an idealized hypermasculine man with whom he could feel protected, experience his own masculinity as being affirmed, and obtain mirroring that buffered his shaky sense of masculine adequacy and containment of his exhibitionistic style. Mr. J had engaged in several relationships with men whom he hoped would fulfill his needs only to be frustrated, with the relationships taking on highly masochistic characteristics.

Treatment gradually revealed severe problems in the father-son dyad dominated by the inability of Mr. J to experience idealizing and mirroring functions with his father. While he maintained a highly successful career, he had a long-standing history of difficulty modulating self-esteem and regulating tension. He employed a highly exhibitionistic and controlling style of relating to people. When the treatment focus shifts to underlying self-pathology it is important to realize that the self is still working on the integration of the seropositive status and for the clinician to remain available to address concerns when they arise.

An example of refined understanding of the meaning of the problem within the transference/counter-transference continuum occurred several months into the treatment. Mr. J had cancelled his Monday appointment. The next day he called and in an apologetic, almost pleading tone, asked if I could see him that evening. When he came in he was preoccupied, anxious, and angry with himself for not being able to stop drinking as his physician had recommended. (Exploration revealed he had only drunk three glasses of wine that week.) He went on to say that his father had called after reading an article and had questioned if he was eating properly and proposed vitamin supplements. He was touched by his father's concerns, but did not change his eating patterns or run to the health food store and obtain the vitamins his father recommended.

Mr. J's associations revealed that he was worried that his physician, father, and subsequently myself would be angry with him for not following advice and treatment recommendations. The physician because he had not stopped drinking, his father because he had not taken his advice, and myself because he had cancelled his session. These three idealizing relationships with males that he was struggling to maintain, who knew about his distress over testing positive and were offering help, had served to modulate his anxiety. The threat of disruption of the selfobject bonds via his transference fear resulted in growing anxiety and preoccupation with contracting AIDS. Essentially, if he disappointed us by not following our advice, and we became angry, he surely would contract the disease and die, and it would be all his fault.

Mr. J experienced considerable relief as we understood his current distress in terms of disappointing the males he was beginning to idealize. This led us into his intense sense of masculine inadequacy that evolved as he reached latency. There were many tear-filled sessions as he related how painfully insecure he felt, and the fantasies he developed to soothe himself and compensate for his insecurity. His painful insecurity was contrasted by his fantasy of superman standing behind him as he practiced the piano, turning the pages as he played, while reassuring and protecting him from harm. This fantasy became eroticized as he entered adolescence, and as he entered adulthood his search for a partner was colored by this fantasy, only to be repeatedly disappointed by men who met the fantasy physically but emotionally were unable to sustain him.

Over the course of his treatment, Mr. J's T-cell counts held above the 500 level. His general presentation changed considerably. He gradually appeared more calm, comfortable, and confident. In social settings dramatic changes began to happen. Previously in social situations with other gay men, he found himself feeling painfully insecure, that he was not "butch" enough, that other men would find him lacking in some way. This was gradually replaced by a quiet confidence. He found himself feeling as if he fit in, and rather than being a "wallflower" he was actively engaging others in conversation. In the context of dating he came to the point of deciding that he would tell other men of his antibody status before he had sex with them. "It has to do with personal integrity. That has become real important to me."

MOVING ON

HIV and 12-Stepping

In clinical work with HIV-related problems we may encounter clients who are struggling with overcoming a substance addiction and/or compulsive sexual behavior. It is not unsual to find both problems in the same person. It is highly problematic to conceptualize sexual behavior as an addiction, though there may be some similarities. The key difference lies in that substances are something taken into the body, whereas sexuality is a central part of the person's biological and mental endowment. In compulisve sexuality we see the person's sexual fantasies take on a life of their own, often taking the person farther and farther from human relationships. In substance abuse, the body develops a need for continued infusion of the substance. Generally we do not think of helping a substance-addicted person return to more appropriate substance use. Whereas in a sexual compulsion, one does hope that the person can come to enjoy his sexuality in more life-affirming and relationship-enhancing ways.

From a self-psychological perspective, both problems can be viewed as a reflection of self-deficits, and attempts at soothing and modulating affects. Kohut (1978) stated, "the addict craves the drug because the drug seems to him to be capable of curing the central defect in his self. It becomes for him the selfobject that failed him." In the wake of HIV infection, with shaken self-esteem, vulnerability to fragmentation and often volatile affect states, the person may turn to substances or to sex only to find these behaviors increasingly running, and often ruining, his life. The loss of the sense of future and deep despair may often fuel the reliance on substances or sexual activity as efforts for relief and temporary bolstering of self-esteem. However, as illustrated in the study results, the sense of future often expands and contracts. While the loss of the sense of future may fuel an ever-increasing reliance on substances or sexuality, the expansion of the sense of future may also propel the person into treatment for the addiction and into the world of 12-stepping and sobriety.

In Shelby (1992) I discussed clinical work with Mr. S and Mr. C. In the course of treatment both men sought inpatient treatment for their substance addictions, returned to treatment following hospitalization, became active in 12-step groups, and are still going strong. Mr. C's reliance on IV cocaine increased dramatically during a period when he was depressed and despairing, convinced that death was imminent. When he found that his T cells had actually risen considerably he became frightened, realizing that he indeed was not dying, and that he either had to get treatment for his substance abuse or it, rather than HIV, would soon kill him. Mr. S went into substance abuse treatment as his depression began to lift, self-esteem began to stabilize, and he became more and more aware of the self-destructive nature of his drug abuse and parallel sexual compulsion.

There is often an integral interplay between drug use and sexual fantasy or activity. Substances often intensify sexual fantasies and encounters, and in the case of sadistic or masochistic fantasies "loosen" defensive structures enabling the person to engage in them with another person rather than merely fantasizing. In some cases, individuals appear to become addicted to substances while pursuing their sexual fantasies, the substance addiction gradually coming to dominate the person's existence. There also appears to be an interplay between the psychoactive nature of some substances and the virulence of the sexual fantasies. In essence, the more "strung out" the person gets, the more masochistic and/or sadistic the sexual fantasies may become.

Speaking in the language of drive theory, Lauffer (1976) offered the concept of the central masturbation fantasy, "the fantasy whose content contains the various regressive satisfactions and the main sexual identifications" (p. 300). The central fantasy given its regressive nature often has a perverse flavor. Stoller (1985) described this aspect of mental life as often reflecting a humiliation and the attempt to master it by eroticizing the humiliation, in a sense turning defeat into triumph. Ornstein (1991) described sexual fantasies as efforts at self-healing. In a similar vein, Goldberg (1975) emphasized perversions as attempts to soothe and modulate painful affect.

The clinical issue is: what does the central masturbation fantasy reflect for a particular client? If we view the central fantasy as a reflection of a self-deficit, a narcissistic injury or unfulfilled longing, then we can come to understand some of the central ways our clients experience themselves and others, and what they are missing and longing to obtain from another person. Often the deficits and injuries lay in the realm of gender identity or the gender self. From a self-perspective, *when* the fantasy emerges is central in that it is viewed as a sign of fragmentation, or overstimulation and an effort to restore cohesion. Both factors are important: the issues that trigger the fantasy, and the narcissistic deficits, or longings that its theme represents.

The self-esteem deficits that often underlay and fuel these extreme forms of sexual behavior and fantasy are often enhanced by the narcissistic injury that accompanies testing positive for HIV. Any sense of being damaged and undesirable is enhanced, and the sexually transmitted nature of the illness only adds to any shame and guilt in the sphere of sexuality. While some men may retreat considerably from sexuality after testing positive, individuals who have long relied upon sexual activity to bolster self-esteem and maintain cohesion may find themselves seeking more sexual encounters with others. One can view any increase in substance abuse, compulsive or increasingly fetishistic sexuality, as attempts to maintain cohesion in the face of the fragmentation that often accompanies testing positive.

In Shelby (1992) I related the early phases of the treatment of Mr. S. The case account left off with his entering an intensive inpatient substance program tailored to the needs of gay men and lesbian women. Though an intensely vulnerable man, when Mr. S encountered a supportive environment he was able to make tremendous psychological gains. He became intensely involved in the inpatient program and upon return, became very involved in the 12-step community. For the first year after his hospitalization he was seen three times per week, and attended a 12-step meeting every day. For the first time in his life he found a sense of belonging to a peer group emerging. In self-help groups and support groups the emphasis is on helping each other with a problem. In the childhood experience of many gay men, negotiating peer groups was often highly painful. They found themselves uncomfortable with "boy stuff" and may have been ridiculed and called a sissy due to their lack of athletic skill and differing temperament. Hence, membership in the group was difficult because of their "problem."

When an individual's experience of the gay community is for the most part in the context of bars, and ultimately sexual pursuits, a degree of failure, cynicism, and alienation may come to dominate the individual's experience. As Stoller, (1985) points out: ". . . I do not find heterosexuals in the mass to be more normal than homosexuals. When it comes to the expression of sexual excitement, *most* people, whatever their preference, often appear to be quite hostile, inept, fragmented, gratified only at a considerable price, and deceptive with themselves and their partners. Are there reliable reports to the contrary?" (p. 97). Despite its excitement and allure, the playing field of sexual pursuit often takes considerable narcissistic toll as disappointments mount. Many men become experts at picking out good sex partners, but not necessarily good prospects for an enduring and sustaining relationship. Membership in a helping group is a powerful buffer against accumulated disappointment and accumulated cynicism, and offers a venue to gain other experiences with gay men as mentors and friends in a common pursuit of helping each other maintain sobriety and the renewal of the self's growth.

In intensive psychotherapy with individuals involved in 12-step programs, it is useful to conceptualize each as a therapeutic endeavor, though with different goals and means. In psychotherapy, we follow the transference, helping the client understand the unique meanings painful events and encounters have for them, assisting them in the process of renewed growth in a highly personal way. Often we attend to difficulties people encounter in their 12-step meetings when old meanings are activated. Twelve-step groups provide an important structure-building experience for people. They provide a philosophy for achieving and maintaining sobriety and the ongoing experience of others struggling with the same problems being helpful and supportive of individual efforts. For men who are positive they provide the experience of being engaged in an ongoing effort, an ever-evolving process that often serves to buffer the tenuous sense of future. Often, people who felt themselves to be failures find themselves being viewed as leaders, with much wisdom to offer others in the pursuit of sobriety.

Mr. S

Prior to entering inpatient treatment, Mr. S's substance abuse primarily occurred over the weekends. He found the weekends and their lack of structure to be a painful and lonely time. From Friday evening on, he was using cocaine and alcohol, out in the bars in pursuit of a man who fit his sexual fantasy, or recovering from the effects of the previous night's binge. Mr. S's fantasy focused on a taller, bigger, older, darker, bearded or mustached, slightly threatening man who would dominate him, yet also be kind and affirming of his masculinity. While his fantasies contained themes of dominance and surrender to anal intercourse, and at times fisting, there was also a predominant desire to be taken care of, to surrender to the care of a man who he trusted and idealized.

However, Mr. S rarely found a sexual partner. In the course of the evening, he would find himself anxious and uncomfortable, alienated, and "on the outside looking in" in the bar setting. He was often afraid to approach people for fear of making a fool of himself, of finding that the man he was attracted to found him lacking. He would do cocaine to increase his excitement and bolster self-esteem, then drink to modulate the effect of the cocaine. Many a time he found that when he did approach someone, he was too high and intoxicated to carry on a conversation. Often he would return home alone, frustrated, disappointed, lonely, and high. He would then engage in highly masochistic masturbatory activities that included anal stimulation and piercing of his nipples and genitals. Alternately, he did have several fuck and drug buddies, where the ritual was for them to inject him with cocaine and then proceed to engage in activities that tended to revolve around Mr. S's submission to the desires of his partner. Again, the theme of submitting to, of being intensely taken care of by a dominant male was prominent.

The longing to be lovingly dominated by another male was in sharp contrast to his experience of his father, by whom he felt neglected, intimidated, belittled, and punished unfairly. A prominent childhood memory was that of his father becoming enraged and chasing him with a riding lawn mower. He ran into the house to hide, begging for protection from his mother, who retorted that she was not going to protect him. He was terrified that his father was going to kill him, yet could find no place to hide or protection from his wrath. When he was found by his father he was beaten mercilessly with a belt. Mr. S recalled the preoccupation with needles and piercing first surfaced during the time his mother became increasingly regressed and depressed prior to her suicide. Mr. S was left with a strong feeling of being bad, that there was something wrong with him, that the contempt and disregard he felt from his father were all his fault.

Another prominent theme was Mr. S's mother's anxious preoccupation, if not panic, as he reached puberty. He recalled being sent to the doctor when his pubic hair emerged and sensed his mother's anxiety, feeling that something bad was happening to him. He began to feel acutely ashamed about his body and the changes that were happening. Shortly after being sent to the doctor, his mother took him to the barber and ordered a crew cut. Mr. S again felt acutely ashamed and weird as other boys his age were beginning to wear their hair longer, not shorter. That summer at camp, he did not take a shower for fear of being seen naked, nor did he remove the baseball cap he wore to hide his short hair. In the midst of his anxious misery over his emerging secondary sex characteristics, Mr. S's mother committed suicide, and he was placed in the care of his father.

Subsequently a complicated constellation evolved in his experience of his father: longing for his approval and support, terror that his father would harm him, rage and contempt for his father's inability to be a benign, consistent, and level-headed parent. Money was a powerful tool in his family. It could be plentiful and overstimulating or angrily withheld. It seemed to Mr. S that the more he wanted something, the more precious it was to him, the more likely his father was to deny and withhold the funds to purchase the item or adventure. Mr. S was left feeling that he was "begging for crumbs" from his father, locked into a desperate attempt to gain his approval and mirroring, something his father appeared incapable of doing. Yet Mr. S kept trying, only to be bitterly disappointed.

These themes were prominent throughout Mr. S's treatment. In the wake of the loss of his therapist to AIDS and his own beginning antiviral treatment, Mr. S turned increasingly to cocaine, and the anxious search for a benign male to offer comfort and reassurance. This selfobject need was already sexualized, but became more so in the midst of his turmoil. In thinking about what was repeatedly played out over Mr. S's weekends, we see a frightened and fragile young man, out searching for a relationship to take comfort in. The profound sense of being damaged secondary to the HIV infection in addition to pre-existing self-esteem issues, and the loss of his therapist to HIV, fueled the intensity of his search but also complicated it, as he felt he was offering damaged goods to potential selfobjects. With the repeated frustration of his fantasy of finding a man who could tend to him, he returned home and in the wake of his disappointed hope, he became further fragmented, engaging in masochistic masturbatory activities.

As he stabilized in his recovery, Mr. S related considerable shame around his past sexual activities and the physical damage he had done to himself through his self-inflicted piercing of his nipples. This was understood and worked through along the lines of his frustrated search for a strong male, with whom he could feel protected, comforted, and affirmed. When he was unable to find such a person, he blamed himself, was flooded with feelings of not being good enough, and turned upon himself. There was considerable guilt and shame around these activities, along with feeling that he had brought being positive on himself though their pursuit. When people are struggling with these issues it is often helpful to work along the lines of forgiving themselves for their past sexual pursuits, and working through the guilt, shame, and humilitation that fueled the activities and fantasies in the first place.

A strong idealizing, mirroring transference emerged. The treatment hour was viewed as an important calming, soothing, and structuring encounter. There were many shaky times during his first year of sobriety, disorganizing conflicts emerged in the course of Mr. S's negotiating the 12-step community, sponsors, and his work. These were handled within the context of the transference and his self-deficits. When not recounting problematic encounters with others, he was recounting his progress in his sobriety, in getting to know himself and integrating ideas and concepts from his various groups. He clearly gained a great deal of encouragement from my interest and quiet delight in his progress.

Gradually, Mr. S related that for the first time, a sense of direction in his life was emerging. Indeed as one listens to his history there was a lost, wondering quality about his life and career development, yet he had managed to secure a responsible and well-paid job in his area of expertise. It was clear as the treatment unfolded, that he was offered little guidance, support, and encouragement from his parents who were preoccupied with their own significant psychopathology, marital conflicts, and substance abuse. He painfully recalled many times of looking to one of his parents for support and affirmation, only to be repeatedly disappointed. This repeatedly frustrated need extended well into childhood as he tearfully recalled calling his father whenever he got a raise, promotion, or "even a good dental check up," only to hear a rather unimpressed reply or no response at all.

In problematic encounters with others, Mr. S was often left with an acute and profound sense of being bad. This led to many problematic interactions in his workplace in that when the sense of being "bad or wrong or lacking" emerged, he became disorganized and enraged. We gradually were able to relate this to his encounters with his parents, where problems and painful feelings were ignored or squelched rather than worked through. Time and time again he was left feeling that events were his fault, that he was bad. When the dangerous feeling of bad emerged in the present day he would on one hand become enraged with the person who he felt was calling him bad or questioning his ability, on the other hand become involved in desperate attempts to convince the person that he was not lacking or that he was not bad.

Gradually, over his treatment of several years, Mr. S's anxious, at times agitated presentation, was replaced with a quieter, calmer, and more reflective style. As he progressed in his recovery he was often called upon to give the leads at meetings and his thoughts and ideas were consistently well received. He was also sought out as a sponsor. The treatment relationship and his encounters with others gradually expanded his capacity to be with people in an ever-wider range of experience. Periodically he would marvel at how his experience of self had changed. Recently Mr. S related: "It's hard to put into words. My T-cells have never been lower, I have had shingles twice, and in all probability, I am going to die from an AIDS-related illness some day. The weird thing is that despite being positive and all of that, I have never felt better about myself. I feel calmer. For the first time in my life I have hope–not hope that I am not going to die from AIDS–but that everything will be okay no matter what happens."

Mr. C

In Shelby (1992), I discussed the earlier stages of Mr. C's treatment. Though he stabilized considerably over the initial course of his treament, Mr. C's life in general had a highly chaotic flavor about it. It became clear that there was something going on that he was just not ready to bring into the treatment relationship. He became increasingly depressed and elusive, often canceling sessions. When he did appear for an appointment he was able to relate that the despair was returning, he was sure that his counts had fallen, and that death was imminent. Mr. C was so certain that this was the case that he was terrified to phone his physician and inquire about the results. Eventually he called only to find out that his counts had risen considerably. As described earlier, Mr. C then realized that HIV was not going to kill him imminently, but his drug use would if he did not get help for it. At this point he "confessed" to me the extent of his IV cocaine use and how it had dramatically increased over the last few months as he grew more despairing. He realized that his addiction was now running his life and he was terrified: terrified of the degree that he was involved with the drug, terrifed to do anything about it, and terrifed that I, and his physician, would humiliate him because of it. There were many missed sessions, and fleeting messages left for me during this time. The idea of inpatient treatment in a gay/lesbian program was introduced and Mr. C made initial inquiries in between highs.

After a missed appointment I called him at home and Mr. C answered. He related his struggle over deciding to go into the inpatient program. After some discussion, I pointed out that he knew if he did not go into the program the drugs were going to kill him, that he had told me he did not want to die, so the only thing left to do was go. That afternoon he left for the program and began his long process of recovery. Mr. C later related the importance of the phone call for him. I happened to call just as he was shooting up; it was the first time a modulating person had intervened in his shooting ritual.

As we talked he looked at his "works" and his swollen, bruised veins. Shooting changed from a sacred, eroticized event to an act of destruction. He panicked, picked up the phone, called the program, and was on his way.

On return to the treatment relationship following the inpatient program, and a stay in a halfway house, the treatment relationship changed considerably. We began to meet twice a week, and Mr. C actively went about setting up his recovery matrix. Mr. C also introduced into treatment the ongoing sexual abuse he experienced with his stepfather from the time he was 13 to 16 and an isolated rape at the hands of his step-grandfather at age seven. He also revealed the extent of his sexual compulsion: engaging in anonymous fellatio in baths and bookstores numerous times in the course of a week. While using cocaine, his ritual was to get as high as possible, go to the baths, and seek out partners to fellate. He reported the act of fellating another man had a hypnotic effect. He would become lost in the act, feeling a sense of union, power, and relief.

A more complete picture of Mr. C's childhood emerged. His mother was a chaotic, overwhelmed woman prone to alcohol and prescription drug abuse, who devalued men, yet desperately sought them out, tending to latch on to fairly dysfunctional partners in the process. His father left the family when Mr. C was four or five, and had minimal contact with the chidren. Mr. C recalled how he was very concerned about his mother's well-being, very tuned into her emotional ups and downs, yet never feeling successful in his efforts to bolster her brittle self-esteem. When stressed, his mother was quite hostile, punitive, and physically abusive. He recalled numerous childhood illnesses, during which he felt some sense of being tended to, but if his illness threatened to disrupt a family outing, he was invariably left alone.

School was an anxious and painful time for him. A reading learning disability hampered his ability to learn in a conventional setting; he was called a sissy, mocked, and beaten by his peers. To his horror, his mother remarried when he was in latency. He did not trust the man from the start, and his fears were confirmed when, within hours of moving into the house, new, even stricter rules were established. Severe verbal humiliation and often physical abuse were meted out to those who disobeyed or failed to perform a task adequately. The stepfather as well often mocked Mr. C, calling him a sissy, and belittling him in general.

When he was about 13, Mr. C "seduced" his stepfather. During a large, extended family gathering in the backyard of the home, Mr. C found himself alone in the swimming pool with his intoxicated stepfather. Mr. C found himself fondling his stepfather's genitals; the man offered no resistance, and encouraged Mr. C to continue. Both were caught up in the excitement of a sexual act occurring while the rest of the family went about their party. The sexual relationship evolved into numerous acts of Mr. C fellating his stepfather and periodic anal intercourse, often while Mr. C's mother was at home. There were many times that Mr. C recalled sneaking into the parental bedroom, waking up his stepfather and engaging in sex with him while his mother slept. Outside of the sexual relationship, the verbal humiliation and belittling continued. As he grew older, Mr. C's stepfather "passed him on" to other pedophilic men.

Mr. C felt great shame, guilt, humiliation, and horror as he related the account of his sexual relationship with his stepfather. He was not sure whether it constituted sexual abuse as he recalled initiating the contact. There was some relief at my pointing out that it is the adult's responsibility to say, "no." My offering that the sexual relationship was an attempt on his part to get some sense of an affirming, sustaining relationship from another man was met with tears and relief. He tearfully recalled a series of failed and disappointed attempts at relationships, how all of his life he had hoped that this man would be it, that someone would love and respect him. Instead he found himself feeling used, and in various ways being told or feeling that he was just not good enough. He came to feel that all he had to offer was sex, that he had nothing else to interest another man.

Mr. C was aware of the eerie similarity between sneaking into the darkened parental bedroom and fellating his stepfather, and his searching the darkened corridors of baths and bookstores for men to fellate. Sex had become an important and central modulator for him. Mr. C had limited ability to feel or manage affect, especially sadness. Whenever he felt threatened by an affect state, he would head for the bookstore. In frustration he related that he "acted out" when he felt sad, depressed, lonely, happy that things were going too well, or that things were going badly. Early in his recovery, he made an attempt at attending a 12-step group for sexually compulsive men, only to find himself so overwhelmed that he feared it threatened his sobriety. Consequently, the sexual compulsion was put "on hold" while Mr. C solidified his sobriety through the many relationships he developed in the 12-step community.

The relationship of Mr. C's self-deficits to his experience of HIV infection were expressed in a number of ways. He related a long-standing wish of wanting to just lay down and die, a passive suicidal fantasy that first emerged as a young child. Often more generalized depressive and despairing states were expressed in terms of it being just too hard to keep on fighting the infection, that enough was enough, he just wanted it to be over and done with, so he could rest. Another aspect concerned his fear of dying alone. Though he wanted to be surrounded by family, he feared that they would be abandoning or overstimulating. He could not fathom his mother or sibs being attuned to his needs, hence he retreated to his isolated position. Once again he felt abandoned and isolated in the face of great emotional need. In the several years after achieving sobriety, Mr. C's T-cell counts continued to hold steady at relatively high levels. While there was some reassurance in this, it also symbolized for him the need to continue to seek relief from his great psychic pain and distress, and periodically, just how tired he was, that his life had been such a struggle, and that no complete relief appeared to be immediately in sight.

Almost two years passed before he was ready to take on his sexual compulsion. In the meantime the foundations were being laid in the treatment relationship to address the tremendously painful affect surrounding the abuse, and most important, the deep sense of betrayal and consequent deficits in the ability to develop idealizing relationships. My previous experience had been that often sexual compulsions modulate considerably as an idealizing transference emerges. The selfobject transference serves to modulate the affect states and provide cohesion to the fragile self. However, with Mr. C the deficits in the idealizing sphere were so great that considerable work had to be done to enable the capacity to idealize emerge once more.

The topic of working with survivors of childhood sexual abuse is complex and great diversity and controversy exists in how best to approach the treatment of these clients. The approach taken with Mr. C was that the issue was the consequent disruption in selfobject bonds and resulting self-deficits. In Mr. C's case the loss of his father, rape by his stepgrandfather at age seven, and consequent sexually, emotionally, and physically abusive relationship with his stepfather shattered his capacity to idealize men. Given the chaotic, acting-out nature of his family in its several transformations, the central adults in his life tended to modulate their affect states by either inappropriately relying on their children for support or by acting out their rage in the form of physical abuse. Consequently, in addition to the trauma of sexual contact with an adult, severe deficits already existed in Mr. C's capacity to tolerate and modulate affect states.

The two years following Mr. C's return from his inpatient stay involved for the most part listening for what interaction with another person had overwhelmed him, helping him to tolerate the feeling state, and understand the meaning of the event. Gradually, he became much more steady and resilient, and a better judge of who in the 12-step community would make good companions in that they could tolerate and respond to his affect states and needs. Many times he related how he was struggling to "stay with me" in the sessions. If the topic or interaction felt too threatening he would "blank out," trace the outlines of objects in the room, or count—distractions he developed as a child in an effort to manage his intense pain, confusion, and sadness.

He lived in fear of sexual feelings emerging in the transference which initially limited his capacity to relate his sexual fantasies and experiences. As we worked this through he related his initial shame at having periodically eroticized the relationship, along with his fear that the sustaining aspects of the treatment relationship would be destroyed, and eventually, that the eroticization also served defensive purposes, that when he felt threatened by me, sexual fantasy served to make the relationship less threatening and more manageable.

As he approached the subject of revealing the extent of the sexual abuse in his childhood, he felt great fear that he was about to destroy his family, and would lose what little he had. This was understood as a reflection of his predicament in childhood, that even though he was having sex with his mother's husband, revealing the abuse would probably result in the stepfather's expulsion from the family, and his mothers' rage at him for destroying the tenuous family constellation.

As the treatment continued, Mr. C increasingly found himself uncomfortable with his sexual activity. He was troubled by the disparity between the reality of his sexual life and his longing for a partner where the relationship was held together by mutual love and respect. Eventually, Mr. C "hit bottom." He came in and announced that he had enough and was planning on joining a 12-step group for sexually compulsive men. What Mr. C found was that he was very anxious in the meetings, that he continued to have difficulty staying out of the bookstores and that he became increasingly sad, depressed, and withdrawn. As we talked about this constellation, it became clear that he was not able to build the supportive matrix in the area of his sexual compulsion, as he had in the area of his substance abuse. The shame, depletion, and horror secondary to the sexual abuse felt so entwined with his sexual compulsion that he was overwhelmed at the very thought of other people knowing about his history, let alone believing that someone, especially another man, could help him with it.

Mr. C appeared for a session looking sad and shaken. He asked if I had a dictionary. He related that he had been thinking about the term "mentor" that I had used before to describe an aspect of relationships with other men that had been sorely missing in his life. As he read the definition he began to weep, relating that he was beginning to understand what he had missed, and beginning to understand what he was grieving for all of these years and intensely so as of late. He then looked at me and reflected on how he did have a mentor in myself, and that I had given him a taste of what was missing in his life. He went on to say how he was afraid that he did not know how to let me help him in this area–that relationships with men and his sexuality felt like a mine field. It was hard to believe that we both could survive going through it.

Before the next session, Mr. C dreamed that he was a child and back in the house he grew up in, though it was deserted and the windows boarded up. He was alone with his stepfather who was drunk and had tried to rape him, but had passed out instead. When Mr. C went to the kitchen to look for a knife, the knives were gone except for the knife sharpener. He took the knife sharpener and plunged it up his stepfather's nose. Mr. C reported feeling shaken by the dream, and that he had spent the rest of the night reading a book. However, his affect was brighter, more relaxed and spontaneous than it had been for several weeks. I pointed out that in his dream he had slain the dragon, that perhaps he was beginning to feel that he could talk about his experience in a broader way, and not become overwhelmed. Mr. C then related his preoccupation with the knife versus the knife sharpener and how he had stuck it up his stepfather's nose. He had stuck him with a phallic object rather than a cutting, slicing knife.

This led to his fascination with large penises, how they intrigued and frightened him. Intrigued because of their power and virility, frightened because of the pain they caused. He began to sweat profusely as he related how his stepfather had been preoccupied with penis size and made many references to it. As he was passed on to other men by his stepfather, the size of the man's penis came to symbolize how much hurt he was going to feel when they began to fuck him. Mr. C then began to cry as he associated to the rape by his stepgrandfather when he was seven, he recalled the cutting pain as the man inserted his penis into him, and the fear that his insides were being torn and cut to shreds. From then on he felt broken inside. For many weeks he had trouble controlling bowel movements, and was terrified that his insides were damaged beyond repair. All of this suffering occurred in isolation, as he was too terrified, ashamed, and confused to tell anyone, and given his family's style of relating, he had no faith that anyone would help. As the session came to a close Mr. C smiled and said, "I can't believe it. I am doing the work. I am letting you help me."

Mr. C then was able to go about setting up his "recovery matrix" in the area of his sexual abuse and consequent sexual compulsion. What emerged and worked for Mr. C was not the usual Sexual Compulsives Anonymous 12-step approach, but rather a series of friendships, retreats, massages, and other bodywork activities that tended to his deep pain and despair over the way he was treated as a child. To his surprise, the more he felt tended to in the area of his abuse and deep psychic pain, his need to modulate these feelings with sexual activity with strangers declined markedly. He also found his hope and optimism regarding his ability to face the hardships of disease progression increasing markedly.

Moving On

Mr. G: Mourning and HIV

In Shelby (1992) I discussed the earlier phases of Mr. G's seven year psychotherapy, and the often considerable impact of the death of a partner on the surviving partner's experience of self and his own HIV infection. HIV-positive surviving partners are faced with the incredibly complicated emotional tasks of mourning the loss of the relationship, sorting out the often strong tendency to identify their infection with the illness and death of their partner, and maintain their own ongoing process of living in the face of their own HIV infection and need to tend to its psychological impact.

The early phases of Mr. G's treatment had centered on providing a relationship that facilitated his mourning process. His life was shattered by the death of his partner: the loss of the selfobject dialogue was acutely destabilizing. Gradually Mr. G's confidence began to stabilize, and he became aware of just how lonely he was. He had become very isolated in the years since his partner's death, but was overcome with anxiety when he ventured out into the gay community. He had few gay friends to help with this process of re-engaging. I had maneuvered him into a group I ran for positive men. He gradually became involved in the group, and several members helped him engage with the larger HIV-positive community in the city.

By his sixth year of treatment, Mr. G had become an integral member of the group, and developed a friendship with another group member. In the course of the group, the partner of another member died. Mr. G repeatedly reached out to the grief-stricken member, conveying his understanding of the depth of his loss. His friend enlisted him to help lead a smaller group for men who needed extra help and support while they were joining a large support/ educational organization for men who test positive. During a session following one of these groups, Mr. G related that a young man who was very shaken, anxious, and overwhelmed had come to the group and he had spent a great deal of time with him; listening, reassuring, and answering his many questions. Mr. G reflected on his sense of amazement and accomplishment–that he had helped someone with being positive–an issue that he himself had felt so helpless about. I pointed out that he had also helped a group member mourn–another experience that had left him feeling helpless.

Several weeks later, his friend asked Mr. G to accompany him to the hospital to visit a friend on the AIDS unit. Mr. G was anxious at first but went along and spent several hours visiting with the patients. The session following his visit proved to be productive and intense. Initially, Mr. G related his sense of mastery at having gone to the hospital where his own partner had died six years before. Since the visit, he had felt very spontaneous, happy, and engaged. How different it was from the time when his partner had been hospitalized. There was no AIDS unit then. There had been a great sense of anxious mystery. This time on the unit, things felt more normalized. Gay men were visiting with each other. There was a sense of belonging. Gradually, as his associations deepened, Mr. G's affect became more sad, and somewhat frightened. He related how in the past he had become very shaky and overwhelmed if he even looked at or went near the hospital. Instead, he had walked in, visited other men and walked out. His assumption was that the next time he entered the hospital would be during his first AIDS-related illness. He would be acutely ill, on a stretcher, gasping for breath, going to meet the same fate as his partner.

I sensed there was more–something still deeper–and urged him to continue. He went on to relate a solemn vow he made the night his partner died: never again would he be happy; that happiness would no longer be a part of his life. I reflected on the penitential quality of the vow, like a monk depriving himself of worldly pleasures, locked away in his cell, flagellating himself for his sins. Mr. G began to cry, "I killed him, didn't I? I am the one who gave it to him. Why should I have what he can't?" Mr. G was both horrified and amazed. As he spoke these words, he began to realize the extent to which his life had become organized around his partner's death and the responsibility he felt for it. Eventually he asked, "My God, what have I been doing to myself all of these years?"

The often elaborate networks of relationships or supportive matrix that HIV-positive men form often provide much more than "support." Strong selfobject bonds often form in groups of positive individuals. In negotiating these relationships, men are often exposed to different ways of viewing and adapting to situations and feeling states that come with being positive. Strong idealizing and twinship bonds may emerge. The relationship with Mr. G and his friend has very strong twinship elements. The two shared similar career and family backgrounds, and as each recounted their adventures together there was a clear sense of delight at having found a friend that each other made sense to.

A fascinating aspect of the matrix that many infected people form is that in assisting someone in a difficult aspect of his experience a person may be learning a new perspective or reworking a painful aspect of his own. Given the many losses to AIDS, in Shelby (1994) I proposed that a culture of mourning has evolved. Not necessarily a static state of mourning where the accumulation of grief is so profound that people's losses and sorrow are not tended to, or minimized, but a dynamic process of making sense of the loss through dynamic relationships with others.

Though many of the people of an individual's selfobject matrix may be in mourning themselves, they can still facilitate the process for each other. In responding to the grief of another group member, Mr. G was also acknowledging and reworking his own grief. Mr. G's friend was visiting the hospital in his role as a member of a committee whose task it was to look after ill members of the large social/educational group. He had done this because of his own fear of, and inexperience with death. He felt that by being around ill and dying people, he would feel less anxious as his illness progressed. In inviting Mr. G along, he had no idea of the impact it would have, or how it would help Mr. G bring into focus deeply rooted and influential meaning structures regarding his partner's death and his own illness.

Mr. G's realizations in treatment are an illustration of my earlier assertions that in seropositive surviving partners, one often sees a powerful combination of continued idealization of and identification with their infection with the partner's illness and death. Illusive, but highly influential meaning structures can evolve that become central organizers of the surviving partners' experience of self. Though in the course of treatment we had touched on these issues many times, it was not until through interaction with his selfobject matrix that Mr. G was able to bring his vow and its impact so directly into his conscious experience.

In the months since his hospital visit, a great deal happened in Mr. G's life. On a visit to his parents, he came across his high school yearbooks. As he read the inscriptions, he saw evidence that others viewed him quite differently than he had assumed. He was clearly well-liked, in some cases idealized, was considered funny, brilliant, outgoing, and was voted "most likely to succeed." "Who was this person?" he asked. Again he was amazed and shaken. The disparity between other's experience and his remembered experience of himself as a child and as an adolescent were considerable. Two distinct but highly interrelated lines of association followed. The first related to his questioning if he had "made himself over" in the wake of his partner's death (his assumed responsibility, his vow, and his own serpositivity). Had the severe damage to his self-esteem resulted in his remaking his own history? The second line was related to his emerging sexuality. Back in high school, it had been a deep, dark secret that no one knew about; certainly not the people writing in his yearbook. What would they have written if they knew about it? He realized that these two areas of meaning had converged. His partner's death and his own infection had concretized his secret evolving sexual orientation and his sense of being weird, different, if not evil.

Over the next few months, Mr. G re-established contact with several old high school buddies who were also gay. To his delight he was warmly received. As his T cells approached 200, Mr. G began to consider retirement. He had ample resources through disability policies. He found during a week's vacation when he stayed in the city that he was able to keep busy and to entertain himself. I interpreted this along the lines that he did not have to become ill and die as his partner did, but rather he could take charge of the situation and determine how he wanted to approach his life in the face of his illness. He also obtained DDC (Hivid) and began combination drug therapy. He was surprised that he had approached the new regimen with a sense of calm, radically different from the great turmoil when he began AZT. Again, I pointed out that he was viewing himself in a much different light since his realization of the extent that he had organized his illness around his partner's death.

Mr. G's friend who had engaged him in the larger group and invited him to the hospital was diagnosed and was acutely ill for several weeks. Mr. G found himself very engaged with his friend; there were many long phone calls and visits. He reported that the whole experience of his friend's diagnosis and illness was very calming, rather than a wrenching experience. He found himself feeling considerably less frightened of illness and death.

Mr. G's brother visited him for several days. While he found himself having a great deal of fun, and enjoying the visit immensely, he also found himself engaged with his brother in long conversations about death and dying, and trying to make sense of these experiences. His brother, a professional firefighter, faced death every day. He had numerous "close calls" and experienced the death of colleagues and people he had hoped to save. Again, Mr. G found the conversations calming, and was delighted at the depth to which he and his brother could understand each other. Mr. G also stopped smoking. He reported that he had realized the connection between smoking and his partner. During his illness, his partner was simply unable to smoke. His partner had wanted Mr. G to stop as well but he was unable to do so. The smoking periodically became a source of conflict. Mr. G felt ashamed that he was unable to stop for his partner's sake. Mr. G related that he realized what had prevented him in the past: that if he was unable to stop for his partner, how could he stop solely for himself?

Concurrently, Mr. G found his memories of his partner changing. They were not focused on his partner as ill and dying, but rather on his partner as alive and living. He found himself consistently better able to access memories of their many travel adventures and shared interests. Mr. G reported he was more able to smile when thinking of his partner, rather than become filled with empty longing and a sense of dread.

Mr. G gradually became more adventuresome. His previous vacations since his partner's death had been spent with family or alone. Now he contemplated different trips, and signed up for a course in an area that he had always found fascinating. Throughout my work with Mr. G there was a highly bright, inquisitive, and adventurous aspect about him that was eclipsed by his vulnerability and pull toward isolation. After he had worked through the previously described events and their complicated meanings, his sense of curiosity and adventure increased markedly. He decided to go on a vacation with his friend from the group. The two men took great delight in planning and organizing the trip. Mr. G decided that while on vacation, he wanted to learn to roller blade.

Much of his vacation was spent learning to roller blade. He found himself delighted with the adventure of blading around the island, and caught up in the physical and emotional "high" of the activity. Upon return he was clearly delighted with himself and the sense of mastery he found with the new activity. He reflected on the confidence in his body integrity he experienced as he found himself able to negotiate more complex maneuvers. He contrasted this with the way had come to feel about his body as infected, fragile, and vulnerable to infection. He also contrasted his newfound athletic prowess with the painful uncertainty he felt so many times in athletic activities as a child.

He also began to reflect on the changing nature of our relationship. At first I had felt like a lifeline, but gradually he found himself "checking in" and filling me in on the events in his life. He also reflected on the great adventure of his seven-year treatment, how so much had happened, so much of himself felt transformed. He began to contemplate termination. In working through the idea of terminating, he immediately came upon his assumption that there would be no termination to his treatment, that I would see him through his own illness and death. He reflected on just how tenuous and limited life often felt contrasted with his ongoing stable health and the great sense of personal growth. He marveled at the fact that seven years after his partner's death, he was still alive and feeling able to terminate his psychotherapy. So many times he had felt the end was near, only to have life continue to unfold.

Moving On

Mr. L: Mourning and the Ability to Use the Matrix

An aspect of clinical work with HIV-related problems often involves enhancing people's ability to utilize sustaining and affirming relationships that are available to them. The combination of self-destabilization, and past selfobject disappointments may hinder some people from seeking out support and reassurance from others. The acutely painful affects and the acute vulnerability of the self when a person is grieving the loss of a central relationship, often makes for difficulty in feeling sustained by the matrix of supportive relationships.

As we often observe in clinical practice, an old self-injury or constellation of deficits may be awakened in one arena of a person's life, then played out in another. This process is often observed in a person's attempts to negotiate an HIV-related problem. As the following case illustrates, while the dynamic playing out of past disappointments in self and others was central, the bottom line for the client is the desire to feel understood, to feel a part of rather than cut off from important relationships. While the impulse to attack and destroy may be present, the hope is for reconnection and reassurrance.

At the time of this sequence of events, Mr. L was a 39-year-old surviving partner. He and his partner of 16 years were members of a group I ran for HIV-positive men that was also a source of data for the study which this book is constructed around. The two men were members of the group for approximately one year before Mr. L's partner died after a fairly quick and, toward the end, gruesome illness with lymphoma. Mr. L is a kind of rigid, MBA, banker type: very cut and dry, shy, almost concrete, but when comfortable very warm and likeable. His partner was a very popular educator, well-read and bright. His partner, during the time he knew he was positive and during the illness, tended to be almost hysterical in the context of the relationship, but presented himself as very "together" publicly and in the group. In the context of the relationship, Mr. L took the "calm down, everything will be all right, we will make it" stance, while his partner was often acutely anxious, depressed, and plagued by somatic preoccupation and fantasies of the worst order.

Several weeks after his partner died, Mr. L requested individual sessions. He came dressed almost exactly as I was dressed, often during the sessions appearing like an eight year old that had just found a new "big brother." At that point he was not acutely distressed, but he related that he sensed what was coming, affect other than a delighted gleam was prominently absent. He quite directly stated that he was looking for someone to help guide him through the next few months. He had never been alone; he moved at 22 from his parent's home into a home with his partner. He related that he felt his partner had helped show him the way, how to grow up, and could always help him "sort things out." Now he was alone facing some big decisions without the person he had always relied upon. Further associations revealed that he felt his partner was the smarter, better educated one. Though Mr. L had his own series of degrees, his partner had tended to devalue them–they were in business, whereas his were in more esoteric, "real knowedge" areas. Mr. L tended to agree. Clearly he idealized his partner a great deal, though devaluing himself in the process. He was also establishing with me a relationship with many of the same selfobject characteristics as that with his deceased partner.

Parallel to issues related to mourning, the following history evolved. He was the "middle" child form a large Irish Catholic family. He felt he was the "black sheep"–though rigid, he was in many ways the "loosest" of his family. He had not revealed his sexuality or the nature of his relationship with his partner to his family until his partner's diagnosis. At that time he revealed "everything"–that he was gay, that his "roommate" was his partner and was ill with HIV-related cancer, and that he was seropositive.

Mr. L described a long history of difficulty expressing affect, never remembered his dreams, and often became concrete, and slightly combative, when attempting to relate private, affective, or transferential phenomena. Further elaboration revealed that as a child he viewed himself as the troublemaker of the family, often fighting with his younger brothers. For a period of several years, he always accompanied his parents because they would not leave him alone for fear that a fight would break out. The nature of the arguments centered around a great sense of injustice. His younger sibs were allowed to do things that he and his older sibs were punished for. He was horrified at their rambunctious, destructive behavior and felt it was his duty to bring them into line as no one else seemed inclined to do so. He embarrassingly related how deprived he often felt. As the middle child, he got the hand-me-downs, while they got new toys and clothes. His father, who he experienced as distant, was enthusiastically involved with the younger children, but tended to ignore Mr. L and the older sibs. As he observed his father take an active interest in the younger children's athletic pursuits, Mr. L found himself wondering what was wrong with him that his father was spending so much time with his younger brothers and not with him. Though he related his getting punished for his behavior with bravado, he was embarrassed and uncomfortable with the affect around feeling deprived, depressed, and neglected. What became clear was that he was a child whose distressed affect was not responded to, but his acting up was.

Two months after his partner's death, Mr. L fell silent in the group, rarely talking about his loss, or the sadness, loneliness, and feeling lost that he was relating in his individual sessions. The group would periodically check in with him but he related that all was fine. This coincided with a period when group was into learning to enjoy themselves again, often going out as a group to a bar. A great deal of time was spent talking about the good old days, how they used to feel so comfortable going out and partying, but now, felt inadequate and alienated out on the party circuit. Mr. L went along on these outings and was considered the life of the party.

In the midst of this, a mutual friend who had been very close to his partner came over to Mr. L's home to pick out photographs of his partner for a memorial page in the yearbook of the school he had taught at. She had helped out a great deal during his partner's acute illness and was present at his death. She began to cry as she looked at old photographs. Mr. L panicked. He wanted so desperately to cry with her, but was afraid, and "hid" in another room. Shortly after this event he became acutely depressed. He felt incompetent, a failure, he missed his partner terribly, and only felt comfortable sitting on the tombstone across from his partner's grave, smoking cigarettes and drinking a coke. He felt terrible that he had not cried, that he had betrayed his partner, and feared that he was disappointing me because he had such difficulty crying in my presence.

He then became enraged with the group. "They are fooling themselves. They are trying to pretend none of this is real. Just because they can go out and party is not going to make it go away." He wanted to tell the group off, point out their folly, but feared he would be bashed and would destroy the important connections he found with the members. He found himself feeling increasingly alone, and isolated in the group.

In individual session, while he was able to express his anger, he became defensive when I pointed out that he was also feeling acutely alone, cut off, distressed, and feared expressing the depth of his distress. He then became angry with me saying that I was defending the group and "taking their side." I pointed out his experience in his family, that while he often got angry and was bashed for his acting up, rarely were the underlying feelings addressed or responded to. Now he was in a similar position. In order to feel understood and reconnected, he needed to express his sadness and sorrow, but he was used to getting angry and being punished. We had to find a way for him to let the group know just how bad he was feeling.

He initially responded that he could not do it, that it would be a burden on them, ruin their good time. If he talked about it he would cry. I pointed out that during his partner's illness he had cried often, and the group responded. Eventually he said, "I am going to do it. Will you help me if I get into trouble, if I start getting mad?" At the next group I provided an oblique opportunity and Mr. L gradually let the group know how bad he was feeling. He cried as he related just how lost, confused, and vulnerable he felt, that he was not the "surviving partner poster boy" he felt the group saw him as. Several members of the group related their concern for how he was "really" doing, but that they did not want to push. Another member who was also a surviving partner related his own discomfort when people held him up as a shining example of coping with loss, when inside one feels so sad and distressed. Despite his fears of rupturing his ties with the group, Mr. L found himself again feeling a part of the group, understood and responded to. Mr. L's distress and depression eased markedly over the next few days.

Moving On

Mr. N: Failing to Live Positively

In the study results, the term meltdown was used to describe the periodic depression and deep discouragement that many men encounter as they negotiate the experience of being HIV-positive. The experience of a meltdown is often acutely painful and frightening. As described earlier it often includes the fear that death is imminent and that it is their fault, along with the profound sense of being overburdened and just too tired to continue the fight. Often a profound feeling of having lost all ground regained since learning he was positive emerges along with the fear that he will never get it back. While these feelings are painful unto themselves, when men are engaged in support groups or larger support organizations, other group members may be frightened of the distressed individual's affects and fears and have considerable difficulty helping them to feel sustained. Thus, people may feel increasingly isolated from sustaining relationships at a time of great need.

Mr. N sought treatment after several months of feeling increasingly sad, isolated, depressed, and frightened. His experience was summed up in, "I am a failure at living positively. I was able to go on for quite a while, but I just can't anymore. I just want to get it over with. My friends at the group tell me to get over it, to stop thinking this way, but I can't." Mr. N related how he had been a founding member of a local social/support/informational organization for men who tested positive. For several years he had been an active member and developed several important realtionships. The theme that had evolved in the group was that of "living positively" of thinking about one's infection in optimistic terms, taking an active role in medical treatment, and in general, adopting and maintaining a fighting spirit toward the infection.

While this was the group theme, or party line as Mr. N called it, another important and devastating process was occurring. Several of the founding members of the group had recently died, and several more were becoming increasingly ill. Mr. N was strongly identified with many of these people as they had been the ones that helped him feel more confident and less devastated and frightened by his own infection. He was deeply shaken by their loss and became increasingly depressed and discouraged. When he tried to express these feelings to other group members he felt attacked for not "talking the party line."

Further exploration of Mr. N's current situation revealed considerable depression and isolation. He had few friends to begin with and had lost several positive friends in the last year, including one that he felt particulary comfortable with. He had not worked in several years and was living off of his investment income. Mr. N had lost his job due to cutbacks in his area of expertise shortly after testing positive. Though he was clearly a skilled investor and had done quite well financially as a result, he felt deeply ashamed of the fact that he did not have a "real job." In trying to understand his shame, it became apparent just how frightened he was of social interaction, and performance. He was terrified of the idea of looking for a job, the scrutiny that he would be under, and the fear that employers would find out that he was positive lurked in the background. His days were spent watching the stock market and various TV shows, with the meetings of the support organization his main social outlet. Now he was feeling cut off from the group because of his failure to "live the party line." Mr. N felt very uncomfortable in social relationships and just being out and about in his neighborhood. Though he felt a degree of comfort in his increasingly isolated existence, his home was beginning to feel like a prison.

Gradually, Mr. N was able to relate the depth of his sadness and discouragement, and the degree to which he felt irreparably damaged. It was clear as we spoke that he was concerned and watchful that his expression of his feelings were not a form of heresy for which he would be chastised, if not cast out. He was especially frightened of his desire to "give up and to have it all over with," his fear being that if he thought that way, death would surely be imminent, that he would die quickly, just as his friend had done. Given the depth of Mr. N's depression, a medication consult was initiated, and he began to take antidepressant medication. The response was quite good: he felt the "nasty edge" of his sadness and self-loathing diminish, and continued to work in individual therapy.

Mr. N was greatly relieved as I pointed out that "positive living" was certainly a good approach to being positive, but that the issue was how one maintained the stance, that in my experience and philosophy, acknowledging and tending to the sadness, discouragement, and fear was the best way to enhance and maintain optimism—not denying, minimizing, or attempting to drive away one's fears. As the treatment progressed, Mr. N was able to more fully mourn the loss of his friend that appeared to trigger his depressive episode.

They had known each other for quite some time, and Mr. N found a great sense of acceptance with him. Whereas Mr. N often felt that he had to be careful about what he said or felt, his friend was always accepting and encouraging. Mr. N was shocked and frightened by the suddenness of his friend's illness and death. He had contracted hepatitis, gone into acute liver failure and died within a number of days. Mr. N had tended to experience his friend as hearty and stalwart. If his friend could die that suddenly, than surely he could as well.

Something about Mr. N's experience in the group appeared to be recapitulating an earlier experience. As he talked about his family, it was clear that he felt like the "black sheep." His father and sibs were all successful, heterosexual professionals that had "children and real jobs." Growing up, he always felt different from his sibs and many of his peers. He developed a seizure disorder as a child. The subsequent medical intervention and restriction on his activity helped to confirm his feelings of being different and weird as well as damaged. As he entered young adulthood and began to act on his homosexual orientation and fantasies, the sense of being weird and different became even more solidified. Mr. N was also plagued by the feeling that he had failed his parents, not lived up to their aspirations. He had turned out to be a "funny uncle" not "one of the boys" like his brothers.

In the support organization he found that he was accepted and being different and "damaged" were the norm. For the first time in his life he began to feel comfortable in groups and found himself able to socialize more easily with others. When his depression frightened the other members and he was chastized for feeling that way, Mr. N felt his world come crashing down once more. He felt that he had also failed at being HIV-positive. As the treatment progressed, Mr. N became less isolated, and once more became active in the group. He also began to talk with his family more about his being positive and attempted to educate them about the disease in general and his experience with it. To his surprise the family was responsive and supportive and he subsequently became more involved in the lives of his nieces and nephews. As he began to take his young relatives on outings to museums, parks, and plays, he was consistently amazed that they indeed liked him for who he was.

On one outing he was taken back when a niece asked quite candidly, "You are just HIV-positive, right, you don't have AIDS?" A frank discussion ensued, and all were left feeling reassured. In the session that followed Mr. N reflected, "Gee, I guess I am not the funny uncle after all. I am a nice uncle, that they just plain old like, and are worried about."

Over the next year, Mr. N's T cells continued to drop, despite the addition of combination therapy. He related his changing medical status to his sibs, and in general their response was quite reassuring. While he found his declining counts very discouraging he also was able to take advantage of his resources and travel. With quiet acceptance he related. "This is probably going to be my last good summer. I had better take advantage of it." Over the course of the summer he visited several friends in different parts of the country, many he had known since college. He was open about his medical status to all, and was warmly received and supported.

On his last trip, Mr. N became aware of difficulty with blurred vision, but intially wrote it off as a problem with his new lens prescription. When problems with memory became acutely apparent and his vision declined dramatically he was hospitalized for tests which eventually concluded PML. During the initial weeks of his hospitalization Mr. N was amazed at the response of his family and friends. He had always wondered if his family would be there for him when he got sick. They were and he was tremendously reassured. Mr. N was amazed and grateful when a brother whose wife was a nurse familiar with HIV offered to care for him in their home and arrangements were made for him to be transferred. However, Mr. N's condition declined in such a way that home health care would be too difficult. As Mr. N continued to decline, his family gathered around and several of the friends he had visited that summer came to visit him. Despite his fears of dying alone and rejected, he died surrounded by his family.

The Big Bang

Mr. K: "The Unrepentant Sinner"

As the epidemic progresses, I have found my practice to be less dominated by men in the throes of a protracted fragmentation fol-

lowing testing positive but rather by men who experience a profound loss of coherence farther into the experience, usually when
their T-cell counts decline to the 100 to 200 range. The study results
indicated that not all men experience the profound loss of coherence
detailed in *The Twilight Zone* soon after testing positive. Some
people will not become acutely disorganized until their counts decline to the point they begin taking antiviral medication, they experience the loss of an important relationship, or counts decline into
what they feel is an acute "danger zone."

Several factors may account for this. A central one may be that as
the epidemic progresses, being HIV-positive is much more com-
monplace in the gay community and considered an aspect of the
norm, hence there is not as much anxiety culturally transmitted. The
other factor of course is individual constitution–the structure and
resiliency of the self. In thinking about how the mind tends to
manage the psychological impact of HIV infection, it may be useful
to think in terms of the concept of the vertical split in the self posed
by Kohut. As Goldberg (1974) notes: "The split-off area of the
psyche has been described by Kohut as analagous to the mechanism
of disavowel. . . . Not only do the split-off parts of the self not
communicate with one another so that one does not know what the
other is doing, but the feeling states are clearly different" (p. 341).
If we think about the progression in men's experience of testing
positive we see considerable anxiety, fear, if not terror, damaged
self-esteem, and loss of a sense of future dominate the person's
existence, then quietly recede. People to varying degrees become
re-engaged with their lives and may for the most part conduct their
lives as if nothing is wrong. As men continue to live in the face of
HIV, the sense of continuing to live in the world, and the sense of
one's self as dying and leaving the world can become two distinct
self-experiences.

It is when people are no longer able to maintain this split that
they often become depressed and disorganized. (Some HIV clinicians have proposed the term "supportive denial" to conceptualize
this constellation.) Disease progression–decline in T cells, mild to
moderate or bothersome symptomatology such as fatigue or thrush–
impedes the person's ability to maintain the split and anxiety, depression, and a feeling of having "fooled one's self" may emerge. I

am not proposing this "defensive" maneuver in pathological terms, but rather as a naturally evolving attempt on the mind's part to integrate being positive, but to also remain engaged with life.

Men who test positive or for the most part are on any point in the continuum of infection are faced with the challenge of keeping engaged with life and going on living while they are faced with the knowledge of infection and the possibility of death. Hence the challenge is to keep on living while, on some level, one feels that they are dying. We see this often confusing aspect of the psychological experience of infection and illness, often right up to impending death.

The profound experience of feeling like *Damaged Goods* often is accentuated by previously existing self-esteem issues. Old meanings around feeling "not good enough" or "bad" and the difficulty of past selfobject relationships to modulate them may be activated and come to dominate the person's experience of infection. Depending on the nature of these meanings they may at times interfere with the person's ability to accept the infection, to seek and follow through with appropriate treatment, and to feel that one has the right to respond to the infection with medication.

When Mr. K entered treatment he was quite depressed and shaken. He had just turned 30, and was in a relationship for about one year. In the previous few months his T cells had slipped into the 100 range and he was becoming profoundly fatigued as he attempted to maintain his employment. He had stopped taking antiviral medication because it left him feeling weak and nauseated. He was afraid of becoming ill and dying and was panicked at the idea of disease progression. There was a sense of profound discouragement and sadness as he related his current life. Mr. K felt backed into a corner. He was increasingly exhausted at work, often coming home and going straight to bed. As he related his current fatigue it was difficult to sort out what may be related to his depression versus the infection. He had been hospitalized for depression approximately 18 months prior. He did not follow through with outpatient treatment and antidepressant medication. He felt betrayed and enraged with the church. He desperately wanted the comfort that religion had once provided him, yet felt it was not obtainable. Mr. K related that he was a fighter and a do-er, that he had always been able to overcome obstacles in his life. He had taught himself to read when no one else could, and he left the little town he grew up in and made a career for himself in the city. But he felt his fighting spirit was slipping away. In general, he appeared on the verge of a major depressive episode.

A prominent theme concerned his anger at his parents–especially his mother. Often their phone conversations would erupt into angry battles. Mr. K related that he was raised in a Southern fundamentalist religion and that his parents refused to accept his being gay. In their eyes he was a sinner and there appeared no way around it. He was becoming increasingly enraged–he wanted his parents support and acceptance. Here he was dying of AIDS, and rather than offer reassurance and love, his mother was worried about his being a sinner and what the neighbors would think. Another prominent theme was his feeling used. He felt used and taken advantage of by his previous physician and therapist in previous attempts at psychotherapy. He felt that they were more interested in the money than in helping him. He also felt used in several previous relationships and from his descriptions was involved with several highly devaluing men who took considerable emotional and financial advantage of him. He felt used and taken advantage of at work as well. He found himself often doing the work of other employees, was the one called upon for overtime, and usually complied, even though he felt tired and sick. Though he was talented and skilled in his profession, I did not get the sense that he really believed in or valued his own ability.

In regard to his infection, he felt profoundly discouraged. He had switched doctors and was relieved that his new doctor who had also made the referral to me, took time to listen and left him feeling tended to. He had a history of starting and stopping his antiviral treatment. He would begin taking the medication, start feeling sick and discouraged and then stop, often without really discussing the difficulties with his physician. Instead he would approach the physician about another problem he was having. He was profoundly discouraged as well by the mounting costs of his medical bills. In general it felt like he was kind of going along with treatment recommendations, but not enthusiastically engaged.

Several months into treatment his depression had lifted considerably. He related that this treatment felt different, that he felt I was really listening to him, and responsive to his concerns. We had discussed the possibility of his retiring and taking advantage of the disability benefits through his employment. He felt profoundly relieved by this, feeling that I had given him permission to explore the possibility. He knew it was an option, but was having trouble with feeling that he really deserved–or was sick enough–to take advantage of it. Mr. K had talked with his partner about his fear that his partner was disappointed in him, that he was not pulling his own weight financially or with the household chores. His partner reassured him that this was not the case, and Mr. K was relieved. In general he appeared to be more engaged with managing his infection, exploring his future options for retirement, and talking with his partner about his fears as well as possible plans for managing his infection and potential plans for the future.

After several weeks of feeling consistently better physically and emotionally, Mr. K arrived for his session appearing sad and discouraged. He related that he had gone off the medication again, that he hated taking it, and that he was beginning to feel sick again because of it. There had also been another angry phone conversation with his parents. They had previously offered to help out financially, but had balked when he requested help. Instead of an offer to help in any way possible as he had hoped, his mother said there was no money to give him at all. He attempted to focus on numerous somatic complaints, but I steered him in the direction of his experience of the medication and disappointment with his parents.

Mr. K related that every time he took his medication, it was a reminder that something was wrong with him. He felt bad. "Every time I take a pill, it's like someone telling me that there is something wrong with me. I just feel bad that I have brought this all on myself." He went on to relate how as a child he felt bad and defective. He had a reading learning disability, was taken for testing to different specialists, but no one ever explained to him what was wrong, or offered strategies for learning to read despite his disability. He recalled how his mother often said, "We know he is not stupid, but . . . ." He felt there was always this air of concern and "yes, but . . . " about him. He was more comfortable with adults and often tried to engage in conversation with the adults but felt repeatedly rebuffed. He felt painfully inadequate compared to his brother who was a star athlete, whose bedroom was full of trophies. He desperately wanted the affirmation that his brother received, yet never really felt it. All he wanted was his parents to say, "You are okay." A profound sense of being bad and damaged was emerging, and he could find no one able to modulate the feeling.

He recalled being desperately eager to please, a tendency that continued to this day, especially so with adults and authority figures. Yet he never really got what he was looking for. He was active in the fundamentalist church his family belonged to, and he himself at one time believed in the rigid interpretation of right and wrong, of sin or redemption that the church espoused. As he entered adolescence, he related how he began to argue with his Sunday School teachers, especially if he felt he and his fellow students were told they were "wrong" if they did not believe the doctrine being presented. The arguments appeared to escalate as he became increasingly aware of his attraction to boys and men. I reflected on the arguments he was having with his mother and how they seemed to be escalating. I wondered if he was trying to convince himself that he was not deeply bad, and hoping that she would say something to modulate that feeling state.

Mr. K began to look quite shaken. He reported that I was on to something and he was struggling to stay with me, but he kept "blanking out." I began to speak for him. I offered that perhaps he himself felt like a sinner because he was gay, and that AIDS was God's retribution, that he was looking for someone to convince him that this was not the case, and desperately looking to his mother to absolve him. Mr. K was quite shaken, gripping the couch, holding his breath, and terrified. He said, "Go on, you're getting it. I am here, it's hard, but I am here." I pointed out that in the way fundamentalists operate there is nothing worse than being an unrepentant sinner. If you are an unrepentent sinner, you can be cast out, spit upon, devalued, erased.

By this time, Mr. K was white as a sheet, he again stated that he kept "blanking out," but was struggling to stay with me, to hear my words. He began to relate how indeed he did cling to wondering if he was a sinner, if he was going to hell, if there was no hope for him. As much as he hated to admit it, he did feel like an unrepentant sinner, and that there was no hope for him. He felt trapped in this deep sense of being bad, that there was no way out. At the end of the session he related some relief, but also that "there was more to this." Over the next few sessions we put into words the central ways he had led his life. On one hand he felt like there was something wrong–bad–about him. His desperate attempt to please adults and others was an effort to convince himself that he was not bad, hoping that acknowledgement of his efforts and skill would help buffer this central feeling. Yet at the same time, his deep questioning of himself prevented him from owning his abilities and taking pride in his work, it also left him susceptible to abusive relationships. He became very sad as he related how much of his life had been desperate attempts to please others in the hope that it would somehow save him from the deeply ingrained feeling of being bad and a sinner. A deep split had formed in his experience of self. On one side he was bad–a despicable, unrepenting, homosexual sinner; on the other he was eager to please–ever the good boy hoping for praise for doing things just right, yet feeling disappointed over the lack of affirmation. He related how at different points he found himself indulging in the bad, "If I am a sinner, and damned, well, I am going to be one hell of a sinner," or indulging in the efforts to please. Neither one felt real, or affirming; he always felt trapped.

Over the next few weeks he related several traumatic incidents in his life, including a rape when he was first exploring his sexuality. Mr. K had met a man and eventually had sex with him several times. One evening he found the dorm curfew approaching. He said he had to leave or else he would be in trouble at school. The man became enraged, beat, raped, and threw Mr. K out of the house. This too he had taken responsibility for, thinking that if he were back at the dorm at the Christian college he was attending, the rape never would have happened. After the rape he felt his world collapse; he became withdrawn, insecure, and confused. He related how he had slowly "come out of his shell" in late adolescence, found his social skills blossoming, and was well liked by his peers. After the rape, his confidence collapsed, he blamed himself, and being at the school he was, he felt there was nowhere safe to turn. He feared if he went to his friends he would be rejected as a sinner; if he went to the college counselors, he feared the same fate. Mr. K was taken aback when I pointed out that he was only trying to follow the school rules, and his attacker's rageful response to his need to leave was quite crazy. He replied, "Gee, you are right. I was just a college kid; I had to follow the rules. I did not do anything to deserve what he did."

As we began to think about his life in these terms, he became brighter, more assertive at work and in his relationship. His somatic preoccupation began to lift, as did his feeling sick in response to the medication. For the first time in his life he began to believe in himself, and his abilities. He began to feel a sense of gratification and accomplishment, to really hear and take in the compliments of others. However, he was aware that doubts still lingered over his unrepentant sinner status. He was somewhat ashamed to admit that the doubts still lingered. I pointed out that the way fundamentalist churches operated, those who offer different views are suspect, if not actual agents of the devil. He was somewhat embarrassed to admit that indeed that was the case.

Fortunately an event happened in the family that helped him see this religious dynamic, that had become a family dynamic, as it was played out in the current day. His sister had developed cancer as an adolescent, had recovered, and become the state cancer "poster girl," giving talks to other children with cancer and appearing at fund raisers. Mr. K loved his sister greatly, though he reported some jealousy at the way she had been held up as a tragic victim of a deadly disease in sharp contrast to the way his HIV infection was responded to. The sister had decided to divorce her physically and emotionally abusive husband. The parents responded to her situation much the way they had Mr. K's. She was told to work it out, that divorce was a sin, and that she was now ruined in the eyes of the church. They refused any financial assistance; they would not assist her in her sin.

Mr. K was enraged when he heard of this, calling his parents and angrily pointing out that they were doing to his sister what they did to him. Their kids have real problems; his sister was distraught and in pain; he was dying, and all they get is being called sinners. He found himself beginning to believe in a stronger way that his belief of being bad and a sinner had as much to do with his mother's devaluation as it did with church doctrine. Far from his feared total rejection by his parents, he found them taking him more seriously after this conversation. His father especially was concerned about how he was feeling, what medications he was on, and where he could learn more about AIDS.

Mr. K found his depression and somatic concerns continuing to lift. He was no longer bothered by the persistant nausea that for so long had gone with his antiviral medication, and he found himself feeling less fatigued. When problems at work arose, rather than trying to fix them by working around problematic employees, he pointed out the problems to his supervisors. He told his immediate supervisors of his HIV status and how he just did not have the energy he once did and that he was thinking about disability. To his surprise they were very supportive, affirmed how valued he was, and offered to adjust his work schedule. Mr. K also found himself not wanting to go on disability just yet. For the first time in his life, he found himself hearing people's compliments and beginning to appreciate his own skills. He was beginning to feel satisfied and take delight in what he was able to create. That felt too precious to give up just yet.

As the treatment progressed, he found himself feeling more and more comfortable with and accepted by his family. A long visit home proved to be very healing and reassuring. He felt his parents delight in him, that his parents were showing him off to friends and relatives. He was even able to attend services at the church he was raised in and to his relief did not feel personally attacked and enraged. Mr. K also found himself taking his medication regularly and not being bothered by the familiar nausea. As he reflected on this he said, "You know, I have come to feel that I really want to live as long as possible, that maybe I am worth saving after all."

SUMMARY

This chapter has been an attempt to "bring it all together." The results from the study, though powerful and illuminating in their own right, could very well stand alone in some contexts, for example, for the HIV-positive person who reads this book in an effort to make sense of his experience. However, if we are working in a clinical context we need an additional perspective–a theory about how human beings come to feel the way they do and experience their lives the way they do. We need a clinical theory to help us translate the theory about what it is like to know one is HIV-positive into the realm of clinical intervention. Thus, the psychology of the self helped to translate the general range of experience presented in the results chapters to the realm of personal meaning and its transformation presented in this chapter.

In my years of working clinically with and researching HIV-related problems I have been repeatedly awed and humbled. The contrast between the devastating effects on the self and the process of adult development that HIV infection brings, contrasted with the often remarkable personal growth I have observed in my clients, has been a source of continual inspiration. Clearly human development does not come to a stop in the face of a life-threatening illness. In fact, in many cases, with the right environmental influences, HIV infection appears to spur on a consolidation of the self and a continued process of finding meaning in life, often up through its final moments.

For clinicians who have read this book, I hope you have found it helpful. While we often work with a client through many stages of HIV infection, I know of no other place where the many phases, component aspects, and transformations of the experience of knowing that one is HIV-positve are chronicled. Many of the ideas presented in this final chapter are questions that have struck me and I have struggled with over the years. You may have a different perspective on them, or questions of your own, but again, I hope my efforts are helpful in your clinical endeavors. There is much work yet to be done. Many more people will seek our help as they attempt to manage their lives in the face of HIV.

For the HIV-infected people who have read this book, again I hope it has helped you make sense of your complex experience. You more than others know just how hard it is to live with HIV. Hopefully, by reading just how hard it can be to live with HIV, your triumphs as well as those days when all seems to have gone to hell will be validated and you will find reassurance that you are not alone.

Bibliography

Baker, H.S. & Baker, M.N. (1987). Heinz Kohut's self-psychology: An overview. *American Journal of Psychiatry.* 144 (1), 1-9.

Borden, B. (1991). Beneficial outcomes in adjustment to HIV sero-positivity. *Social Service Review,* September.

Cohen, J. & Abramowitz, S. (1990). AIDS attacks the self: A self-psychological exploration of the psychodynamic consequences of AIDS. In A. Goldberg (Ed) *The Realities of Transference, Progress in Self-Psychology,* V6, Hillsdale, NJ:The Analytic Press. 157-171.

Faigen, S. (1988). Teaching concepts about transference and countertransference in the field. Paper presented at Fieldwork Supervisors Meeting, Loyola University School of Social Work.

Glaser, B. (1978). *Theoretical Sensitivity.* Mill Valley, CA: The Free Press.

Glaser, B. & Strauss, A. (1967). *The Discovery of Grounded Theory: Strategies for Qualitative Research.* Chicago: Aldine Publishing Company.

Goldberg, A. (1974). A fresh look at perverse behaviour. *International Journal of Psychoanalysis.* V56, N3, pp. 335-342.

Goldberg, A. (1990). *The Prisonhouse of Psychoanalysis.* Hillsdale, NJ: The Analytic Press.

Hays, R.B., Catania, J., McKusick, L, & Coates, T.J. (1990) Help-seeking for AIDS-related concerns; A comparison of gay men of various HIV diagnoses. *American Journal of Community Psychology.* 18, pp. 743-755.

Hays, R.B., Turner, H., Coates, T.J. (1992). Social support. AIDS-related symptoms and depression among gay men. *Journal of Consulting and Clinical Psychology,* V60, N3, 463-469.

Kennedy, L. (1979). Generalizing from single case studies. *Evaluation Quarterly,* 4, pp. 666-678.

Kohut, H. (1972). *The Analysis of the Self.* New York: International Universities Press.

Kohut, H. (1978). Preface to *Der Falsche Weg zum Selbst, Studien zur Drogenkarriere*. In: P. Ornstein (Ed.) *The Search for the Self*. New York: International Universities Press.

Kohut, H. (1984). *How Does Analysis Cure?* A. Goldberg & P. Stepansky (Eds). Chicago: University of Chicago Press.

Lauffer, M. (1976). The central masturbation fantasy and its relation to treatment. *The Psychoanalytic Study of the Child*. 31, pp. 297-328.

Lincoln, Y. (1992). Sympathetic connections between qualitative methods and health research. *Qualitative Health Research,* 2(4), pp. 375-391.

Lincoln, Y. & Guba, E. (1985). *Naturalistic Inquiry*. Newbury Park, CA: Sage Publications.

Muslin, H. (1985). Heinz Kohut: Beyond the pleasure principle: Contributions to psychoanalysis. In J. Reppen (Ed.) in *Beyond Freud: A Study in Modern Psychoanalytic Theorists*. Hillsdale, NJ: The Analytic Press. pp.203-230.

Ornstein, A. (1991). Sexual Fantasies: Efforts at Self Healing. Paper presented at: Between Patient and Therapist: Perspectives from Self-Psychology, March 1-3 Cedar Sinai Hospital, Los Angeles, California.

Ostrow, D.G. Monjan, A., Joseph, J., Van Raden, M., Fox, R., Kingsley, L., Dudley, J., & Phair, J. (1989). HIV-related symptoms and psychological functioning in a cohort of homosexual men. *American Journal of Psychiatry,* 146, pp. 737-742.

Palombo, J. (Personal Communication, February 24, 1988).

Perry, S.W., Jacobsberg, L.B., Fishman B., Weiler, P.H., Gold, J, & Frances, A.J. (1990). Psychological response to seriological testing for HIV. *AIDS,* 4, pp. 145-152.

Saari, C. (1986). *Clinical Social Work Treatment*. New York: Gardner Press.

Saari, C. (1991). *The Creation of Meaning in Clinical Social Work*. New York: The Guilford Press.

Schwartz, H. & Jacobs, J. (1979). *Qualitative Sociology: A Method to the Madness*. New York: The Free Press.

Shelby, R.D. (1992). *If a Partner Has AIDS: Guide to Clinical Intervention for Relationships in Crisis*. Binghamton, NY: The Haworth Press.

Shelby, R.D. (1994). Mourning within a culture of mourning. In M. Forstein, S. Cadwell & R. Burnham (Eds.) *Therapists on the Frontline of AIDS,* Washington, DC: APA Press.

Strauss, A. & Corbin, J. (1990). *Basics of Qualitative Research.* Newbury Park, CA: Sage Publications.

Stoller, R.J. (1985). *Observing the Erotic Imagination.* New Haven:Yale University Press.

Wu, H. (1990). Psychosocial factors in biological and psychological outcome in AIDS. Doctoral Dissertation, Northwestern University.

Index